Ethnic Identity and Development

Ethnic Identity and Development

Khat and Social Change in Africa

Susan Beckerleg

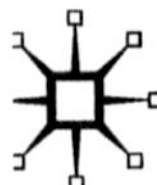

ETHNIC IDENTITY AND DEVELOPMENT

First published in 2010 by PALGRAVE MACMILLAN® in the United States—a division of St. Martin's Press LLC, 175 Fifth Avenue, New York, NY 10010.

Where this book is distributed in the UK, Europe, and the rest of the world, this is by Palgrave Macmillan, a division of Macmillan Publishers Limited, registered in England, company number 785998, of Houndmills, Basingstoke, Hampshire RG21 6XS.

PALGRAVE MACMILLAN is the global academic imprint of the above companies and has companies and representatives throughout the world.

ISBN: 978-0-230-62310-1

Library of Congress Cataloging-in-Publication Data is available from the Library of Congress.

A catalogue record of the book is available from the British Library.

Design by Scribe Inc.

First edition: June 2010

10 9 8 7 6 5 4 3 2 1

Printed in the United States of America.

Contents

Illustrations

Figures

Tables

Acknowledgments

Most of the data on khat presented in this book were collected between 2007 and 2009 for a project funded by the UK Economic and Research Council (ESRC), "Khat and Social Identity in Uganda" (RES-062-23-0560). I thank the ESRC for supporting this research. In 2004 and 2005, I was a member of a research team of a study, "The Khat Nexus: Transnational Consumption in a Global Economy." This was also an ESRC Award (RES-143-25-0046), and I gratefully acknowledge the support received to carry out fieldwork in Kenya and Uganda.

I thank Brill for granting permission to publish parts of the article, "From Ocean to Lakes: Cultural Transformations of Yemenis in Kenya and Uganda," which first appeared in *African and Asian Studies* in 2009.

I thank Professor Gillian Hundt from the University of Warwick for her guidance, support, and academic collaboration since 1994, when we started working together. At the University of Warwick School of Health and Social Studies, I also thank Alison Cowling for the efficient management of my grant and Bola Ole for her work in setting up a SPSS (statistical package for social sciences) database and entering the results of a questionnaire administered to khat users in Uganda.

In Uganda, I thank Musa Almas for his work as driver, guide, interpreter, and key informant, hence combining several jobs and multitasking. I also acknowledge his hard work and resourcefulness in seeking out and interviewing khat users in different settings.

Dr. David Basangwa, a leading Ugandan psychiatrist at the national Butabika psychiatric hospital and founder of a drug and alcohol unit at the hospital, is thanked for his ongoing support of my research. Christopher Muhoozi and Godfrey B. Asiimwe of the History and Development Department at Makerere University are also thanked for their support, contacts, and assistance in the dissemination of findings. Andrew Mugisa of the Toro Development Agency in Fort Portal is thanked for keeping an open mind on khat, for organizing a consultative meeting in 2008, and for continued assistance.

Given that khat may be banned in Uganda by the time of publication, many people involved in the khat industry would not welcome inclusion in the acknowledgments of this book. Most names have been changed in the text in the interests of maintaining confidentiality and protecting rather than penalizing those who helped me with their frank responses. However, the following individuals involved in the Ugandan khat industry assisted me more than once, and I believe might enjoy, or at least not mind, seeing their name in print: Issac Kizito, Denis Kasujja, Mama Mbale, Mama Saidi, and Mama Abdul. All the other unnamed khat farmers, traders, and consumers are also thanked for answering my questions and allowing me to get in their way as they worked or to share their leisure time as we chewed together. Ugandan government and community leaders are also thanked for consenting to be interviewed and for answering so many questions.

Chapter 1

Introduction

Catha edulis or khat is a tree that grows wild across much of Africa and Asia, favoring altitudes of between 5,000 and 6,500 feet above sea level. Khat production has its origins in Yemen and Ethiopia, and consumption of khat as a stimulant has been a part of social life in these countries for at least a millennium. Cathinone, the main psychotropic ingredient, is largely responsible for the stimulating effects achieved by chewing the plant. These effects are similar to, but weaker than, those produced by amphetamine use. The cathinone present in the plants' leaves and stems starts to break down as soon as it is picked, but if ingested within thirty-six hours of harvesting, khat activates the central nervous system, producing mild euphoria succeeded by a more contemplative, quiet state and followed by sleeplessness and alertness. While alertness is sought by long-distance drivers, watchmen, and students studying for examinations, sleeplessness is undesirable for most consumers and is sometimes countered with alcohol or, less commonly, diazepam consumption.

Controversy bedevils the substance, with one camp arguing that use of khat has serious ill effects on the health, sanity, and social well-being of consumers and their families. Medical studies have identified a large number of health problems associated with khat consumption, from gastrointestinal problems to tooth cavities, oral cancer, and insanity. A second camp denies that khat does any significant harm and point to the generation of incomes for producers and traders of the plant in Kenya and Ethiopia, both countries with successful khat export markets.

Khat has many names and local nicknames and, in the academic literature, many ways of spellings the word. Although "khat" is the standard spelling used in academic writing, many variations are found in journal articles including, qaad, kat, and tchat. The Yemeni Arabic, *qat*, is the probably the original version of the word, with khat a bad transliteration of qat (Gebissa, 2004; Kennedy, 1987). In the countries where khat is consumed it goes by other names: *chat* in Ethiopia, in Kenya *miraa* or *murungi*, while in Uganda, khat is widely known as *mairungi*. In this book, I use the word khat unless I am quoting text that uses other spellings or other words.

The main geographical focus of this book is Uganda, where khat production consumption is a new phenomenon and a growing cause of disquiet to the authorities. The story of Ugandan khat is one of changing economic fortunes and new social identities. Uganda has been dogged by decades of violence, much of it with a strong ethnic dimension. Yet, throughout the turmoil of the 1970s and 1980s, khat production and consumption spread throughout the country. During this period many people fled their home districts, resulting in the high degree of ethnic "scrambling" that characterizes the population today. In Uganda, small-scale khat producers, agents, and wholesales from many ethnic groups supply consumers from equally diverse backgrounds. The distribution of khat operates on the basis of personal contacts, and it provides a modest living for numerous men and women. The industry is self-regulating and operates in the face of opposition from many local authorities and from the police.

Ugandan khat production, trade, and consumption has, until now, been largely undocumented. I first spotted khat on sale in Uganda in 2003 when I was visiting the capital Kampala. In 2004 I returned to Uganda to carry out research as coinvestigator on a UK study titled "The Khat Nexus," which considered khat as a newly globalized commodity. As part of the same project, I had also carried out a study of khat in Kenya and visited Rwanda to assess khat use there. We published the results in a coauthored book, *The Khat Controversy* (Anderson et al., 2007), as well as in various papers in social science journals. In 2007 I obtained funding to carry out a study of khat and social identity in Uganda and most of the data on Uganda presented here were collected during fieldwork between July 2007 and July 2009.

I employed the usual range of social science methods: key informant interviews with officials, khat farmers, traders and with elderly people who remembered how khat came to Uganda; a questionnaire survey to khat consumers; and, of course, the principle method of social anthropology, participant observation. In this case participant observation involved chewing khat and sitting for hours in retail outlets. By feeding back findings to key Ugandan audiences, such as health workers, local government officials, and university students, more data were generated from the questions and discussions arising from my presentations.

Internationally, khat has come to be closely associated with Somalis. During the early 1990s, when war in Somalia caused the exodus of refugees that continues in the present day, khat consumption started to spread across the world, following the migratory patterns of Somali asylum seekers. Countries with significant populations of Somalis have responded in different ways to the khat importation. The United States led the way in 1993 when cathinone, the main active ingredient of khat, was categorized as a Schedule 1 drug, indicating that it is considered to have a high abuse potential for users and no accepted medical use. This scheduling of cathinone puts khat on a par with other illicit drugs such as heroin, LSD, and ecstasy (Varisco, 2004, p. 104). The move to proscribe the main active ingredient of khat appears to have been in response to the experience of the United States in Somalia, when their troops were driven back from Somali soil by militiamen allegedly high on "khat" (Anderson & Carrier, 2006). As khat started to enter the global public consciousness, it was as a substance that caused aggression and had fuelled war in Somalia (Randall, 1993). In East Africa, Somalis are closely connected to khat, in Uganda as initiators of production, in Kenya as domestic traders and exporters, and everywhere as consumers.

Yemeni migrants, who became "Swahili" in coastal Kenya and Tanzania and are known as "Arabs" in Uganda and Rwanda (Beckerleg, 2009), also played a role in promoting khat production in Uganda and in spreading consumption in Kenya. Hence, the story of khat in East Africa is one of peaceful interaction between migrant Somalis and Yemenis and local people. In the first three chapters, I trace changing the ethnic identities of Somalis and Yemenis in East Africa, the role of khat in their lives, and how they taught Ugandans to cultivate khat and to harvest it from the wild. Subsequent chapters trace the ways that indigenous Ugandans, like other East Africans, developed a local khat industry that is an important example of local economic development, achieved in the face of government indifference.

Khat use in Uganda is an example of the growing national hedonism that embraces listening and dancing to loud popular music, drinking in bars, watching English league soccer, and engaging in sex with multiple partners. These forms of recreation are a reaction, for people living in southern and western Uganda, to earlier decades of violence and social disruption, as well as a sign of increasing national prosperity. Most Ugandans now aspire to leisure and recreation in ways that would have been impossible even ten years ago. The survey I conducted with 210 consumers shows that a wide range of people, drawn from diverse ethnic groups, now chew khat. A similar process, whereby khat chewing has spread to all ethnic groups and has become a popular activity among youth, has also occurred in Kenya and Ethiopia (Carrier, 2005a; Gebissa, 2008). The spread of khat use in East Africa has caused concern among local leaders, many of whom seek to ban the substance. In the final chapter, I assess the impact of khat production, trade, and consumption on both national and personal development in the main African countries where khat is produced, namely, Uganda, Kenya, Ethiopia, as well as in Yemen where it probably all started.

Chapter 2

Somali Identity and Khat

In the nineteenth century, Arabs from Zanzibar arrived in the kingdom of Buganda on the northwestern shore of Lake Victoria and introduced Islam to the court, where the affairs of the kingdom were conducted and visitors received. They found a hierarchical polity that was slave owning, clan based, ritualistic, and ruled over by the *kabaka* (king). Shrines where *lubaale* (gods) and the spirits of deceased kabakas resided were important ritual centers that underlaid the secular power of the kingdom. Nevertheless, the Ganda, the people of Buganda, were interested in Islam and many converted to this new religion. In the 1860s British explorers arrived and were closely followed by British Protestant and French Catholic missionaries (Bennett, 1986). Wars followed the introduction of these new religions, as Ganda clans fought among themselves and with the neighboring kingdoms of Nkore and Bunyoro. The result of these wars was British domination over the kingdom of Buganda and of a wider area that collectively came to be known as Uganda.

The earliest fleeting reference to a Somali connection to Buganda relates to a war between Muslims and the colonialists in 1888. Martin (1976) has identified a Somali trader who was active in Buganda politics at this time: "During the Muslim coup in Uganda in 1888, which terminated in the deposition of the Kabaka Mwanga, a leading role was played by a trader who was both an emissary and a close personal friend of Sayyid Barhhash—Sulayman al-Jabri al-Barawi. At this time a leading member of the Qadiriya in Buganda, Sulayman had begun his career as a trader from Tabora, a town where the Arab majority were of the Hinawi faction. Sulayman opposed the European Christian missionaries at the Kabaka's court with some success in 1887 and 1888" (Martin, 1976, p. 167).

Sulayman's last name, al-Barawi, indicates that he was a native of Barawa on the southern Somali coast. As a member of the Qadiriya brotherhood, al-Barawi was a follower of Shaikh Uways, also a native of Barawa. Indeed, according to Kassim (1995), "The Uwaysiya, a branch of the Qadiriya brotherhood (*tariqa*) founded by Shaikh Uways, were involved in the Muslim resistance to European colonization in Buganda in the 1880s, and in German-controlled Tanganyika in the 1890s" (Kassim, 1995, p. 33).

In Somalia the Qadiris made use of khat to keep awake during lengthy, *dhikr* sessions, where Quranic phrases that mentioned or praised God were repeated for hours on end. This practice was opposed by the rival Salihiya brotherhood, led by Sayyid Muhammed, also known as the "Mad Mullah." Martin writes that in 1895 Sayyid Muhammed returned to Somalia from Mecca, preaching reformist doctrines and preaching against the use of all substances, even tea: "He attacked the use of tobacco, intoxicating drinks, tea, and coffee, and he castigated persons who chewed *qat*" (Martin, 1976, p. 180). Khat incurred the particular attention of Sayyid Muhammed: "His fulminations against *qat*, which many Qadiris used to keep awake at their *dhikirs*, led to a confrontation between Sayyid Muhammed and certain of the religious leaders of the town [of Berbara]" (Martin, 1976, p. 181).

Hence, khat was not just consumed but was important in Islamic ritual, among Somali Qadiri in nineteenth-century Somalia. Ethiopian Muslims in the province of Harerge used khat in a similar manner. According to Gebissa (2004): "For centuries, it has been a standard practice for those who participated in religious ceremonies held at the Muslim shrines in the province to spend long hours of the day and night chewing while praying to Allah" (Gebissa, 2004, p. 11).

The late nineteenth and early twentieth centuries saw the so-called scramble for Africa. The Mad Mullah fought the British in Somalia, while in Uganda the Ganda and Nyoro peoples also resisted European colonial forces. Somali territory was also divided at the time. According to Goldsmith, "The arbitrary colonial division of Africa in the late nineteenth century partitioned the Somali population into five different regions: the largest portion of Somali territory fell under Italian control; the British took the northern extension of Somaliland to insure [*sic*] a supply of livestock for their base at Aden; and the environs of the port of Djibouti became a French enclave. A large slice of Kenya's Northern Frontier District, formerly Galla territory conquered by the Somalis during the nineteenth century fell under British administration, and the Ogaden region of Somalia's western flank were officially ceded to Ethiopia" (Goldsmith, 1997, pp. 480–481).

KHAT, RELIGION, AND COLONIAL POWER

From at least the late nineteenth century, khat was being imported to Somali areas from the Harerge region in Ethiopia. The ethnic Somali territories that received khat included the southern areas that later became Italian-controlled Somalia, the British protectorate of Somaliland in the north, and the French port-state of Djibouti. Prior to the construction of a railway from the Harerge to the port of Djibouti in 1902, camel caravans were the main form of transport carrying khat (Gebissa, 2004, p. 13).

In 1921 the British authorities in Hargeisa, the capital of British-controlled Somaliland, passed a law forbidding the cultivation, import, and sale of khat (Gebissa, 2004, p. 79). From 1921 khat was smuggled to British Somaliland from the Harerge in eastern Ethiopia, and by the early 1930s Somali traders were engaged in smuggling khat from Ethiopia through Somaliland to Djibouti (Gebissa, 2004, p. 54). Yemeni traders in Djibouti and other trading ports along the long Somali coastline boosted the demand for khat in the early twentieth century. Imports of Yemeni khat from the port of Aden partially met demand. All measures applied by colonial governments to curb khat consumption failed. In both South Arabia and Africa, regulation of khat was tried and failed. Hence, "Attempts by the colonial authorities to ban the sale and consumption of khat—Djibouti (1956–57), Somaliland (1921–57), Aden (1957–8), and Kenya (1945–56)—proved unworkable and were quietly abandoned" (Klein & Beckerleg, 2007, p. 240).

As khat use started to spread among urban Somalis, it lost any religious connotation, and by the 1940s chewing was primarily a secular activity of progressive young male Somalis, as Gebissa outlines in his history of khat (2004):

> As Somalis moved to towns, they formed social clubs and self-help societies, whose membership consisted of the new elite. Their goal was to promote interest in secular education, to exhort Somalis to overcome clan divisiveness in the name of Islamic unity and to seek appropriate privileges for civil servants. Over time traders, coffee-shop owners, personal servants of British officials, truck drivers and the foreign-educated elite began to develop new interests and aspirations. They subscribed to the ideal of a united and independent Somalia. In their clubs, the

> intelligentsia discussed politics and began to chew khat. Young men began to participate in regular afternoon chew sessions. (Gebissa, 2004, p. 81)

Such clubs were also a key factor in the development of a Somali national consciousness that sought to ultimately unite all Somali territories in one state. Barnes links the growth of the "Greater Somalia" idea to the social clubs and professional societies that developed in British and Italian Somali lands in the 1940s (Barnes, 2007). Goldsmith points out that the flag of the now defunct Republic of Somalia, a five-pointed star on a blue background, represents Somali aspiration for a united Somalia (1997, p. 463). Khat chewing was linked at this time to Somali identity, and this factor hindered all attempts by European powers to regulate chewing. Abdullahi notes that Somalis sensed hypocrisy in the move against khat: "Various attempts to curb the use of qat have produced little success. The British tried to stop it in the 1950s when they governed the north. However, the Somalis saw it as an injustice and a double standard since the British were drinking whisky and alcoholic beverages" (Abdullahi, 2001, p. 153).

INDEPENDENCE, INSTABILITY, AND DISUNITY

Somalia gained independence in 1960, but not all the five ethnic Somali regions were included in the new nation (Meredith, 2006). In a 1960 referendum of the population of Kenya's northeastern, Somali-dominated province, 90 percent of voters opted to join Somalia (Goldsmith, 1997). The Ogaden region of Ethiopia also fell outside Somali borders, and the former French territory of Djoubuti remained apart. Hence, Somalia was made up of the former Italian-controlled area and British Somaliland. In 1969 Siad Barre took control of the country in his capacity as one of a group of army officers who had seized power (Goldsmith, 1997). Barre, like the British, made a futile attempt at controlling khat. As Abdullahi has noted: "Qat was again banned in 1983 by the government of dictator Mohamed Siad Barre. Unluckily, this last attempt was a half-hearted step by the government aimed more at depriving Somali guerrillas based in Ethiopia from hitching rides on qat trucks, and commerce in qat continued under the hands of the supporters of the regime. The Barre government publicly permitted qat use in its last days in 1989" (Abdullahi, 2001, pp. 153–154).

The demise of the Barre government ushered in, in the early 1990s, a period of war and instability that persists to the present. Somalia fragmented into small territorial units based on clan membership, under the shaky authority of elders, warlords, and businessmen. Khat chewing of supplies flown in from Kenya and overland from Ethiopia became associated with the civil war (Randall, 1993). Anderson and Carrier (2006) report that the banning of khat in the United States in the 1990s occurred partly as a reaction to the failure of Operation Restore Hope, when, in 1993, U.S. troops invaded Somalia with the objective of restoring peace by putting an end to the clan-based war that was tearing the country apart. They were forced to withdraw and the war continued unabated. At that time, it was noted by U.S. authorities and other observers of the conflict that the fighters combating U.S. troops were all chewing khat. It was all too easy to link khat to the violence characterizing the region and to take action by making khat use illegal in the United States (Anderson et al., 2007). However, little could be done to control khat imports to Somalia, where there was little or no law and order.

Somalis living in the former British Somaliland asserted a separate identity in 1994 and declared themselves an independent state. Somaliland, however, remains unrecognized by any other government. Khat use is not only legal in Somaliland (Anderson et al., 2007; Klein & Beckerleg, 2007) but also was used by delegates to a major conference that was to decide the "destiny" of Somaliland in 1993 (Walls, 2009, p. 384). "The conference lasted more than four months, and throughout that time, semi-official debates and meetings were constant. They assumed various forms, from more formal chaired meetings where two or three parties would be invited to take part in a debate on a given issue, to direct negotiations between clan or sub-clan representatives, as well as myriad qaad-chewing sessions" (Walls, 2009, pp. 384–385).

Somaliland remained relatively peaceful, and khat was used by politicians to woo their supporters in the 2003 election (Anderson & Carrier, 2006). By contrast, no general elections have been held in Somalia. Following earlier attempts to control khat use in the twentieth century, one more attempt was made to ban khat in Somalia. In 2006 the Islamic Courts' movement took control of much of southern Somalia. One of their actions was to ban khat, which was, and is, imported daily in large amounts from the Meru region of Kenya (Anderson et al., 2007). The rule of the Islamic Courts was short lived, as they were deposed in December 2006 after fierce fighting with Ethiopian troops who were operating with U.S. support (Barnes & Hassan, 2007).

SOMALIS AND KHAT REAPPRAISED

The form of Islam practiced by the conveners of the Islamic Courts is very different from that of the Sufi style rituals of the Qadhiri Brotherhood of the late nineteenth century. But even then there were tensions over competing forms of religious observance between the Qadhiri and the stricter Salihiya brotherhood, led by the Mad Mullah Sayyid Muhammed. One of the issues they clashed on was khat use, so that for over a hundred years there has been a Somali discourse on khat. In the mid-twentieth century khat was used by young, urban men with a secular orientation and a taste for nationalistic politics. Therefore, although it is widely claimed that Somalis have no tradition of khat use, its use has been closely tied with both Islam and politics across the region since before European colonial incursions started. From the twentieth century, Somalis in the diaspora, be it Nairobi or New York, have taken up khat chewing as a badge of identity. Their khat use has caused controversy and concerns for their mental health as well as for national well-being wherever they live (Klein & Beckerleg, 2006). Somalis, due to their recent tragic history as refugees across the world, are the ethnic group now most closely associated with khat use. The association of Somalis with khat certainly applies to Uganda.

UGANDAN SOMALIS

Somalis, particularly those originating from British Somaliland, have been consuming khat since at least the nineteenth century, and Ugandan Somalis are no exception. Indeed, an early Somali visitor to Uganda was an Islamic scholar and member of the khat-using Qadhiri Brotherhood from southern Somalia, who helped the Ganda people fight British colonialism. Yet Ugandan Somalis play down their cultural links to khat. The history of Somalis and of the place of khat in forging their cultural identity in Uganda as well as in Somalia is complex. Ordinary Ugandans who link khat to Somali cultures tell a diffferent story.

In Uganda, whether the Somalis like it or not, khat consumers from diverse ethnic backgrounds associate the origins of the khat-chewing habit with Somalis, often citing the "happy goat" story. This story told by khat consumers all over the world relates how a goat herder was tending his animals when he noticed that they had become very frisky and "busy with the women goats" (Rushby, 1999, p. 28). The goat herder realized that the goats had been eating from a particular bush and tried the leaves himself. Of course, it was a khat bush. In other settings—London, Ethiopia, Kenya, Yemen—the goat herder is usually a Yemeni or an Ethiopian, a wanderer in a region where khat consumption goes back centuries (Gebissa, 2004; Varisco, 2004; Weir, 1985). Kennedy names the goat herder as Awzulkernayen and notes that the story is sometimes set in Somaliland (Kennedy, 1987, p. 62). The Somali herder in the version of the story told in Uganda discovers khat in Somalia, where he is perceived to be a recent immigrant, a stranger who introduced the foreign habit of khat chewing.

LUGARD, THE NUBI AND SOMALIS IN UGANDA

Khat use may first have been introduced to the kingdom of Buganda, in the heart of the region that was to become Uganda, by Sulayman al-Jabri al-Barawi, who fought with Muslim Ganda against the British in 1888 and is therefore the first recorded Somali in Uganda. The second named Somali to visit Uganda was in the employ of a British commercial agent, Captain Frederick Lugard, and acted as his bodyguard and confidant. The story of Lugard's bodyguard has become an important reference point for the claims of the Ugandan Somalis. The chairman of the Ugandan Somali community, Din Hassan, told Irene Nabusoba of *New Vision* newspaper in 2007, "We have been here for about 120 years. We came at the same time as the Nubians. We have intermarried with the locals, adopted their cultures and contribute to the county's economic development" (Nabusoba, 2007, p. 14).

> The vice chairman of the Ugandan Somalis, Abdulahi Roble, added that Din Hassan's grandfather, Jama Ali, led the first group of Somalis to settle in Uganda while working as Captain Frederick Lugard's bodyguard in 1909 (Nabusoba, 2007, p. 14). Roble, when interviewed by a journalist from the Ugandan daily newspaper, *The New Vision*, explained how Somalis came to settle in Uganda:Roble said there were about 70 Nubians and 50 Somalis who were employed by the British colonialists.
>
> Most of them worked as askaris. After the First World War, they retired and settled mainly in Bombo, Old Kampala, Kisenyi, Jinja and later spread to other parts of the country.
>
> "Being cattle keepers and Muslims, the colonialists gave them contracts to slaughter meat in the country," Roble revealed. (Nabusoba, 2007, p. 14)

The Somalis, as long-term residents of Uganda, are keen to claim deep roots in the country. However, they might do better to claim al-Bawari, who helped the Buganda kingdom to fight the British as their illustrious forbearer, rather than Lugard's interpreter and assistant who served British colonial and commercial interests. The identity and curriculum vitae of the interpreter is set out in a biographical note by Perham, the editor of Lugard's diary kept during his two years in Uganda: "Dualla Idris (1862–) A Somali from Habr-Awwal; lived in America as a boy; 1879–84 in Congo with Stanley, and travelled to England with him; 1887–8 accompanied Count Teleki's expedition and acted as an interpreter, caravan leader and intermediary with native tribes; 1890–2 with Lugard in Uganda as interpreter and confidential assistant; a Muslim; spoke Somali, Swahili, Arabic and English fluently, and had some knowledge of a number of tribal languages of E. Africa" (Perham, 1959, p. 409).

Dualla was probably a Somalilander and Habr-Awwal not a place but his clan affiliation. Writing on the clan structure of Somaliland, Walls writes, "The Isaaq and Daarood are both composed of a number of clans. In the case of the Isaaq, these include the Haber Awal, who in turn divide into several sub-clans, the biggest of whom are Sa'ad Mussa and 'Iise Mussa" (Walls, 2009, p. 376).

Whatever his clan affiliation and home area, Dualla was available for employment in the service of Europeans. Lugard signed Dualla on in Aden in 1890 while he was en route to Mombasa, where he started the long and perilous trek to Uganda on behalf of the Imperial British East India Company. Apparently, Lugard greatly valued Dualla: "This man, whom Lugard, writing in 1893, described as 'the most energetic, valuable native I have ever met, thoroughly trust-worthy and very conscientious and willing,' spoke English, Arabic and Swahili as well as his own language" (Perham, 1956, p. 193).

Movement around East Africa was by caravan, a long and arduous journey on foot. On a caravan journey, the European leaders walked or were carried on sedan chairs by porters. They were accompanied by servants, armed guards, and porters whose jobs were to carry supplies such as food and gifts for chiefs encountered *en route*. Fabian (2000) has recounted how the arduous journeys resulted in many Europeans being "out of their minds." Lugard, however, appeared to have retained his full faculties. Perham has edited Lugard's diaries and, according one entry he assembled a large caravan that, besides Dualla, included more unnamed Somalis: "Lugard left Mombasa on 6 August 1890, starting by the Sabaki route. His caravan comprised 3 Europeans, 66 Sudanese and Somalis, 285 Swahili (porters, *askari* and servants)" (Perham, 1956, p. 206).

During the two years Lugard spent in Uganda, he managed to subdue the Ganda people and to establish British dominance. The extraordinary circumstances in which he brought about these feats were well known through European newspaper reports at the time. Lugard successfully recruited the Sudanese army made up the people who were to later to be widely known as the "Nubi," Sudanese soldiers who had been abandoned by their leader Emin Pasha, an unusual and, in the minds of Europeans, exotic character.

Emin Pasha was a German convert to Islam and the governor-general of Sudan, a region under the control of the Egyptians and therefore, ultimately, the British. In the 1880s, the uprising to the Madhi in Sudan had forced Emin Pasha and his Nubi troops (Johnson, 2009; Leopold, 2007) south into the area of Equatoria, now part of northwest Uganda. Accompanied by wives, concubines, children, and camp followers, the Nubi settled in Equatoria and lived off the land. The area of Equatoria was disputed by the Belgians under King Leopold and by the British, in the guise of the Imperial British East India Company. But Emin was not destined to remain stranded in this remote region and was rescued in a daring adventure by the journalist Henry Stanley. Emin was brought out of Equatoria, and his troops were abandoned under the control of one of their officers, Fadl el Mula Bey, and left to their own devices. Leopold surmises that "the remaining soldiers presumably exploited their superior fire-power over the local people, while at the same time becoming increasingly integrated into the host population" (Leopold, 2005, p. 121). These soldiers, known as the Nubi or Nubians, split into two groups: the main group under Fadl el Mula Bey were regarded as rebels and supporters of the Mahdists by the Europeans and a smaller group led by Salim Bey, which had been left behind by Stanley. Lugard approached Salim Bey's group in 1991 and recruited them to fight with the Ganda against the Kingdom of Bunyoro (Leopold, 2005). "It was Salim's people who were approached by Captain Frederick Lugard of the IBEAC in 1891. By then Kabaka Mwanga's kingdom of Buganda had become a prize for which European nations were fighting tooth and nail through trade, arms and religious rivalry" (Leopold, 2005, p. 123). But this did not occur without a battle, a battle where Lugard relied on his Somali interpreter, Dualla, and other Somalis. Perham, based on Lugard's diary entries, recreates the scene:

> The Somali scouts chosen for their dash and pluck for this dangerous work, which most men refused, now fell back into line. The Maxim was brought up. Lugard had, as we know, little skill and no faith where

> this clumsy proto-type of the machine-gun was concerned. Moreover the box of reserve ammunition was not there and Dualla was beside him, maddening him with his hysterical clamour. At 4 o'clock he advanced with his little group, holding fire as long as he dared until he saw some of the enemy hordes outflanking him along the hills to the left. He therefore fired the Maxim into a dense mass of the enemy. To his relief the machine responded and mowed down a group of men. (Perham, 1956, p. 270)

After this battle, Salim and his men joined Lugard and marched on Buganda. Indeed, the Nubi faction led by Salim served the British, even without pay, for a number of years (Moyse-Bartlett, 1956, p. 51). When Lugard departed from Uganda in 1892, he left behind the Nubi, a fighting force serving British interests, but took the Somalis with him. An excerpt from Lugard's reads, "I have taken a few men without arms. *All* the Somals, 39. This reduces expenditure by £1000 a year about, and they are continually sick and discontented especially now that Dualla is going, so Williams asked me to take the lot" (Perham, 1959, p. 310).

Dualla and the other Somali men serving under Lugard left Uganda in 1892 and were, therefore, not the first Somalis to settle in Uganda. Lugard (and Dualla) departed, but the changes he brought about in the Buganda kingdom still resonate today. In 1892, in the name of the Imperial British East Africa Company, Lugard imposed a settlement that included the parceling of land along religious lines. Land ownership in Buganda was granted to clans and powerful individuals who were Muslim, Protestant, and Catholic (Hanson, 2003).

Somalis and the King's African Rifles (KAR)

By the time Lugard had recruited Dualla in Aden, Britain already controlled Somaliland: "Britain signed treaties of protection with the northern clans between 1884 and 1888. This was the beginning of the British Protectorate of Somaliland" (Abdullahi, 2001, p. 20).

Aden too was under British control, as part of a plan to protect British interests in India. Thus, Abdullahi reports that "British interests on the northern Somali coast as well as the Yemeni coast were motivated by their strategic plan for their more valuable colony of India, especially after the opening of the Suez Canal in 1869. Aden in Yemen was to be a coaling station for ships en route to India and a garrison city for the troops guarding it. In turn the Somali coast was to be the feeder of the troops in mutton" (Abdullahi, 2001, p. 19).

Somaliland was governed from India and "the Indian connection continued for fourteen years after which Britain became more involved in Somaliland due to the war in the Sudan" (Abdullahi, 2001, p. 20). The war in the Sudan was with the Mahdi, which forced Emin Pasha and his army into the region that became northwest Uganda.

The Indian-Somali connection was apparent in 1890 when Lugard, traveling through Kikuyu land Kenya, found that "Grant cannot make himself understood and the Somalis only speak a few words of Hindustani except Jumar who is away with Dualla" (Perham, 1959, p. 333).

The first evidence of Somalis serving under the British in Uganda dates from 1898. The Uganda Rifles was set up by Lugard and continued after his departure. Somali soldiers who were probably recruited from British Somaliland were stationed in Uganda. As Farley notes, "The Uganda Rifles were reorganised in 1898 comprising the Indian troops and seven companies of Swahilis, Somalis and Baganda and loyal Sudanese, who were now given an increase in pay, receiving Rs.18 per month" (Farley, 1959, p. 25).

A few years later, in 1902, the King's African Rifles (KAR) was formed and the sixth battalion was made up of Somalilanders (Moyse-Bartlett, 1956). In the early days, the KAR worked toward establishing Pax Britannia in remote parts of East Africa.

In 1917, the KAR were fighting Swahili and Abyssinians in the Turkana area bordering Kenya and Uganda, and Moyse-Bartlett notes that "Rayne set out with Raikes and 50 Somalis of 'A' Company" (Moyse-Bartlett, 1956, p. 441).

In 1921 the headquarters of the fifth battalion of the KAR was transferred from Kismayu in southern Somalia to Meru in Kenya in order to be better placed to administer the Northern Frontier District of Kenya (Moyse-Bartlett, 1956, p. 456). Meru District is the main producer of Kenyan khat, but in the 1920s it had yet to become a major commercial producer (Goldsmith, 1994). The Northern Frontier District is the overwhelmingly ethnic Somali area that later voted to join Somalia (Goldsmith, 1997).

From the 1920s the Somalis serving in the KAR were organized into a camel corps. This corps was made up of 219 Somalis and 104 men from Nyasaland (Moyse-Bartlett, 1956, p. 461). In order to ensure loyalty to the British crown and not specific national interests, it was usual to have battalions made up of more than one nationality or ethnic group.

During the 1930s, at the height of the world depression, the KAR was reorganized to have bases in the Turkana region (Lake Rudolf), in Uganda (Bombo), and three bases in Kenya: "It was expected that the Northern Brigade would station one battalion on the frontier west of Lake Rudolf, with a company at Bombo for internal security, one battalion on the frontier east of Lake Rudolf, with headquarters and one company at Meru with a company at Wajir, and the reserve battalion at Nairobi" (Moyse-Bartlett, 1956, p. 463).

In 1935 the Italian invasion of Abyssinia (now called Ethiopia) from Eritrea and Somaliland destabilized the region (Moyse-Bartlett, 1956, p. 466), and in 1938, plans for the defense of Kenya in the event of an invasion by Italy were drawn up: "For the immediate defence of Kenya in the event of a war with Italy, all frontier detachments were to be withdrawn from the line Wajir-Marsabit; 5 KAR was to mobilize at Isiolo, 4 KAR to move to Garissa, with two companies at Malindi, 3KAR to mobilize at Nairobi and send a company to Mombasa for local defence" (Moyse-Bartlett, 1956, p. 471).

It was during World War II that Somalis serving in the KAR started causing trouble. Hence, according to Moyse-Bartlett (1956), in 1943 there was unrest in Moshi, Tanzania, caused by the desertions of Somali troops in 71KAR. The trouble spread: "As in all Somali units, however, a spirit of unrest had now developed, caused mainly by the fear that Somali troops would be treated on the same lines as other Africans. It was this that made so many Somalis reluctant to serve outside their country and gave rise to spasmodic requests to for the grant of Asian status" (Moyse-Bartlett, 1956, p. 577).

In 1944, while World War II was still in progress, the Camel Corps was disbanded after looting of arms and ammunition at Burao, Somalia. In all, 140 men went missing (Moyse-Bartlett, 1956, p. 578).

Hence, from the work of Perham on Lugard (1959) and Moyse-Bartlett on the KAR (1965), the role of Somalis in the British army in Eastern Africa can be traced. As the previous quotations demonstrate, during the first half of the twentieth century, Somalis in the employ of the British served first in the Uganda Rifles and then from 1902 in its successor, the KAR, and were stationed in Uganda and Kenya. During these forty-six years, from 1898 to 1944, there were two world wars and numerous regional wars where the European colonial powers jostled for power in Ethiopia, Eritrea, Somalia, Somaliland, Tanzania, and beyond. The Somalis were stationed and lived alongside men from across southern and eastern Africa. However, even as the Somalis were serving in a force called the King's *African* Rifles, they perceived themselves as separate from other Africans.

The Nubi troops, or the Sudanese, as they referred to themselves, were also beset by identity issues and in 1940 drew upon the circumstance of Somalis to argue their case. Johnson (2009) reproduces a portion of a letter from Union of Sudanese, sent to His Excellency, the governor in Council, Nairobi: "The Sudanese are and have been for centuries, Mohamedans speaking as their mother tongue the Arabic language, living in their social economy like other Mohamedans and it is submitted that they should be treated like other Mohamedan Communities, viz. that for taxation purposes they be classed as non-natives and pay as Arabs, or Somalis pay—there would be no objection in principle to paying as Indians or other Asiatics. It is not the amount of tax, but the principle, which is felt to be irksome" (Johnson, 2009, p. 123).

In an endnote of the paper Johnson is dismissive of Somali claims for nonnative status: "Despite the direct comparisons the Sudanese made with the Somalis, as fellow Muslims their circumstances were fundamentally different, as Sudanese arguments for special status rested primarily on their military service and the loss of their homeland while in British service, and only secondarily on religion. Somali claims to non-native status seemed to have rested on a feeling of innate racial superiority" (Johnson, 2009, p. 129).

Changing Somali Ethnic Identity

Somalis, then, have a long history of disassociating themselves from other Africans, and the problems of the KAR are just one manifestation of the tangled threads of Somali identity. The proximity of the Somali coast to Arabia, their adherence to Islam, and their distinctive appearance have all caused ambiguity over the origins and ethnic identity of the Somalis. The colonial racial ideologies that produced the Hamitic myth of separate origins for some Africans fuelled the Somali sense of separateness and superiority of other Africans. Abdullahi sums up the colonial theorizing on race as follows: "Early theories mostly speculated on a view called the Hamitic myth under which Somalis were characterized, by virtue of not closely corresponding to a standardized image of the African, as being relative newcomers to Africa whose ancestors crossed over from Asia and mixed with the former inhabitants. This was a view based on the nineteenth-century European view of inhabitants of Africa as a monolithic group; any variation between African groups was then to be explained in terms of African migrations" (Abdullahi, 2001, p. 11–12).

The Hamtic myth, explicitly or implicitly, allows writing on Somalis, and their neighbors the Ethiopians, to be treated as Asians: "Orientalism is a term usually applied to Asiatic cultures, but Somalia and Ethiopia have often been lumped together with 'oriental' societies, in opposition to their 'Black' or 'Bantu' African neighbors" (Ahmed, 1995, p. 160).

Thus, Richard Burton, the great Victorian explorer and linguist, wrote about the Somali region as part of the Orient, an archaic term usually denoting Asia. In *First Footsteps in Africa*, Richard Burton "contributed much to orientalist scholarship and directly included Somalia as part of the orient" (Ahmed, 1995, p. 158).

Ahmed cites the following from *First Footsteps in Africa* as an example of Orientalism: "Daughters as usual in Oriental countries, do not 'count' as part of the family: they are however utilized by the father, who disposes of them to those who can increase his wealth and importance" (Burton, 1856, p. 86; cited by Ahmed, 1995, p. 158).

Early colonial scholarship resonated with Somali notions of identity that typically portrayed Somalis as seeing themselves as a homogeneous ethnic group with a common culture based on nomadic pastoralist and a common religion, Islam. Claims by some clans that they were descended from Arab forbearers allowed, and allows, many Somali to consider themselves Arab (Mukhtar, 1995).

Just as further south along the East African coast, the Swahili posed problems for colonial classifiers but were often accorded Arab status (Caplan, 2007). The Somali wanted similar "privileges," and in the 1920s, Somalis insisted on their own racial classification. Besteman notes, "During the 1920s, for example, there was a great effort on the part of Somalis and British administrators to have the classification of natives into racial categories revised so that Somalis could be categorized as Europeans or Asians rather then 'black natives,' as Somalis considered themselves derived from Arabia, not Africa" (Besteman, 1995, p. 50).

Being Arab, and therefore Asian, was also a status issue. Declich notes that Hersi, in a 1977 thesis on "The Arab Factor in Somali History," "has shown how, under British colonial rule, Somalis preferred an identity associated with the higher status ascribed to 'Asians' over that associated with 'Africans'" (Declich, 1995, p. 192; Hersi A. A. PhD thesis 1977 UCLA).

Hence, throughout the twentieth century, Somalis have been promoting their ethnic identity as Arabs and as a homogeneous people in terms of ethnicity. "Too often the people have been represented as homogeneous—the ideal nation-state. The central government actively promoted the idea that the Somali Republic was the most homogeneous in Africa and one of the few in the world" (Abdullahi, 2001, p. 7).

Contributors to *The Invention of Somalia*, edited by Ahmed (1995), seek to set the record straight on the diverse origins and livelihoods of Somalis by discussing the identity of the agriculturalists of the Juba Valley and the traders and maritime farers of the long coastline of the Indian Ocean that stretches from Djibouti to Kenya. As Abdullahi points out, "The Somalis are a people of a predominately pastoralist culture, even if their ancient cities have maritime traditions spanning several millennia" (Abdullahi, 2001, p. 8).

The notion of the Somali ideal nation-state, indeed of the state at all, has been illusive since the 1990s. However, the Somaliland progress toward peace and stability has been substantial. Yet it is a country that has largely failed to attain international recognition (Walls, 2009). From the late nineteenth century, the Somalis were divided into five groups: the northern Somalilanders, their neighbors in French-controlled Djoubuti, the southern inhabitants of Somalia, the Somalis of the Ogaden region of Ethiopia, and the Somalis of northern Kenya. Most of the Somalis serving in the KAR came from British-controlled Somaliland. They shared the common Somali self-perception of being set apart from the Africans with whom they served.

SOMALI IDENTITY IN UGANDA

Somalis in Uganda have turned the conventional notion of Somali identity on its head and are campaigning for recognition as an indigenous tribe. They also want to be granted land and, in making their case, they compare their circumstances to the Nubi, fellow former members of the KAR. The Ugandan Somali community is correct in claiming that they came originally as members of the KAR. Upon discharge from the KAR, Somali men were allowed to settle where they wanted in British East Africa, and some set up home in Kenya and Uganda. Their campaign for recognition as Ugandans centers on their claim to be indigenous Ugandans, a claim that, in turn, rests largely on the recorded presence of Dualla Idris, the interpreter for Lugard, in Uganda in 1890. In February 2009, interviews that I conducted with members of the Somali community revealed their aspirations to be recognized as indigenous Ugandans. I met Abdi above a shopping complex that also housed the Somalilander-run money transfer business, Dahabshil. Abdi explained that the first Somali was Lugards's interpreter, and that other Somalis came to Uganda in the 1890s as members of the KAR and then stayed. He had also heard of the Camel Corps, although he did not know any details. The Somalis have a sense of grievance because they were not allocated land. Under the British, Abdi explained, the Nubi were allocated land at Bombo and Entebbe, but the Somali were given nothing. Many Somalis live in the Kampala District of Mengo near the Kabaka's palace and the parliament of the Buganda kingdom because that is where they congregated, not because there was a special allocation of land for the Somalis.

Next I met Hassan, the proprietor of a bonded warehouse for imported cars, and a man considered within his community to be a knowledgeable Somali elder. Hassan reiterated that Somalis, unlike the Nubi, were given no allocation of land in Uganda. However, they had been granted, along with Pakistanis, the main mosque in Nakesero, at the heart of the commercial district of Kampala.

The process of parceling out land in Buganda, started by Captain Lugard in 1892 in the name of the Imperial British East Africa Company, is still causing friction in the twenty-first century. Much of the Buganda land carved up in 1900 (Hanson, 2003; Kasozi, 1996) is still controlled by the Buganda kingdom. The Somalis point out that Nubi discharged from the KAR were allocated land in the towns of Bombo, Entebbe, and Hoima, while they got nothing. This is indeed the case: "Very many of the [Nubi] soldiers were absorbed into civilian life, and their followers remained in large settlements which are still very evident, notably at Bombo, Hoima and Entebbe" (Farley, 1959, p. 25).

The Somalis are seeking land within the kingdom of Buganda, but for nearly thirty years the Buganda king, the Kabaka, was absent from Uganda. Under the leadership of Milton Obote, and with Idi Amin as his henchman, the Kabaka was driven out in 1966 and the kingdom of Buganda abolished. President Museveni restored the Kabakaship in 1994, and the Somalis took this opportunity to write to the Kabaka requesting that they be granted land. The Kabaka did not reply.

The second point of concern for Ugandan Somalis is their status in the country and their right to Ugandan passports. According to Hassan at the bonded warehouse, in the 1960 constitution, a few years before independence was achieved, Somalis were automatically counted as citizens of Uganda if they were born in the country. Museveni came to power in 1986, and it was under his rule that the government changed the constitution so the Somalis are now no longer treated in the same way as indigenous Ugandans. At one point, their Ugandan passports were revoked. A member of the Somali community told me that they had considered employing a lawyer, as he put it, to "sue the government." Rashid referred me to a lawyer who had been retained by the Somali community. The lawyer explained that the key issue was whether the Ugandan government counts Somalis as indigenous Ugandans. The attorney general had given an opinion that Somalis could be citizens by birth, like other nonindigenous Ugandans. After this opinion had been expressed, there was no need for any court case. The attorney general's opinion had cleared for Somalis to apply for Ugandan passports, and each individual would have a file in the relevant office. The lawyer explained that the system was not open to abuse because a recently arrived refugees would not have a file or would have left any trail of being a Ugandan.

Ugandan Somalis and Khat

Prominent Ugandan Somalis claim links to Lugard via Dualla and to the KAR, but not to khat, as part of their heritage or culture. It does seem to be the case that khat use was uncommon or nonexistent in Uganda at the start of the twentieth century. Memoirs and travelers' accounts of Uganda in the late nineteenth and early twentieth centuries make no mention of khat, although they do frequently mention alcohol and sometimes cannabis use by caravan porters. Lugard does not mention khat use by Dualla or other Somalis in his company or by caravan porters. Similarly, Bell (1949), in his sometimes gory account of elephant hunting with a large caravan of men in the 1920s in northeastern Uganda, refers to alcohol but not khat. A very different character, the missionary doctor Albert Cook (1945), traveled extensively in Uganda from 1897 to 1940, but *Uganda Memories* does not include khat. Similarly, Rockel, in his study of caravans as "carriers of culture" (2006), makes no mention of khat, although he reports that caravan porters transporting ivory to the coast indulged in cannabis and alcohol use.

Harvesting Wild Khat

The first Somalis settling in Uganda probably came from Somaliland as members of the KAR. Upon discharge they were free to settle anywhere in British East Africa. They sent for wives from home and set up businesses in the transport and catering sectors across Uganda. Although Ugandan Somalis shy away from embracing khat as part of their ethnic identity and culture, most Ugandans assume that Somalis introduced khat consumption to Uganda. The idea that Somalis discovered khat chewing and that it is indigenous to their country probably gained credibility in Uganda because Somalis were largely responsible for the spread of khat there. The oral histories I collected from elderly Somalis who had served in the KAR and from their descendents confirm their early role in promoting khat production. For example, Rashid, an elder sitting in "Little Mogadishu" in the Kampala area of Mengo, remembers how he and his fellow Somali khat chewers would pay local Ganda men to go into the bush to collect wild khat for them. In the town of Mbale in eastern Uganda, near the border of Kenya, I was told by two young Somali men that their grandfathers used to chew khat harvested from the wild area of the mountains of Karamoja, lying to the north of Mbale. A Somali called Mohammed Musa used to bring the khat to Mbale, but it was for Somali and Yemeni consumption only.

Somalis also settled in the Karamoja region, the area where, in the 1920s, large-scale elephant hunting was continuing and where Ethiopian incursions, including slave raids from the north, were threatening Pax Britannia (Merard, 2007). Bell, the elephant hunter, does not refer to khat consumption in the area, but it was certainly growing wild in the region. Mahmoud is a Somali Ugandan khat trader, who was born in the trading center of Moroto in Karamoja, with relatives in Nairobi. He explained to me that his father came to Uganda with the KAR in the 1940s and settled in Moroto. Somalis in the area did not keep animals because the local Karimojong pastoralists would steal them, so Somalis became business people instead. When the Somalis first arrived in Moroto they found Yemeni and Indian traders already there. It was Yemenis and Somalis who discovered the wild khat trees and taught local people to first harvest and, later, cultivate khat.

Adam, another Ugandan Somali khat trader from Karamoja, claims to know when and how Somalis started extracting khat from the wilds of Karamoja. In 1943 a Somalilander was stationed in the British army at Morita at the base of Mount Kadam. He recognized khat trees growing wild and taught the local Karimojong pastoralists about it. Adam was vague about names, and the information is almost certainly repeated hearsay. However, during a visit in March 2009 to the remote trading center of Namalu, near Mount Kadam, interviews with local men who harvest and sell wild khat indicate that there may be truth in Adam's version of events. They explained that Morita is a place at the back of the Mount Kadam, near Nakapirpirit, where there used to be Somali shops, police barracks, and an airstrip.

Namalu is the location of a trading post, administrative center, and Italian mission. In March 2009 it was busy with truckers delivering food aid to the drought-stricken Karimojong. There was a café selling quite a range of dishes and crowded with truck drivers. Outside were youth selling ***namalu*** khat from a kiosk. I talked to an elderly Karimojong man, Sagadi Iddi Juma, who said that he had been chewing khat with Somalis since 1962. In fact, consumption does not necessarily lead to knowledge about khat; he was not particularly well informed, but several young Karimojong traders who sat in on the interview contributed information that eluded their elder. The group said that khat is harvested from the wild in three places in the Karamoja region: Kadam Mountain, Napak Mountain near Iriri, and near Kaabong in the mountains further north. Sagadi added that khat with red leaves also grows on Mount Moroto, but it is not harvested because it gives the user a headache, and there was one person, "an Arab called Amoudi," who used to chew it. Sagadi and the assembled group of traders were of the opinion that Somalis from Kenya "showed us the khat that God, and not the Somalis, put on the mountain." Sagadi, in order to bring his point home, recounted a version of the "happy goat" story (Rushby, 1999).

East African Khat Connections

According to the Ugandan Somali men I interviewed between 2007 and 2009, other Somalis, unconnected to the KAR, were also living in working in Kampala and across Uganda from the early twentieth century onward. They came to trade in livestock and in the meat and skins derived from the goats and cattle that they had herded; they also set up butcher shops, general stores, and cafés. For example, Abdullahi, one of the elders of the Ugandan Somali community, reports that his ethnic-Somali father came from Ethiopia to Uganda as a goat trader and butcher. His father was familiar with khat and told Abdullahi that, when he would chew khat at fifteen-years-old, it would make him "lazy and dizzy."

Across Uganda, Somalis are most well known as transporters of people, goods, and fuel. Wealthy Ugandan Somalis own large bus companies and a string of fuel service stations, as well as being importers of used, reconditioned vehicles usually from Japan. Less well-off Somali men often work as long-distance drivers, an occupation ideally suited to khat chewing and, according to many Ugandan, the literal carriers of the khat habit. These Somali men may have brought the khat chewing habit to Uganda from Somaliland, which is situated near the major khat-producing region of Hararge in Ethiopia (Gebissa, 2004). Khat consumption is now widespread in Somaliland; a study on khat consumption in Somaliland found that 30 percent of Hargeisa residents chewed khat. According to the Somali National Well Doing Organization (SOVOREDO, 2002), the first time khat was used in Somaliland was in 1910, when it was imported from Ethiopia and Yemen (Anderson et al., 2007, p. 77). However, khat use in Somalia and Somaliland, at least among adherents of the Qadhiri brotherhood, dates from the nineteenth century.

There is also a strong Kenyan connection between khat and Somalis. Many Somali men serving in the KAR had been stationed in Kenya, and some of those in Isiolo, near the main khat-growing area of Meru. One office bearer of the Ugandan Somali community claimed that retired Somalis from the KAR in Isiolo had brought khat seedlings from there to Uganda. Another successful businessman said he had moved to Uganda from Isiolo in the 1940s, an area "given to Darood/Haarti and Isaaq Somali clans" by the British colonial government of the Kenya. He added that khat was taken to Uganda from Kenya on donkeys by Somali traders, who were interested in ivory and other goods. Isiolo is the first place outside the immediate growing area of Meru in northern Kenya that the khat producers marketed their khat. This commodification of khat first occurred in the late nineteenth century, starting in 1885, according to Goldsmith, who traces the history of the marketing of Kenyan *miraa*, as khat is known there, in detail (1994, p. 101). Goldsmith links the growth of Isiolo to the growing trade of Somalis livestock and skins for Meru miraa in the early decades of the twentieth century: "The Somali ascendancy in the cattle trade spurred the growth of Isiolo town, on the interface of the highlands and arid regions to the north, making it the major commercial administrative center for the Meru's pastoral neighbors. The Somalis were relatively recent arrivals in the area, but their appetite for miraa is longstanding and legendary. Isiolo thus naturally became the major destination for Meru miraa, and became the major re-export market for miraa sold in northern Kenya and beyond" (Goldsmith, 1994, p. 102).

The Meru khat market continued to grow and, during World War II, was further stimulated by "the quartering of Somali soldiers in Nanyuki and Isiolo" (Goldsmith, 1994, p. 102). These soldiers were members of the KAR and some subsequently settled in Uganda. From at least the 1940s, Kenyan khat from Meru was imported to Kampala. Supplies came in by road and later by plane. "Little Mogadishu" in the Mengo area of Kampala is still the only place in Uganda where expensive Kenyan khat from Meru is sold. However, in the 1930s, khat bushes appeared in Kampala, and these plants appear to have been imported from Meru by a Somali.

THE KIBULI CONNECTION

Kampala is a city of hills. The Kampala neighborhood, Kibuli, is perched on a hill overlooking the central business district. A white and green mosque declares the nature of the area. Kibuli was part of the land granted to Mbogo, a Muslim member of Ganda royal family under the 1900 agreement between the British and the Ganda that parceled out land in Buganda. "Mbogo built his headquarters at Kibuli on part of the land he was given for his collaboration" (Kasozi, 1996, p. 2). Kibuli is a major center of Islamic and secular learning, rivaled only by the Mosque and Islamic institutions located at Old Kampala, on another hill overlooking the city.

The Muslim leaders in Kibuli are linked through kinship to both the Ganda royal family and Ugandan khat production. Indeed, Kibuli is the source of the khat plants that are now grown commercially in southern Uganda. Knowledgeable khat traders in Kampala point to Kibuli as the original source of khat in the country. They mention two names, Mtajazzi as the first person to grow khat and Sheikh Semakula as the pioneer of commercial production. There are several versions of how Mtajazzi first got a hold of khat plants. The most popular version has Mtajazzi going as an Islamic scholar to Zanzibar and bringing back khat seedlings. Other stories recount how he returned to Kampala from Yemen, or even Cairo, carrying khat seedlings on long dhow voyages across the Indian Ocean. Such informants have missed the crucial facts that khat requires altitude to thrive (Gebissa, 2004; Maunda, 1999), and that the Zanzibar town is on a low-lying island, that Cairo is also low lying, and that khat seedling are unlikely to survive a long sea voyage.

In the 1920s Mtajazzi came to the Kampala from the Comoro Islands, part of the Swahili world where many migrants from Yemen had settled. He married the sister of Sheikh Semakula, who was still alive in 2004 when I met her. She recalled that they had khat planted in the garden at home in Kibuli and that Somalis came to visit. Some of Mtajazzi's descendants still live in the section of Kibuli now called Mtajazzi but do not recall many details about how khat came to their neighborhood. However, in 2007, Mtajazzi's son, Omar Mukassa, a journalist, approached on my behalf his very elderly aunt, Mwanaidi

Mzee, who did remember who had first brought khat to Kibuli. The story Mwanaidi told involves a Somali.

During the 1930s, khat came from Meru in Kenya to Kampala by train. Somali businessmen also used the train to come from Kenya for trade in beads, pearls, and other goods. They used to bring their own khat for personal use. Mtajazzi mosque was built in 1933. Around 1935 Ibrahim Mogan came to Kibuli as a friend of Mtajazzi. He was a dealer in skins and hides and lived in the Kampala area called Mukalitunzi (meaning "in the pine trees") near the commercial area of Kisenyi where foreigners congregated. Mogan spoke Arabic and Swahili as well as Somali. He was also the consul or ambassador for the Somali community in Uganda.

Mogan said to Mtajazzi, "The land is fertile. I will bring khat to plant. In Somalia we have khat." He brought the seedlings by train packed in earth in a wooden box about two meters long and one meter wide. The seedlings were planted behind the house among the banana plantation and next to the mosque.

In the 1930s distant relatives of Mtajazzi came to stay with him. When they went home they took khat seedlings and planted them in Kitola, to the east of Kampala.

Among Mogan's circle there were Arabs called Binanam and Mohammed Nashir, who were also in the skins and hides business. They were friends of the Ganda prince, Badru Kakungulu, who lived in Kibuli, and with Mttajazzi, who was connected to the prince by marriage. The group of Somali and Arab traders visited Mtajazzi in Kibuli regularly. Somalis from Kisenyi would come to Mtajazzi and buy khat for their own use. Then they started paying the gardeners to slip them extra supplies that they could sell to fellow Somalis and to Arabs in Mukalitunzi, which was a growing settlement where traders from Kenya lived. Mtajazzi decided to uproot the khat. Apart from the Somalis, most Muslims were saying the khat was makruu, meaning a practice not preferred by Islam.

In the 1940s Sheikh Semakula came from the Muslim-dominated area of Butambala to Kibuli. His sister was married to Mtajazzi. Semakula was the Imam leading the prayers at the main mosque at Kibuli and later became the Mufti, dealing with Islamic legal affairs for Uganda. His brother-in-law, Mtajazzi, gave him khat seedlings and he took them to Butambala. Every Friday Semakula came for lunch with Mtajazzi, who told his lunch guests that, in his opinion, khat was mkruu. But Semakula decided to continue promoting khat cultivation. Somalis were now referred to Butambala for khat supplies.

In the 1940s Ibrahim Mogan married in Kampala but fathered no children. He fell sick and decided to go back to Somalia. He set off with his Burundian servant but died en route when he was more than half way home. The servant took Mogan's body to be buried with his people. He then returned to Kampala with Mogan's bankbook. Mogan had left most of his wealth to his servant, and Mtajazzi helped him access the money. The servant then returned safely to Burundi. "We have family there and they informed us that he arrived home," Mtajazzi is reported to have said.

Many of the details of this story have been impossible to verify. Why did Ibrahim Mogan import khat by rail, probably from Kenya? He was perhaps unaware that khat grew wild across Uganda, or perhaps he preferred Meru khat to anything that Uganda could produce from its wilderness areas. So it seems Mogan transported seedlings by rail from Kenya and gave them to Mtajazzi, a leading Muslim, who in turn gave seedlings to Sheikh Semakula. Yet nobody in the Ugandan Somali community has heard of Ibrahim Mogan, and nobody knows anything about consular ties in the 1930s and 1940s, formal or informal, with either Somaliland or Somalia. There are no records and people's memories, apart from Mwanaidi's, do not stretch to Ibrahim Mogan. What is certain is that khat was planted in Mtajazzi's home in Kibuli and that Semakula took seedlings to Butambala in the 1940s. Abdullahi, a leader of the Somali community, said that the name Mogan indicated that a Somalilander of Isaaq clan, probably living in Kenya but originally from Hargeisa.

It is, however, certain that production of khat in central Uganda stems from seedlings brought by Mtajazzi who lived in the Muslim enclave of Kibuli in Kampala. In the 1940s Sheikh Semakula, who was the brother-in-law of Mtajazi, took seedlings and planted in Butambala. From there, khat spread to farms across the country, the subject of Chapter 4.

Chapter 3

Yemeni Migrants

Traversing Forest, Mountain, and Desert

Somalis were not the only migrants to promote khat production and consumption in Uganda. Yemeni migrants, many working as traders of skins and hides, spread across the country and, in the mountains they traversed, identified wild-growing khat. These men had moved from one poor Arabian country, Yemen, which was controlled by Britain, to another part of the British Empire in Africa. Most analyses of migrants within the British Empire consider the situation of people that have moved from a poor country to Britain a much richer one (Gardner, 2002; Hall, 1990; Jenkins, 2004). The movement of people from a poor to richer countries, often to the former colonial power, usually leaves the migrants socially and economically disadvantaged. Yemenis in Uganda attained economic success and high social status, while men settling in Kenya succesfully integrated with the Swahili. As Yemenis forged new cultural identities in East Africa, they used khat consumption as an ethnic marker.

Yemeni Immigration to East Africa

While the Somali migrants who settled in Uganda came from other parts of the East African region, and many first came to the country in the service of the British as members of the King's African Rifles (KAR), the situation of the Yemenis was different. For Yemenis arriving in East Africa the physical journey and cultural distance was longer than for Somalis, who are indigenous to the region—periodic claims to be Arabs or Asiatic, notwithstanding (Declich, 1995, p. 192). By contrast, the Yemenis who crossed the Indian Ocean and traveled into

Uganda were operating without the institutional support or hindrance of the British colonial administration.

Trade routes between ports of the Indian Ocean have been operating for thousands of years, and there is a long tradition of *dhow* (traditional timber ships) travel, from Yemen to ports in India and the east coast of Africa and the Dutch East Indies. Some traders settled in their ports of call. In addition, between the thirteenth and eighteenth centuries, Yemeni individuals claiming descent from the Prophet Mohammed settled in East Africa, where they were accorded high social status (Boxberger, 2002). Hence, Yemenis, particularly those from Hadhramawt in the south, have a long history of emigration (Boxberger, 2002) and have become part of host societies in as varied settings as Singapore and the steel mills of northeastern United States (Clarence-Smith, 2002). In Britain there are longstanding Yemeni communities in Cardiff, the East End of London, northeast England, and Sheffield (Halliday, 1992).

Using their kin-based and social networks, Yemeni individuals, usually young men, arrived at the East African ports of Lamu, Mombasa, and Dar es Salaam.

From the nineteenth century, when levels of migration from the Hadhramawt region of Yemen increased, young men arriving in ports such as Mombasa and Zanzibar were met by Yemenis who had already migrated or by their descendents. This type of migration can best be understood as a form of "network-mediated chain migration" (Brettell, 2008). Economic theories of migration focus on "push" and "pull" factors (Hollifield, 2008), and indeed, in economic terms, the reasons for emigration from Hadhramawt were linked to two major "push" factors: many people were poor and struggled to make a living on drought-prone marginal agricultural land, and insecurity caused by a series of tribal wars in Hadhramawt from the late nineteenth to early twentieth centuries forced some to leave their lands (Boxberger, 2002). The "pull" factor was much weaker, as life in East Africa was tough and, although many prospered, others ended up working as manual laborers. Indeed, richer Hadhrami migrants tended to settle in the Dutch East Indies or Singapore (Boxberger, 2002).

Hence, unlike African and Asian migrants arriving in Europe or North America in the twentieth century, Yemenis migrating to East Africa traveled from one poor region formerly under British rule to another. In the nineteenth century, many Yemenis, mostly young men traveling alone, made their way to East Africa. At that time, the Omanis controlled the port city-state of Zanzibar and much of the East African coast and dominated, along with Indian vessels, the

Indian Ocean dhow trade. Many Hadhrami emigrants also arrived at the Swahili towns Lamu and Mambrui on what became the Kenya coast. Hence, according to Clarence-Smith: "The Lamu archipelago, outside Omani control until the 1820s and a local centre of boat building, was probably the chief centre of Hadhrami sail shipping" (Clarence-Smith, 2002, p. 253).

As Clarence-Smith explains, Hadhrami craft from the ports of al-Mullaka and al-Shihr also sailed to Zanzibar, the center of the Swahili world at that time: "Dhows from al-Mullaka and al-Shihr brought emigrants, salt fish, salt and onions to Zanzibar in the 1840s, calling in various ports on the way down the coast. They returned with slaves, millet, sesame and sesame oil" (Clarence-Smith, 2002, p. 253).

Hadhrami immigration peaked between 1880 and 1950, the period that Pax Britannia made travel from Arabia to East Africa easier. Thus de Vere Allen writes, "Immigrants from Arabia, from Aden and Hadramawt in particular, flocked to east Africa at an unprecedented rate between c.1880 and c.1950, when transport was cheap and Pax Britannia assured them reasonable security and a better chance of making a living than in their homelands" (de Vere Allen, 1993, p. 240).

De Vere Allen estimates that eight thousand Hadhrami immigrants a year arrived in Swahili ports during this period (de Vere Allen, 1993, p. 241). The vast majority of these immigrants were young men, often unaccompanied (Boxberger, 2002). Until 1967, migrants from South Yemen were able to travel using British colonial passports (Halliday, 1992, p. 76). However, not all those on the move had the correct paper work. Indeed, the number of immigrants from Aden, Hadhramawt, and Yemen is impossible to calculate as many of those immigrants, including some from Oman, slipped in unregistered, as an interview I conducted in Uganda in 2005 illustrates:

Mohammed Ali (Clay) came from Muscat on a dhow when he was about ten years old. They sailed to Mombasa, and when he came ashore, the ship's crew told the authorities that he was the captain's son, so he did not need papers. He went to Karikor in Nairobi where some of his relatives lived. There, he worked making *halwa* (sweetmeats). This was the time of the MauMau uprising. From Nairobi, Clay went into Jinja and from there to Kampala.

Another elderly man recounted how as a young migrant he had traveled from Sana'a, Yemen, to Uganda. In 1946, when he was sixteen years old, Saleh went to the port of Aden. He requested a pass from the British authorities to stay in East Africa, but he traveled originally to Zambia. He went back to Uganda but was caught in Tororo in eastern Uganda without a pass and was told to leave the country. But he slipped away and went to the nearby towns Mbale and then Soroti.

Thus, from the late nineteenth century until the mid-twentieth century, combined "push" factors of poverty and war accelerated the movement of single young Yemeni men who set out to start a new East African life. But the push-pull theory, with its underlying emphasis on economic notions of fleeing poverty to seek fortune (Stark, 1991), cannot explain the success of Yemeni migration to East Africa. Mass migration by Yemenis to East Africa was made possible by the long-established networks that stretched across the Indian Ocean and inland to the Great Lakes region. As Massey et al. conclude, networks not only facilitate but also perpetuate migration, as "each act of migration itself creates the social structure needed to sustain it. Every new migrant reduces the costs of subsequent migration for a set of friends and relatives, and some of these people are thereby induced to migrate, which further expands the set of people with ties abroad" (Massey et al., 1993, p. 447; cited by Brettell, 2008).

Marriage and Integration with the Swahili

Prior to the nineteenth century Arabian immigrants, mostly from Yemen, arrived on the East African coast in small numbers and were absorbed into Swahili society. Some were Islamic scholars or claimed descent from the Prophet Mohammed (*Sharif*). These immigrants were mostly male and married local women. Some descents of these immigrants achieved high status, but they only gained this status after they had been thoroughly integrated into the Swahili cutlure, as de Vere allen explains: "Available evidence indicates that, although Arab immigrants to the Swahili world (and especially sharifs) may have had a better-than-average chance of achieving patrician status, only a limited number of sharifs and a few shaykhs from Yemen and Hadramawt actually settled, and with only one exception their descendents were all well and truly Swahilised before they were accepted as rulers. Otherwise Arab immigration was probably negligible in most areas before c.1700, and did not really assume significant numerical proportions until 1880 or 1900" (de Vere Allen, 1993, p. 245).

In the twentieth century, many Yemeni seamen settling in Cardiff and South Shields in Britain married local Welsh and English women. They were conforming to a pattern long established in East Africa, where the vast majority of migrants were men. These Yemeni men, mostly from Hadhramawt, married local women. According to Le Guennec-Coppens, "In most cases the first to arrive had to contract alliances outside their own group, whereas in the Hadramaut a rigorous tribal endogamy was imposed by the society's hierarchical system. Of necessity, they married women of different origin and status; in order to achieve their identity they naturally preferred alliances with Hadrami women, even if of mixed blood or humbler origin, but they often married Africans and sometimes slaves" (Le Guennec-Coppens, 1989, p. 190).

Male migrants joined a network that linked people of Yemeni origin along the East African coast, as well as inland (Le Guennec-Coppens, 1989). Although marginalized from Swahili society at first, Yemenis integrated quickly due to their hard work and adaptability. The new migrants married and settled down in Swahili towns.

Le Guennec-Coppans analyzed the marriage partners of members of ten East African Hadhrami lineages (1991). She found that half of the 385 marriages were endogamous to the Hadhami lineages. However, there were differences between the type of marriages contracted by men and women of Hadhrami descent. For men, 44 percent of marriages were endogamous, while 63 percent of women made endogamous matches (Le Guennec-Coppens, 1991, pp. 158–159). These Hadhrami migrants also learned Swahili and dropped the use of Arabic, to the extent that few of their children were able to speak their "father tongue," the first language of their fathers. Swahili, the first language of their mothers and the main local lingua franca, became their main medium of communication. In addition, they contributed to the "transformation of their adopted country's civilisation" (Le Guennec-Coppens, 1989, p. 191), or as Trimmingham had it, Hadhramis were "responsible for remoulding Swahili culture and imprinting it with the dominant stamp it bears today" (1971, p. 22).

Yemeni and Hadhrami immigrants settling on the east coast of Africa became Swahili, if not in their own lifetime, then within a generation or two. They were able to do this because the Swahili are not made up of one ethnic group but of peoples from diverse origins who have adopted the Swahili language and culture (Beckerleg, 2004; Caplan, 2007; Mazrui & Shariff, 1994). Hadhrami immigrants to the Swahili towns can be divided into two broad groups: high status Sharif families who claimed descent from the prophet and impoverished economic migrants who, as laborers from insignificant family backgrounds, were assigned low status within the Swahili social hierarchy. But once settled along the Kenya coast in Lamu, Mambrui, or Mombasa, "how the newcomer's social status increased or diminished thereafter was a question of personal qualities tempered by luck" (de Vere Allen, 1993, p. 247). During the nineteenth century the Hadhrami immigrants to Lamu and other Kenya coastal towns were sometimes referred to as Mshihiri, a low status person within the Swahili social hierarchy. According to Madan's Standard Swahili-English Dictionary (1939, p. 302), Mshihiri is "an Arab from Sheher in South Arabia, usually engaged in manual trades and labour, fishing," and so on. However, not all the immigrants from Shihr were of humble or impoverished origins: "Shatry is the main carpet retailer in Mombasa. His family has been in the business of selling carpets and chests longer than any other family in Kenya. His great grandfather was born in Shihr in the Hadhramaut, and so was his great grandmother who claimed a pedigree all the way back to the days of Mohammed in the seventh century. Shatry calls himself a sheriff, that is, he claims that he is a blood descendent of the Prophet Mohammed. He is very proud of this distinction, and one often sees men come up and kiss his hand in respect " (Martin & Martin, 1978, p. 54).

These days the term "Mshihri" has fallen into disuse and most people of Yemeni and Hadhrami origin in Kenya have attained high status within the Swahili hierarchy, regardless of whether they claim descent from the Prophet Mohammed. Some Hadhrami and Omani Arabs work as laborers, porters, or drivers' assistants, known in East Africa as "spanner boys." One Ugandan of Hadhrami ancestry expressed his shock at having observed poor Arabs carrying out manual labor during a visit to Mombasa in Kenya. Many Swahili of Hadhrami origin have become prosperous Kenyan business people. As Le Guennec-Coppens points out, "They have chosen a new economic orientation, commerce, which has largely contributed to their success: farmers have become grocers, nomads have become butchers" (Le Guennec-Coppens, 1989, p. 190). But, according to Le Guennec-Coppens, the price of immersion in Swahili society was the breaking of links with Hadhramawt: "In order to achieve their social and cultural integration as quickly and as completely as possible within two or three generations, they have cut off all relationships with their mother country" (Le Guennec-Coppens, 1989, p. 191).

It is indeed the case that most second- or third-generation Hadhrami in Kenya do not speak Arabic with any fluency and often have no ties with their fatherland. However, in Malindi (Kenya), an elderly Hadhrami businessman acts as the consul for the Yemeni embassy in Kenya. If a visa for visiting Yemen is sought, it is the consul's job to verify that the applicant is of Yemeni heritage. Visits are made to Yemen, but Saudi Arabia and the Gulf states are more frequent destinations for people who are traveling primarily as labor migrants (Beckerleg, 2004). The avoidance of the flaunting of Arab-sounding clan names is another way of discretely fitting into the Swahili world. This does not mean that clan affiliations have been forgotten.

Some scholars have argued that the original Swahili were predominantly Arab immigrants who brought Islam to East Africa. Drawing on archaeological evidence, de Vere Allen (1993) argues convincingly that the original Swahili were former pastoralists who moved into small urban settlements in what is now Lamu District in the eighth century CE. He writes that the Arab influence on Swahili culture dates from the early nineteenth century when there was increased migration from Arabia. Hence, the Swahili are essentially African but have incorporated peoples from many ethnic groups, primarily Arabs from Hadhramawt and Oman, but also Indians, Portuguese, and Chinese.

YEMENIS AND KHAT IN KENYA

Yemeni khat consumption and production dates back to the late fourteenth or early fifteenth century (Gebissa, 2004; Varisco, 2004). Khat was grown and enjoyed in the northern highlands but was not part of the cultural of the southern Yemeni region of Hadhramawt. Over the centuries, khat use has become not only institutionalized in the north of the country but ritualized through its use in the afternoon group chewing sessions and weddings (Kennedy, 1987; Meneley, 1996; Varisco, 2004; Weir, 1985).

Until the advent of motorized transport, global khat production was limited to a few highland areas, notably in Ethiopia and Yemen, and in the Nyambene Hills of Meru District in Kenya. In Kenya, the people of the Nyambene Hills started marketing khat outside their own district to the nearby town of Isiolo as early as the 1880s (Carrier, 2005; Goldsmith, 1994). As cathinone, the main active ingredient, quickly degrades after the khat is picked, consumption was until recently limited to people living near these production areas. Modern road, rail, and air transportation changed this pattern and had made khat, particularly miraa from Meru, a global commodity (Anderson et al., 2007). As the Meru producers expanded their commercial distribution networks to cover the whole of Kenya, they found a ready-made market from Yemeni migrants in Kenya. Yemenis in Kenya, having intermarried with fellow Muslim Swahili, not only lived in large numbers at the coast but also migrated inland to towns and trading centers across the country where they had also, literally, set up shop.

Muslim scholars in Yemen, where theological debate has centered on whether the plant should be considered an intoxicant, have not universally applauded khat chewing (Beckerleg, 2009b). To some extent the religious debate on khat persists, but the liberal interpretation that permits khat chewing among Muslims gained the upper hand (Kennedy, 1987, p. 108). Hence, Yemeni men and a few women from the northern highlands, arriving in Kenya, came to the area with a memory of khat consumption as a deep-rooted culture practice that appeared to be largely compatible with Islam. By the 1950s, Yemenis were able to buy khat grown in the Nyambene Hills in many Kenyan towns. As the twentieth century progressed, the people that the Yemenis lived among, particularly the Swahili at the coast, the Somalis of northern Kenya, and indeed people of all ethnic groups across Kenya, took up khat consumption, the chewing supplies made available by the enterprise of the Meru producers and marketers (Carrier, 2005a; Goldsmith, 1994). But in this new setting, consumption lacked the ritual and cultural finesse of Yemen. As consumption spread to different districts and ethnic groups, a khat subculture and associated language to describe khat and its effects developed. At the coast, Yemenis introduced miraa chewing to the Swahili they lived among and intermarried with. In the Swahili town of Malindi, Yemeni street-corner coffee sellers introduced miraa to their Swahili customers in the 1960s (Beckerleg, 2009b). By the 1980s, miraa chewing was part of the daily routine of many young Swahili men in the town of Malindi (Peake, 1989).

REACHING UGANDA

In Kenya, immigrant Hadhrami became part of a culture that had long been influenced by Arabia and Islam, to the extent that outsiders conflate the terms "Arab" and "Swahili." The Hadhrami immigrants to Kenya not only became Swahili but also influenced the culture of which they joined. In Uganda, the situation is different.

Contact between the East African coast and the kingdoms of Buganda and Nkore, in what is now Uganda, dates from the nineteenth century. These Arabs introduced Islam to the area and engaged in trade (Bennett, 1986; Oded, 1974; Soghayroun, 1981). The "Arabs," many who must have been thoroughly Swahilized, were in touch with the lakes region of current day Tanzania, Uganda, and Rwanda from the nineteenth century. Posnansky (1975) summarizes the evidence for contact between traders and the peoples of inland Tanzania, Rwanda, and the Ugandan kingdoms of Buganda and Busoga: "Historical evidence is limited to the brief references which concern Islamic traders from the coast who had settled in the Tabora region by 1825, were already trading in Koki in southern Buganda sometime before 1832, reached the kabaka's court by 1844, and penetrated into Busoga from the east by 1853" (Posnansky, 1975, p. 218).

By 1948, British colonial records show that the "Arabs" were a small but visible minority in Uganda. The nationality of these Arabs is recorded as British or "alien," with Arabia also mentioned as a country (Uganda Protectorate, 1951). However, there can be little doubt that most of the Arabs in Uganda at that time immigrated from Yemen or Oman via the Swahili coast. While the 1931 census recorded 515 Arabs in Uganda, by 1948, the number had jumped to 1,475 (Uganda Protectorate, 1951, p. 15). In 1948, among the residents age fifty and up, there were fourteen females and ninety-seven males, probably due to "the Arab male arriving in Uganda and taking an African wife" (1951, p. 37). However, the census found that, inexplicably, males predominated in all age groups: "The predominance of males became more marked in the age group 10–14 years where the ratio was 182 males per 100 females; there was a drop in the ratio in age groups 20–24 and 35–39. Throughout the other age groups there were consistently more males than females with a peak in the age group 40–44, in which the ratio was 490 males per 100 females" (Uganda Protectorate, 1951, p. 37).

The discrepancy in the male/female ratio of the young recorded in the 1948 census cannot be easily explained. However, the overall predominance of males is related to the practice of single male migration from Yemen. Boxberger has described how teenage boys, typically age fourteen to sixteen years, were sent off to make their way in the world with a network of previous settlers as their security (Boxberger, 2002). The following interview that I carried out with Said Amar in 2005 at Kisoro in southwest Uganda illustrates the adventurous lives of many of these migrants.

Said Amar left Mukalla when he was fourteen or fifteen years old and went to Abu Dhabi on a boat. Amar and two other young male migrants went into Oman to buy *ntama* (millet) with rupees—this was the Zaffar area near Yemen. They sent the millet back to Hadramawt. Amar went to ask for a passport, and the official wrote in Arabic, "This boy has finished his studies and is looking for food to live," and, to show that it was an approved, official document, added a big rubber stamp the size of a coffee cup. Amar added, "There were tribal wars going on—my mother and uncles had been shot."

It was the time of World War II, when according to Amar, "the British conquered the Italians, and in Mombasa there was a blackout." Amar stayed in Mwenbe Tayari in Mombasa for six months.

Later, he went north along the coast by bus to Lamu and found a boat from Yemen. It took eight days to sail back to Yemen. The boat was blown off course, so that, as Amar put it, "we were sitting in the water and adrift with no food and water. We were rescued by an Italian ship and reached Gasa'a, a Hadhrami town." Amar took back money to Yemen obtained from ivory trading on this trip and bought land in Hadhramawt. The land agreement was written on a goatskin.

On another voyage, Amar sailed to Dar es Salaam in Tanganyika (now Tanzania) and then traveled by bus onto Kampala to work in cafés. In Mwembe Tayari in Mombasa and in Dar es Salaam, khat was traded by Africans from Nairobi. According to Amar, "If you were caught with khat you were arrested." Amar found a place to stay in a Yemeni *nadi* (club) in Mombasa where "you could sleep for free for three days and then paid three pennies or a *soumni* (sixpence)."

Marriage

Most of the migrants from Yemeni reaching Uganda were men or boys who subsequently formed temporary alliances and marriages with local women. The Uganda census report noted that "Arab refers to those persons who came from the states of Arabia. Included in the Arab figures will be some offspring of Arab-African unions, as the Arab race permits such children to be termed Arab" (Uganda Protectorate, 1951, p. 8).

In Uganda, people with Yemeni parentage are called "Arabs," and people of mixed race are labeled as *chotora* (Kiswahili) or *muwalad* (Arabic; Boxberger, 2002, p. 42). Many migrant men married women of African descent or of mixed parentage. However, other men rejected such alliances and arranged marriages with "pure Arab" girls living in either East Africa or from Arabia. Yemeni fathers may refuse African marriage partners on their daughters' behalf.

Occasionally, when contacts with family in Yemen remain close, Yemeni migrants can send for brides. One Ugandan Yemeni man told me how he had married an African, an Ankole woman, but after a long and fecund marriage, he had decided that he must also marry a fellow Yemeni. A bride duly arrived from Hadhramawt and became his second wife.

Brides are also found in Mombasa, the gateway to East Africa for Yemenis. In Mityana, near Kampala, the Ugandan capital, I encountered a Yemeni woman, born in Mombasa, who had moved to Uganda to marry. Her husband's father was from Taiz in Yemen, while his mother had been of mixed Nubi (descendents of the remnants of

Emin Pasha's nineteenth-century Sudanese army) and Mahri (a tribe from the Yemen-Oman border). One of her daughter-in-laws was also of Hadhrami stock but born and brought up in Mombasa. Until recently some men also came from Yemen to marry girls in Mombasa. One man, born and bred in Hadhramawt, explained how he had flown from Aden in the 1970s to marry his Kenyan-born cousin in Mombasa.

Language and Cultural Integration

Many Ugandan Yemeni men, of choice and necessity, have married African women. If the African wives were not already Muslim, they converted, and most adopted the Swahili language and various Swahili cultural attributes. Migrants from Yemen adopted a pragmatic approach to integration into East Africa. Those arriving in Mombasa instantly adopted Swahili culture and language and, upon arrival in Uganda, already spoke Swahili, cooked and ate Swahili food, and dressed like Swahili people. Consequently, it is difficult for wives and children who have never set foot outside Africa to know anything of Yemeni culture. One man, whose father was a Yemeni migrant and his mother an African, told me that he was taken by his father to visit all the Yemenis in central and western Uganda and told about his clan affiliation. Despite this instruction, he told me that Swahili-South Asian dishes, such as *pilao* and *chapatti*, were "Arab" food.

The "chotara" offspring are part of the Arab community in Uganda but rarely speak Arabic. Most second- and third-generation Yemenis do not know their father tongue, have been brought up by mothers who had adopted Swahili as a language upon their marriage, and use this new language to communicate with their children. Hence, as a mother tongue, the children speak Ugandan-Swahili, a basic trade language often also associated with the military. One Yemeni man termed it "matooke Swahili" after the national staple dish of steamed plantains. The distinguished Swahili-language expert, Snoxall was even less flattering in his description of Ugandan Swahili as "either a form of Kisetla [pidgin Swahili typically spoken by white settlers] or a form of very debased Kiswahindi which was almost a mixture of Indian words and Swahili in a very ungrammatical form" (Snoxall, 1985, p. 23). Nevertheless, Swahili is an official language of Uganda, a country with thirty indigenous languages. Although Swahili is related to other Bantu Ugandan languages, it is not popular as a medium of communication because of its enduring association with the police and army, including invading Tanzanian troops in 1979 who deposed Idi Amin (Kawoya, 1985).

At school and on the streets, Ugandan Yemenis learn the local language used by the dominant ethnic group where they live and often also speak it at home among themselves. Therefore, many Yemeni Ugandans communicate in a mixture of languages so that a single sentence often includes words from up to three languages. Valeri (2007) found a similar situation in Oman among returnees from East Africa. For example, Valeri quotes an Omani man who had been settled in Burundi: "My daughter does not speak French at all; she came from Rwanda to Oman when she was three, she is thirteen today. Personally, I am able to think in French only. On the contrary, my daughter is the only member of the family to be really good at Arabic because she has been educated in the Arabic system. I am forced to speak Swahili with her, or sometimes English. With my wife, it is half French, half Swahili" (Valeri, 2007, p. 490).

Old and New Khat "Traditions"

Men arriving in Uganda from north Yemen came from a region that has a long tradition of chewing khat (Varisco, 2004). They arrived in a country where khat trees and bushes grow wild (Eggling, 1951) but where there was no local knowledge of stimulant properties of the leaves. By contrast to Yemenis from the north of that country, migrants from the Hadhramawt region adopted khat consumption once they arrived in East Africa. Their descendants consider khat as part of their cultural heritage, but the men who arrived in Uganda tell a different story. One Hadhrami man, Yahya, told me that he had never seen khat until he arrived in Aden from his homeland in the hinterland. It was when he arrived in Mombasa as a new immigrant that he adopted chewing on a regular basis as part of the local scene. Omani migrants, where there is no tradition of chewing, also embraced the practice as a part of their new Arab identity in East Africa. Mohammed, who migrated to Uganda from Oman as a young boy, said that he started chewing in Kisenyi, now a slum area in Kampala but once a market area owned by successful Yemeni businessmen.

Networks, Movement, and Khat

Yemeni migrants arriving in Uganda came either with a long tradition of khat consumption or rapidly adopted the practice. The vast majority of these migrants were young men seeking to make their own way in life, backed up by a support system in the form of networks that linked individuals to other Yemenis as they moved around East Africa. Mass migration by Yemenis to East Africa was made possible by the long established networks that stretched across the Indian Ocean and inland to the Great Lakes region. Those arriving in Uganda did not settle but, facilitated by their informal network, continued to move around and, as they did, had access to khat from various sources. For example, Saleh Ali migrated to Uganda from near Sana'a, north Yemen, in the 1940s. Like many other Yemenis, he worked in the skins and hides industry. As he moved around he also managed to get khat to chew. Saleh, when interviewed in 2004, reported,

> I settled in the Soroti area in eastern Uganda where many locals chewed khat. Next I moved onto Kampala, then Masaka and finally Kabale. Everywhere I went I linked with other Yemenis and was able to get work in skins and hides. I married a Mkiga woman in Kabale. In Kampala there was a lot of kangeta (khat) from Meru (in Kenya). At that time Hassan Thabit and Mohammed Nasher and Abdallah Nasher were famous in the skin trade as well as for being qat traders—I knew if I reached Kampala I should ask for them. At that time Somalis sold khat in Kisenyi, Kampala—they had come a long time ago, before British law, at the time of the Kabaka. Somali women were the sellers in Mengo and Kisenyi.

These three men, Hassan Thabit, Mohammed Nasher, and Abdallah Nasher, were all Yemeni migrants and figure frequently in accounts of the khat trade from the 1930s to the 1940s, and one of them, Mohammed Nashir, was also mentioned by Mwanaidi Mzee in her account of how Ibrahim Mogan in Kibuli brought khat plants to Kampala.

In 2009 I talked to Mohammed Nasher's nephew, Salim Abdullah Nasher, in his house in Kawempe on the northern outskirts of Kampala, where the family still own a skins and hides factory. It was Salim's grandfather who came to Uganda from north Yemen, so Mohammed and Abdallah Nasher were second-generation migrants. Salim confirmed that his uncle was part of the circle including Mtajazzi and Prince Badru Kakungulu, but categorically denied that Mohammed Nasher had anything to do with khat.

As we sat in his veranda, he explained that to the best of his knowledge, neither his father nor his uncle chewed khat and definitely did not sell it. They were wealthy people living in Mengo, Kampala, with connections to the Kabaka and to Kibuli. Mohammed Nasher was the first Ugandan exporter of hides and skins. Salim showed me group pictures of eminent Muslims dating from the 1950s. In one, his father was posed next to several celebrities: the academic Ali Mazrui, Prince Badru Kakungulu, and the Aga Khan who was the leader of Ismaili community. Salim confirmed that Mtajazzi and Mohammed Nasher were friends and that Mtajazzi visited the Kawempe house. But the connections went beyond friendship. Salim explained that Mohammed Nasher married a Yemeni woman who did not give birth. He then married Prince Badru's sister, who bore a son, Amin Mohammed Nasher.

Salim suggested that I contact several Yemeni elders who he expected would know more about the history of khat in Uganda. I was already in contact with these men and had discovered that they had only scant knowledge the history of khat in Uganda. Later, Salim sent a text message suggesting I contact Khalid Hassan Thabit of Mityana in order to ask him about his father, a renowned Yemeni businessman who is often mentioned in relation to the khat trade. I knew this was good advice because, in 2007, I had spoken to Khalid, who still lives in Mityana, a provincial town about forty-five miles to the west of Kampala. Khlaid and his sons run a coffee-processing factory, but Khalid's father, Hassan, was in the skins and hides business. When I had spoken to Khalid, he told me that his father had migrated to Uganda from Taiz, a city in north Yemen. For more information on his father's dealings with khat, he had referred me to an elderly man, Hajji Badri.

I found this Ganda man, Hajji Badri, a retired butcher, playing checkers with a young man in a shady spot in the business district of Mityana. Hajji explained that he used to pray with his friend Hassan Thabit in Mityana mosque during the first regime of Milton Obote in the 1960s. They were also linked through their respective trades: Hassan was a trader in skins and hides, while Hajji had been a butcher. According to Hajji, Hassan Thabit had "six to seven" khat trees, grown from seedlings brought from Kenya and planted at his farm near Mityana. Hassan spent time in Kampala, in Kisenyi where khat was, and is, sold but also traveled to Mombasa regularly. Hajji had been given some khat seedlings by Hassan and became a small-scale trader in khat, taking it to Kisenyi in Kampala, forty-five miles to the east of Mityana.

It is interesting that Hajji thought that Hassan Thabit's khat trees were grown from Kenyan seedlings. This is feasible if he had taken seedlings originally brought by Ibrahim Mogan, or other unnamed Somalis, from Mtajazzi in Kibuli. Indeed, regardless of whether Salim is correct in reporting that his father and uncle never sold khat, the memories of the men who knew the Nasher brothers and Hassan Thabit are consistent in linking them to Kisenyi, where they mixed with Somali traders, and to Kibuli, where they were friends of eminent Muslim Ganda men. Some khat reached Kisenyi from Kibuli until Mtajazzi ripped out his plants. Khat purchased in Kisenyi was predominantly used by Yemenis and Somalis, while a few Muslim Ganda took up the chewing habit. Some khat was also imported to Kampala from the Meru area of Kenya. This khat was especially popular with Somalis, many of whom would have been familiar with the Meru product from their time in the KAR in Kenya and particularly in Isiolo (Goldsmith, 1994).

THE INTRODUCTION OF KHAT TO MBALE

Many Yemenis settled in the eastern Ugandan town of Mbale, which lies at the foot of Mount Elgon near the Kenya border. Known as "Arabs," and possibly even "Swahili," they had been in the region since the nineteenth century as traders of, among other things, ivory and, it is also claimed, slaves. Hence, their settlement had caused concern to the British authorities at the turn of the twentieth century. According to Moyse-Bartlett, "Sir Harry Johnson, whose arrangements tended to increase rather than curtail the limits of the Protectorate . . . was disturbed at 'a disagreeable little nucleus of enmity' north of Mount Elgon, due chiefly to a settlement of Arabs and Swahilis at Marich, who were reported to be practicing slavery and exporting illicit ivory" (Moyse-Bartlett, 1956, p. 90).

A type of khat, *zakariah*, is grown on the Mount Nkokonjeru in the shadow of Mount Elgon and sold in Mbale. Zachariah died in 1960 or 1962, but his son is also known as Zachariah. He lives on Mount Nkokonjeru were he grows khat, coffee, and subsistence crops. Zachariah is a member of the Gisu, an ethnic group that also lives in Kenya on the other side of Mount Elgon. The Bagisu people are famous throughout East Africa for lavish male circumcision ceremonies that initiate an entire age grade of boys into manhood (Heald, 1999). Dating it from the year of his circumcision, Zachariah recalls how khat came to the mountain and the role that the Yemenis played in promoting the plant. He told me that

> When my father was young, he went to Mbale to work as a houseboy for Arabs and Swahili families. They told him about khat and came to the mountain with him to look for it. Afterwards my father took khat to them and they said, "yes, that is khat." I remember at the time that

> I was circumcised, in 1954, that my father brought seedlings from the wilderness near Bukwa in Sebei district, on the northern side of Mount Elgon. He planted these seedlings, but in 1960 or 1962 heavy floods caused landslides. I remember that the rain started in the morning and went on for two days. All the khat trees were washed away. This was also the year my father died. I decided to return to Bukwa to get more seedlings, as the Arabs had already climbed the mountain to my house to encourage me to plant khat. I asked them why they eat khat. They replied that "khat is not a bad thing: it does not finish strength; you do not feel pain in the body; and if you have only a little food but chew khat you will not feel hungry." My neighbors came and asked how to grow khat. Now about fifty families have some trees, and they sell the khat that they harvest in Mbale. Most people on the mountain do not chew khat, as they are more interested in drinking.
>
> I used to take khat to the Arab and Swahili weddings. A *taarabu* (traditional Swahili music) singer, Saidi Samla, took me to Nairobi once where he was singing at a wedding. Somalis also came to my house and encouraged me to grow khat. In 1978, a wealthy Somali called Taurat climbed the mountain and asked me to supply him with khat. I still do this. This is the only special order I still have. These days I take my khat to sell to retailers in Mbale.

Although Yemenis in Mbale stimulated the process of taking khat seedlings from the wild and planting them, zakariah remains a very minor khat brand in Uganda.

The Introduction of Khat to Western Uganda

There are extensive khat plantations in Kabarole Distrct in western Uganda, under the shadow of the Rwenzoris, the fabled Mountains of the Moon. But the khat grown in Kabarole did not come from the Rwenzoris but from the east, from the region to the north of Mbale. In the 1920s this was a wild region exploited by elephant hunters and slaver raiders (Bell, 1949), where the Abyssinians had territorial claims and were making military incursions (Moyse-Bartlett, 1956). The indigenous population were the pastoralist Karimojong, who have a long and continuing history of tit-for-tat, cattle raiding with neighboring groups such as the Turkana of Kenya and the Toposa of Sudan (Eaton, 2008). This lawless region was the origin of the khat grown commercially in Kabarole.

In 2004 in the town of Fort Portal, the capital of Kabarole District, I was introduced to an elderly Yemeni, Said Sulyman. He explained to me how the area came to be one of the centers of khat cultivation in Uganda:

> My father, Sulemain bin Ali, was from Yemen. He was an ivory hunter in Karamoja. In 1921 he left Karamoja for Kampala and, in 1927, came to Fort Portal. His brother Saleh was living in Kisumu, Kenya. After Saleh died, Sulemain went to collect his two children and bring them to Fort Portal. This was in 1928, and when he returned to Fort Portal, he brought seedlings from Iriiri (in Karamoja region where they grow wild) with him. These he planted in his *shamba* (garden) at home. Rajab Byarafu, a local Toro farmer who was also a Muslim leader, came to him for seedlings. Sulemain died in 1958.

By 2008 when I attempted to follow up on this story, Said had died. However, I was directed by a Yemeni contact to talk to Feisal, a son of Sulyman bin Ali. Feisal lives in the Nubi area of Fort Portal, between the main road to Kampala and the marram road leading to the local khat plantations. He invited me to his house, a large, run-down bungalow overlooking a small river where young men were operating a car wash. He said that he could not work out who I had spoken to in 2004, but he nevertheless told me a story very similar to the one recounted by the old man, Said:

> My father, Sulyman bin Ali, died in 1958. He did not have a brother. I do not know who the elderly man you spoke to in 2004 was. My father came from Yemen from the "area of Abdallah Ali" [the name of the long-standing president of north Yemen]. My father's tribe was Mugh or Mugkh. Sulyman was a buffalo hunter. He sent skins and horns to Europe. He took the khat seedlings from Habash in Turkana land. Or it may have been Moroto (Karamoja), it was somewhere that eastern side. Sulyman found khat in Turkana. He carried a seedling in a pot to Kampala. He came to Fort Portal in about 1933. But it could have been earlier, like 1928, as the old man had said before. He went to the Toro king and was given land in his wife's name because non-Africans were not allowed to own land. His wife was from Tanzania. She used to travel with him. Afterward, he married an Arab from Mbale and a Karimojong. His neighbor on the other side the river was Darwish Haza, another Yemeni. He took some khat seedlings and planted at his place. Sulyman continued with his work of skins and hides and employed "porters." They were the ones who took khat seedlings to their homes. They were Rajab Byarufu's neighbors and he got seedlings from them, not directly from the Yemenis or the Nubi. Rajab was a CID [plain clothes policeman in the criminal investigation department]. He planted four acres of khat. By the time Rajab died, most

> of the Arabs in Fort Portal had died or moved away. The khat planted here at home and at Darwish's place died. I became a mechanic and was not interested in farming. Abdu Haza, the son of Darwish Haza, opened a clothes shop in the trading center of Kyenjojo on the road to Kampala. My father was 104 years old when he died. He had three wives and seventeen children. Here in this house, my father used to chew on Saturdays.

Although Feisal said he did not know to whom I had talked in 2004, and that his father did not have a brother, his memory may have been deceiving him. I spoke to his niece who lives in Kampala and asked her if the old man I talked to in 2004, or her uncle, Feisal, was correct about Sulyman bin Ali having a brother. She recalled a family story about Sulyman bin Ali going to Kisumu to pick up his brother's child. She also remembered that Sulyman having had three wives, one from Tanzania, an Arab, and a Karimojong. It is not clear what relationship the old man I talked to had to Sulyman bin Ali; perhaps the term "father" indicated that he was a classified as father because he was a fellow Yemeni of his parents' generation. Or, perhaps due to family tensions unknown to me, a half-brother of his father had been "forgotten" by Feisal. In any case, both Feisal's and Said's accounts were almost identical in the key points that explain how khat came west to Kabarole.

New supply systems that ensured that Yemenis and Somalis could purchase khat were set up in western Uganda. From the 1970s, khat from the Kabarole District started being marketed in the town of Kasese to the south of Fort Portal. Before the 1970s the Yemenis who had settled from Kasese obtained khat harvested around the town of Goma in what was eastern Zaire and currently part of the Democratic Republic of Congo (DRC). According to Yahya, a Hadhrami khat trader in Kasese, it was a Yemeni called Hassan who used to bring khat that had been harvested from the wild from Goma to Kasese. At that time, only Yemenis chewed khat. The Goma khat trees were destroyed by lava during the volcanic eruption that occurred in the 1990s, which badly affected Rwandan refugees who had congregated in camps there. From 1976 the Yemenis of Kasese started getting khat from the plantation of the Byarufu family that had acquired seedlings from stock brought by Sulyman bin Ali in the 1930s. Yahya reports that in 1976, he had gone with Ali Abubakr and Mohemmed Isa to see Rajab Byarufu to arrange for him to supply them with khat in Kasese.

Mustafa, one of Rajab's sons, recalls that in 1978 he started taking khat to Yemenis in Kasese. At that time all the customers were Yemeni. They chewed together inside specially designated clubs, sitting on cushions on the floor. They used sugar to sweeten the bitter khat and accompanied it with Arab-style black coffee, served in small cups. Later, as khat consumption spread to other ethnic groups, the situation became chaotic, and Mustafa used bodyguards to prevent fights over the khat distribution. Although distribution patterns have changed, Mustafa still regularly visits Yahya's retail outlet in the courtyard of his Kasese home.

Yemenis, living in the large western town of Mbarara to the south of Kasese, also obtained khat from Goma. Abdu, whose father was a khat consumer, recalls that khat came from Goma and was like "sticks" and was chewed with *perimendi* (candy). It was sold in the Syria Hotel that was run by Yemenis named Almas, Karama, and Mafudh. Karama also ordered khat from Mombasa, and this was called *meru*.

The Goma khat supply stopped in 1979, but the meru khat continued to arrive in Mbarara in small amounts. By about 1984, during the second regime of Milton Obote (the period popularly known as Obote II), khat started to be common in Mbarara, Abdu recalled. Khat was brought from plantations near Kampala in the Mpigi District from Butambala, the area where Sheikh Semakula of Kibuli had pioneered khat cultivation. Khat from the Kabarole District was also available in Mbarara. When Museveni came to power in 1986, khat became more widespread and to be used by people other than Yemenis. "They were from different tribes—mostly Muslim—Myeme, Mkonjo, Muankole, half castes," said Abdu.

CONCLUSION

Yemenis arriving at the Kenya coast not only successfully integrated with the Swahili community but have also shaped it as the bearers of new religious movements, medical treatment, coffee drinking, and khat chewing. Ugandan Yemenis have had a more difficult time finding a comfortable "cultural" niche and associated social identity. The passage from Yemen to Uganda involved passing through Mombasa. The ancient Swahili city port of Mombasa is the symbolic and physical place where the culture and language of Yemen is discarded and replaced with Swahili attributes. Thus, dressed as Swahili people and speaking that language, intrepid young Yemeni men set out to make their fortunes in Uganda, Zambia, Rwanda, and Zaire. Those that settled in Uganda were, thus, presenting themselves not so much as Yemenis from south Arabia but as Arabs from the coast. Many Yemenis in Uganda have retained links with Mombasa, and marriages are often arranged with residents of Yemeni descent from the city who are Swahili speakers (Beckerleg, 2009 b).

In Uganda, Yemenis constituted, and continue to be, a tiny minority group. As Arabs, Yemenis formed alliances with Omanis who were also classed as "Arabs" by the British colonial authorities and later by ordinary Ugandans. The Ugandan Arabs were too few and too scattered to exert the cultural and religious influence that Yemenis enjoyed in Kenya. Arabs in Uganda lived among people of many ethnic groups. They have always been a minority in terms of ethnicity and their hybrid Swahili-Arab culture. In addition, and again unlike the Swahili world, as Muslims, they were usually in the minority. Although respected as Arabs, and as speakers of the language of the Quran, they are followers at the mosque, while indigenous Ugandans are the Imams and givers of sermons.

The political violence and disruption that marred Uganda in the second half of the twentieth century affected Ugandan Arabs as much as anybody else. Some Yemenis left Uganda permanently in the 1970s and 1980s, and among those who stayed, many appeared to have been impoverished since Museveni came to power in 1986, partly due to currency adjustments that were made to limit rampant inflation. Although settled in Uganda for generations, many people of Yemeni descent are on the move: working and marrying in Kenya (particularly Mombasa) or Tanzania or trading in Rwanda and the DRC while others have been "home" to Yemen in order to visit or to settle. Ugandan Yemenis participate in the Yemeni and East African economic and cultural arenas. Such dual lives are one of the hallmarks of transnational migration (Gardner, 2002).

Khat consumption has been an important cultural cement for diaspora Yemenis in East Africa (Anderson et al., 2007). In Uganda, Yemeni men gathered to chew khat in a style that mimicked the conventional khat parties of north Yemen (Weir, 1985). Yemeni men, on their travels as hunters and traders, found khat in the wild and arranged for it to be harvested. They also imported khat from the wilds of Goma in neighboring Zaire (now the DRC). The migrants did not come as farmers and in the early days did not have land. Therefore, they did not become khat farmers. The growing Ugandan khat industry, based on production by indigenous Ugandans, grew out of the combined efforts of Yemeni and Somali migrants to get hold of khat.

Chapter 4

Ugandan Khat Production Spreads

From the 1930s to the 1980s, Yemeni and Somali migrants and their descendants taught indigenous Ugandans about khat. They stimulated khat production in Mount Elgon, in Karamoja, and in Kabarole District. Khat is now grown commercially in most parts of the country, and wild khat is still harvested in the southwest and northeast of Uganda. Since the 1980s new khat harvesting and cultivation enterprises have sprung up in places such as Arua and Lira in the north, started by entrepreneurs who learned about khat from other indigenous Ugandans. The khat produced in these areas comes from stock taken from the wild or, in the case of Arua, from the national botanical gardens at Entebbe. However, the biggest khat production areas are in the south, in the central districts of Uganda, with khat from Butambala and Kasenge supplying the Kampala market and beyond. These khat production areas are part of the kingdom of Buganda, where important traditional crops were, and are, plantains and coffee (NARO, 2001).

Buganda: Land, Social Hierarchy, and Plantains

From the 1940s khat was grown in typical Ganda agricultural settings by mostly Ganda people who lived in a unique political and economic milieu in East Africa (Richards et al., 1973). The kingdom of Buganda has abundant rolling hills, fertile soil, and sufficient rainfall to grow a variety of crops. Plantains, which require little labor and can be harvested year-round, were the stable food of the Ganda people that allowed the population to grow. Indeed, it has been argued that plantain production underpinned the development of the hierarchical polity of Buganda (Hanson, 2003). As Audrey Richards commented,

"[Buganda] was an area in which the cultivation of the stable plantain crop was such that it left many men time to direct the efforts of their fellows. Buganda was also a society in which peasants were accustomed to obey orders and subject to heavy penalties if they did not do so" (Richards, 1973, p. 61).

Plantains helped free up men for warfare, and Buganda had a standing army at the end of the nineteenth century, while women stayed at home and cultivated the plantains (Richards, 1973, p. 289). In the nineteenth century, other farm labor came from slaves who were war captives (Hanson, 2007; Reid, 2007). The system worked well in that people had land that was either theirs or was granted for their use by the *kabaka* or by the chiefs and clan heads (Roscoe, 1965). Food was plentiful and the kingdom powerful, which enriched the Arab and Swahili trading partners from the East African Coast (Bennett, 1986). The arrival of Europeans changed everything. In the late nineteenth century, during Lugard's time, the British gained control over the kingdom of Buganda, with its capital, Mengo, in what is now west Kampala. In 1892, Lugard imposed his land settlement, which divided the land of Buganda. Kasozi outlines how land was divided among different religious groups: "The Protestants received six rich counties. The Catholics received the fertile southern province of Buddu which was far away from the centre of political activities. The Muslims were given three small poor counties sandwiched on one side by the Catholics and on the other by the Protestants. These counties were Butambala, Gomba and Busujju" (Kasozi, 1996, p. 30).

A British protectorate over Uganda was declared in 1894, and in 1900 an agreement was made between the kabaka and his chiefs and Britain. The Uganda Agreement changed the basis of land tenure: the kabaka and chiefs became landlords of vast tracts of land and the people living there became peasant tenants (Fortt & Houghton, 1973).

The "class of private landowners" (Fortt & Houghton, 1973, p. 23) thus created were considered by the British as suitable candidates for the development of commercial cash crop production in Buganda. The British first encouraged the growing of cotton in Buganda and elsewhere in Uganda. Early success was not maintained, but the concept of growing cash crops on a large scale did take hold so that from 1907, "plantation agriculture expanded steadily, until in 1915 there were 104 plantations in Buganda, mostly in Kyaggwe county, growing coffee, rubber and cocoa" (Fortt & Houghton, 1973, p. 24).

COFFEE

Coffee was the cash crop that took off in Buganda. It required less labor than cotton and was well suited to the climate. In addition, before its promotion as a cash crop by the British colonial government, it was already well known to the Ganda people, who kept a few trees near their homes (Musoli et al., 2001, p. 379). The beans were used for chewing and not making a beverage. "Robusta coffee is indigenous to Uganda. Before coffee was developed as a commercial crop, a ritual significance was attached to robusta coffee in Buganda. It was used as an offering to gods and spirits. In the ceremony of brotherhood two beans were taken out of the berry; each man moistened it with blood and gave it to the other to eat. When a visitor arrived at a house, he was given coffee beans to chew before being offered food" (Musoli et al., 2001, p. 379).

Coffee beans, sold by hawkers in Kampala and across southern Uganda, are still chewed by Ganda people (Musoli et al., 2001, p. 434). Coffee beans are also still used in Ganda rituals at shrines that are located in rural areas. Shrines, where *lubaale* (gods) and the spirits of deceased kabakas resided, were important ritual centers that underpinned the secular power of the kingdom.

Uganda gained independence in 1962, and shortly afterward in 1966, the kingdom of Buganda was abolished, ushering in a period of political chaos. After two decades of political violence, President Museveni came to power in 1986 after winning a guerrilla war, or as it is usually referred to in Uganda, a bush war. In 1993 Museveni restored the Buganda kingdom and allowed the kabaka to take up residence in his palace. In contemporary Uganda, Buganda maintains an active role in national politics. Clan-based allegiance, social hierarchies, land tenure issues, and ritual centered on the spirit shrines are defining features of the Ganda people. In 1972 (when the kingdom had been formally abolished) Ray, in his study of kingship in Buganda, found twenty-three shrines across Buganda where ceremonies were being carried out (Ray, 1992). Most Ganda are Protestant, Catholic, or Muslim, but some people have joined the increasingly popular evangelical churches. Yet, despite the vast majority of the Ganda adhering to either Islamic or Christian groups, the pagan shrines are maintained by the kingdom of Buganda. Christian and Muslim Ganda people visit the shrines and diviners and healers certified by the kabaka and his parliament in Mengo, Kampala.

Although the Ganda had long used robusta coffee in rituals at shrines, it was arabica coffee that was planted as a cash crop immediately after the start of the agreement with the British. The government introduced Arabica seeds from Nyasaland (Malawi) in 1900 (Musoli et al., 2001, p. 379). Commercial coffee production in Uganda started in the 1920s and was further promoted in the 1950s (Musoli et al., 2001, p. 381). In Buganda, coffee production rose from 600 acres in 1922 to 30,800 acres in 1937 and to 315,000 acres by 1956 (Richards, 1973, p. 292). After World War II world coffee prices were high, but a slump in coffee prices started in 1955, and by 1961 there was a 70 percent fall in the price of coffee (Richards, 1973, pp. 292–293).

Nevertheless, national production grew to two million bags of export quality coffee by the 1960s, peaking at 3.7 million bags in 1972. Coffee at this time was the biggest export crop, followed by cotton and tea (Aluka & Hakiza, 2001, p. 439). After 1972, civil wars and low producer prices adversely affected production, which did not recover until the late 1980s. International Development Assistance, as part of a structural adjustment program, started funding the rehabilitation of old coffee trees in 1991 (Musoli et al., 2001). By 1996 to 1997 Uganda produced 4.2 million bags (Musoli et al., 2001). Coffee remains the biggest export cash crop in Uganda. Khat is grown alongside coffee, often in the same field, and there is no evidence that coffee trees are being replaced with khat production, as is occurring in Ethiopia.

The Place of Khat in Mixed Farming in Buganda and Beyond

Farmers in Buganda found a ready market for produce in nearby Kampala, a rapidly growing city. During the 1930s onward, some men took up trade and spent time away from their farms (Richards et al., 1973). The railway line from the port of Mombasa on the distant Indian Ocean reached Kampala in 1931 and also increased trade opportunities and communications with East Africa and the rest of the world. This changing economic environment ensured that men from Buganda were well placed to communicate with Somalis and others in Kampala, who encouraged them to plant khat.

All the khat produced in south central Uganda is grown within the kingdom of Buganda and appears to come from the original seedlings brought to Kibuli by Ibrahim Mogan or by other, unnamed Somalis in the 1930s. When, in the 1940s, Sheikh Semakula planted khat on his farm, he introduced a new cash crop to the mixed farming system of Buganda. Ganda farmers were producing plantains, beans, peanuts, vegetables for home consumption and for sale, as well as growing cotton and later coffee as major cash crops (Richards et al., 1973). On some farms the khat seedlings were planted in shady groves among plantains and coffee trees. Others, perhaps those more intent on developing khat as major earner, planted their seedlings on dedicated plots where the bushes and trees were maintained in neat rows. However, there is variation in the style of khat cultivation within the five growing areas scattered from east to west across Buganda.

The farming system of Buganda is similar to that of the main khat production area in Kenya. There, close to Mount Kenya in the Nyambene Hills the Igembe and Tigania, clans of the Meru practice what Goldsmith describes as a form of mixed farming that incorporates "agro-forestry," including khat cultivation, "permaculture," and tea production (Goldsmith, 1994). Khat trees have a long ritual significance in this area, and trees have been grown near homes for hundreds of years (Carrier, 2005a; Goldsmith, 1994) in a manner similar to the cultivation of robusta coffee by Ganda people for ritual use. Trees, including khat, and annual crops are planted together in densely cultivated plots that appear as unkempt "jungles," with rotting vegetation as mulch underfoot. This farming system has enabled an increased carrying capacity of the land and more people to remain in the local agro-khat economy, rather than being forced to seek employment in urban areas (Goldsmith, 1994).

In Buganda many of the khat farms that were established from the 1940s onward share key features with the Nyambene style of production. In both places, khat is grown in mixed small holdings intercropped with food crops including plantains and often in or near forests.

Butambala

In 1966, at the time when Richards et al. were conducting their survey in Buganda, Butambala was a county in West Mengo District (Richards et al., 1973). The name "Butambala" has now disappeared from district maps, but the area is still populated largely by Muslim Ganda people. Butambala was the home of Sheikh Semakula, the friend of Mtajazzi of Kibuli, who took seedlings to his home in Kabasanda in Butambala (now known as Mpigi District). Kabasanda is a village in an area of mixed agricultural production and government-gazetted, or protected, forests where people were not allowed to cultivate, about thirty miles to the south west of Kampala. By 2004, when I first learned about Sheikh Semakula's pioneering work in promoting khat production, he was already seriously ill in a hospital in Kibuli, Kampala. In Kibuli, I talked to his sister, the widow of Mtajazzi, who explained that when she was a new bride she saw khat planted in Kibuli and that Somali visitors came to get hold of it. She also explained that her brother had taken khat to Kabasanda and that his family was still producing khat there. I visited his prosperous home, which was reached down a narrow winding lane that leads off the main road that traverses Butambala. The houses making up the homestead were substantial and the property surrounded by mature khat trees, extending for many acres. Some of the khat was in the form of mature trees, while the more recently planted stock are low, closely cropped bushes that look like tea plants (Anderson et al., 2007). Sheikh Semakula died in 2005, so I never met him. However, it was clear that in taking khat seedlings from Kibuli, he started an industry that has benefited thousands of farmers and traders.

One of the first people to follow Semakula's lead and plant khat was the grandson of Twaibu Magatto, a prominent leader of the Ganda Muslim faction and a "moderate" player in the political events that resulted in the carving up of Buganda along religious lines (Kasozi, 1996). This leader is still remembered, and in 2007, at the heart of the khat industry of Butambala in Mirembe trading center, a mosque built with Saudi donations and dedicated to Twaibu Magatto was opened. Twaibu's grandson, Hajji Magatto, now in his eighties or nineties, lives in Mianzi, on the main road west from Kampala to Fort Portal. In 2007, he gave me a colorful account of his dealings with khat and how it has profited his life. His story is paraphrased here:

> Sheikh Semakula was the first person to grow khat and I was the second. Semakula is my "brother." Semakula went to Egypt to study for twenty years. When he returned he brought khat seedlings with him. In 1947 he gave some of the seedlings to me and told me to plant them, as they would bring me profit. I was living in Mirembe village, Butambala at that time. I planted the khat, but even when the khat had grown high I did not know its worth. Semakula brought three Somalis from Kampala to harvest my khat. They were tailors from a shop on the Kampala Road. After that the Sheikh sent more Somalis to help with harvesting. In 1949, when we were still paying Head Tax to the colonial government, I was selling khat and giving some away to my neighbors. Around then, a man called Abdu started saying khat was *haram* [forbidden by Islam]. Semakula told him to show the verse in the Quran that says khat is haram. Of course, Abdu could not find any such verse. In 1953 I was arrested for growing khat. The government investigated khat and found there was no problem so I was quickly released. I moved here to Mianzi in 1987 but the original farm at Mirembe is still producing khat grown by some of my family members. In about 1991 somebody

from Kampala reported me again, because he said khat is haram. The Mityana District Police Commissioner came and told me not to harvest my khat. Then another official came and said, "Grow khat." In 1994 the district police commissioner returned and asked for seedlings. He took 300 and planted them in Kabale District in the southwest.

Hajji Magatto shares the common misconception that the original khat seedlings came from outside East Africa, in this instance from Egypt. Furthermore, he appears to know nothing of Mtajazzi's role in the advent of khat production. This is unsurprising because in Butambala, Semakula is mentioned repeatedly as the first bringer of khat. For example, in 2007 I visited a khat farm in Butambala that had been planted by Sheikh Ahmed Walusimbi, with seedlings obtained from Semakula who lived close by. His son, Kassim, reported that the Sheikh had died in 1984. The farm is not doing well, as demand for khat from Butambala fluctuates because of the competition from newer plantations in Kasenge, which lies to the south of Kampala. Nevertheless, he reckoned that khat still provides a better income than coffee or vanilla. Kassim attributed recent problems in the khat industry to local religious differences rather than to competition from rival production areas. Hence, Kassim recalled that everything was better in Sheikh Semakula's prime. It was shortly before Semakula died that some mosques starting complaining about khat, and "somebody came from Buddo District to make people hate khat." The campaigner told people that khat was haram. According to Kassim, although about 90 percent of the population of the area are Muslim, local leaders have said nothing on the subject.

A few miles from Kassim's farm, but still in Butambala, is the farm of the late Hajji Abdu Musanje. I spoke to his two widows and to one of his sons. Their khat trees were planted in 1970 with seedlings acquired from Semakula. Traders from Kisenyi in Kampala, including Somalis, used to come directly from their farm to buy khat. Now they take their khat to sell in wholesale market in Kisenyi in Kampala, and the Somalis are consumers, not sellers. All the fifteen or so khat farmers I spoke to in Butambala told a similar story: right up to the 1980s, they were still planting khat, with seedlings obtained from Semakula.

KITOLA

According to the memories of Mwanaidi Mzee, the elderly woman who recalled Ibrahim Mogan, the first area to be planted with khat outside Kampala was Kitola and not Butambala. Kitola is situated off the main Kampala-Nairobi highway, near the Mabira Forest, still in within Buganda. Parts of the area are still forested, but large spaces have been cleared to plant sugarcane that stretches almost to the horizon. The khat farmers live in hamlets beyond the sugar plantation. The khat is planted in sloping fields and is no more than waist high. When I visited in October 2007, nobody mentioned Ibrahim Mogan or Kibuli. One elderly woman remembered that when she married into the area in 1954 there was a small amount of khat in the area. She and several other people said that the original khat seedlings had come from Butambla. Any claims to be the first khat production place in central Uganda are forgotten. Although the acreage under khat has now increased, it is still a small production area, competing with newer enterprises situated near the Mabira Forest in Njeru and Lugazi.

MABIRA FOREST

In the Mabira Forest area to the east of Kampala, Buwola is the main khat production area, supplying the towns of Jinja and even Lira in the north. Child (2009) notes that there are "community enclaves" within the Mabira Forest that earn a living in bee keeping, charcoal production, and the collection of building poles (Child, 2009, p. 250) but does not mention the production of khat. The Buwola farms nestle on a narrow strip of land carved out of the Mabira Forest. Plantains, coffee, and mixed crops are interspersed with khat bushes on almost every one of several hundred homesteads. Buwola is a five-minute drive from the main highway yet is within the area that has been protected as Mabira Forest Reserve land since 1932. According to a local leader and prominent khat farmer, Issac Kizito, as well as several other informants, the land used to belong to the Buganda kings. The Soga people who live to the east of the Forest used to send children to work for the Ganda kabaka. One child, Nadyope, pleased the kabaka, Mutesa II, and in 1954, he was rewarded with land inside the forest at Buwola. Nadyope sold the land to another Soga man, Bwanga. In turn, Bwanga sold on the land to Sudi-Lukwago, a Ganda Muslim, who built a mosque in the area and sold off subplots with title deeds. Now people from different ethnic groups have brought land, and another Ganda man, Luyombya, owns all the land in the enclave that was not sold off as subplots.

Issac, a leading khat producer in the forest, has photograph albums packed with pictures of Yemeni men chewing khat outside his house. He explained that his father started khat cultivation in 1975 after he became friendly with people of Yemeni origin. They started with a few seedlings that were purchased in Kampala. By the 1980s the people of Buwola had started to encroach on the forest that lies at the end of their stretch of cultivated land, within seven miles of the main road. Isaac explained that the people had felled trees and started cultivating without permission. They also planted khat. The loss of trees resulted in a lessening of rainfall. The encroachment of forest reserves was common across Uganda in the 1980s and was particularly prevalent in Mabira, where ten thousand hectares were taken over (Byabashaija et al., 2001, p. 54). In about 1987, after Museveni came to power, according to Issac, they were evicted. This area of land, which is reverting to forest, has wild khat among its species mix. Plans to turn parts of the forest, including the area the people of Bulowa encroached upon, over to sugar production by the company owned by the Indian-born tycoon Metha have been shelved after violent demonstrations in 2007 and an international campaign to save the forest (Child, 2009).

KITI

The family of Sheikh Semakula has become leading khat producers and has pioneered production in diverse areas of Buganda. In Kiti, near the town of Masaka to the west of Kampala, seedlings from Sheikh Semakula have traveled another sixty miles from their Ugandan origins in Kibuli. In Kiti, Semakula's son, Sheikh Yusuf, has pioneered the cultivation of high quality khat. The area is flat farmland and the people are a mixture of Christian and Muslim Ganda. But all the khat farmers we met were Muslim and were described by people in the area as "sheikhs." On Sheikh Yusuf's farm, his son explains that all the family are involved in farming and marketing khat that had been growing on the farm as long as he could remember, about thirty years. They have about one thousand trees (Anderson et al., 2007). Although the original seedlings came from Sheikh Semakula in Kabasanda, the Kiti khat trees look completely different and are tall and thin and very dry looking. They produce small, tender leaves that command high prices.

KYADDONDO

About twenty miles north of Kampala, near the main road that passes the barracks at Bombo and leads to the north of the country, Sheikh Semakula's nephew has established a major khat plantation. Abdu was brought up in Butambala and moved to the area shortly after Museveni came to power in 1986. He planted several acres of khat seedlings from stock taken from Butambla. These seedlings have grown into trees of about the size of an English apple tree. Ladders are used to harvest the leaves. Abdu said that leaving the khat to grow into trees was a way of getting more leaves per tree. These trees are very similar in appearance to the khat farms of Meru in Kenya, where the seedlings may have originated back in the 1930s. So far, Abdu is the only khat farmer in the area.

KASENGE: ROYAL CONNECTIONS?

Kasenge, about half an hour's drive south of Kampala, is the fastest growing khat production area in Uganda. The area is characterized by rolling hills covered with plantains and is home to Ganda people who are a mix of Muslims and Catholics. Kasenge is part of the kingdom of Buganda. Accounts of the recent origins of khat production are confused, and there are several contradictory accounts of how it came to Kasenge. Certainly, however, since at least the 1970s, khat production has been expanding in Kasenge.

Richard, a young man who has recently tried his hand as a khat farmer, told me that khat was brought to Kasenge from Burma during World War II by a man called Gubiri. Gubiri had fought alongside Somalis, who were chewing khat that they obtained in Burma. Richard directed me to Gubiri's home, a farm of mixed crops, including khat. Christopher Gubiri, now in his eighties, lives with his wife, Sarah. They have been married for fifty-four years. When Sarah came to her husband's home in 1953, she found khat planted there, she said. Christopher explains that he was not stationed in Burma but was in Nanuki in northern Kenya for about two weeks before being transferred to Abyssinia to build roads, as part of the "Battalion of the Kabaka, King George." He recalled that it was his great-grandfather who was among the first people to plant khat from seedlings brought by Somalis. The Somalis came from Kampala with Ganda people who interpreted for them. Although his great-grandfather was a pioneer in khat production, a woman called Maria, who died "a long time ago," was probably the first to work with the Somalis in this way. Maria's daughter Miriam was still living in Kasenge. When I asked Gubiri about Sheikh Semakula, he replied that "we know nothing of Semakula. Butambala is a different area, they are Muslims and we are Catholics."

Denis Kasujja, a farmer in Kasenge who sells premium khat branded as *kasujja*, has investigated the history of khat in the area. According to his research, a man called Mudiro, who died sometime between

1920 and 1940, was given five hundred acres by Kabaka Chwa II (reigned from 1897–1939; Kasozi, 1996, p. 5). Mudiro was a friend of Sheikh Semakula, and through him, Mudiro obtained khat seedlings from either Kibuli or Butambla. Mudiro's family has sold most of the land Mudiro was given by Kabaka Chwa. Denis introduced me to Miriam who explained that her father, Mudiro, was a brother-in-law to Prince Badru Kakungulu.

According to Miriam, Mudiro's sister, Assiya, was a wife of Kankungulu. Miriam further claimed that Kankungulu kept khat trees in his home, and that the seedlings were imported from Arabia. Kakungulu was a much beloved Ganda Prince, a leading Muslim and devoted educationalist. No mention of a wife called Assiya is made in Kasozi's (1996) biography of Kankungulu. But although Miriam's version of the life of Kakungulu is problematic, there is evidence that Kakungulu lived near Kasenge during his youth. From 1925 Kankungulu received his secondary education at King's College in Buddo, an area adjacent to Kasenge. "Kankungulu was allowed a house near the school where two of his servants Sadiki Musajjalumbwa and Khalid Sebuttema lived. Sir Daudi Chwa was instrumental in obtaining a house close to the school, just outside the fence to accommodate these servants" (Kasozi, 1996, p. 58).

There is much anecdotal evidence linking Kakungulu to Mtajazzi and Semakula, who were fellow residents of Kibuli. The link with Mtajazzi and Semakula suggests that Kakungulu may also have had ties to Butambala and Kasenge, but there is no clear evidence that this was the case. When Kakungulu died in 1991, his body was buried in a mausoleum in the main mosque in Kibuli, at the heart of the area where he lived for much of his life and interacted with men involved in promoting khat production. The interviews I conducted indicate that he was friends with Mtajazzi, Semakula, and the Nasher brothers who were Yemeni migrants working in the skins and hides industry in Kisenyi. All these men who knew Kakungulu were also associates and friends of Kampala-based Somalis. Indeed Mwanaidi Mzee, who recalled Ibrahim Mogan, claimed that he was a friend of Kakungulu. Hence, there is a possibility that a Ganda prince, Badru Kakungulu, was involved in the spread of khat. He was a friend of Semakula and Mtajazzi and went to school near Kasenge. The daughter of the man said to have founded khat production in Kasenge says it was actually Prince Badru who brought seedlings.

Nobody I interviewed could remember dates relating to the founding of khat or other key events in the recent history of Kasenge. Key informants, including Miriam herself, link the introduction of khat to the area to her father Mudiro. Miriam, for her part, prefers to stress the links her father had to royalty. This is an important part of her family history and she may be unaware of her mother's dealings with Somalis from Kampala. What is certain is that khat was introduced into Kasenge by the 1950s, at the latest. The seedlings probably came either directly from Kibuli or from Butambala.

Since the 1980s, when Museveni came to power, production in Kasenge has been increasing, and farmers are continuing to establish new khat plantations. The khat is grown on mixed farms, but the area is not as rich an agricultural region as Butambala. Nevertheless, Kasenge has several advantages over Butambala: It is nearer to Kampala, thus facilitating the cheaper and quicker transportation to daily markets. The soil, less fertile than in Butambala, appears to favor khat, which is said by many farmers in different settings to grow best on hill areas with poor soil. The Kasenge product is considered superior to khat from the Butambala region and therefore is sold at a premium. Khat from Kasenge is transported for sale all over the country and even beyond to Rwanda and Burundi (Anderson et al., 2007).

In the Wild beyond Buganda

Khat grows wild over much of highland East Africa, at least where forests remain (Carrier, 2005). In Kenya wild khat is harvested from the Chyulu Hills in southeastern Kenya and in West Pokot, near the border with Uganda (Anderson et al., 2007). The collection of wild khat is a small-scale operation dwarfed in Kenya and Uganda by its commercial cultivation. However, some wild khat is the source of the plants assiduously cultivated in parts of Uganda.

While Somalis introduced khat from Kenyan stock to Kampala and chewed khat imported from Meru, Yemenis were better placed to get hold of local, wild khat.

Yemenis from the north of the country had migrated from a region where khat plantations were widespread and were more knowledgeable about the plant than were Somalis, who were avid consumers but had little or no experience of production. The people the Yemenis interacted with were farmers and pastoralists from different ethnic groups living across the country. Khat grows wild in the hills and forests in both the extreme east and west of the country. Yemeni informants mention that their forefathers used to harvest wild khat in many mountainous areas of Uganda, particularly in the southwest: in Kisoro, Rukingiri, and Kiyagali on the Uganda/Tanzania border. During the first half of the twentieth century, Yemenis living in more remote areas of Uganda than Kampala or Mityana also set about getting hold of khat by asking local people to seek it out in the wild and bring it to them. Many Yemenis visited rural areas to buy hides and would see wild khat and just pick the leaves. Chewing did not spread to other ethnic groups for many years.

Botanists at Makerere University in Kampala have alerted me to the differences between indigenous plants and wild plants that had been introduced to an area by humans or animals. The catalog of the national Botanical Gardens in Entebbe lists khat under its Latin name, Catha edulis, as having the local name of mairungi and being a tree of "Tropical Africa" (NARO, 1999) without specifying whether it was considered indigenous or merely wild to Uganda. A survey of the tree species found in twelve major Ugandan forest reserves found Catha edulis growing only on Mount Elgon (Esegu, 2001, p. 6).

Yet an earlier catalog of Ugandan trees, *The Indigenous Trees of the Uganda Protectorate*, included khat, or Catha edulis Forssk: "Tree usually about 20 ft. high, occasionally attaining as much as 80 ft. Bole straight and slender; bark whitish, crown small" (Eggeling, 1951, p. 78). He also lists common and local names for the tree: "Somali tea; khat tea; mutabungwa (Lunyankole); omunyaga ngongo (Lukiga); tumeyondet (Sebei); lutandwe, kitandwe (Lugishu)" (Eggeling, 1951, p. 78).

The names for khat listed are in the languages of the Ankole and Kiga people who live in the southwest of Uganda, while the Sebi and Bagisu occupy the east of the country. There is also a hint in Eggeling's description that khat thrives in settings abandoned by humans: "The tree is the main coloniser of abandoned cultivation and of scrub on Mt. Debasien, and of scrub in expanding woodland in parts of south Ankole" (Eggeling, 1951, p. 79).

Eggeling further notes that khat is common around Ankole, Kigezi, Karamoja, and Mbale, "in mountain forest; 5–8000 [feet]" (Eggeling, 1951, p. 79). In all of these four areas, Yemenis, usually in collaboration with local people, were involved in the exploitation of wild khat, but in each area the success of the development of a khat industry differs.

ANKOLE

Although several Yemeni informants mentioned harvesting wild khat in south Ankole near the border with Tanzania, this supply has now dried up. Since the 1960s large-scale livestock-rearing projects have been introduced in the Ankole region (Muherera & Otim, 2002), and there is very little tree cover remaining. Attempts by local farmers to grow khat near the town of Mbarara, the capital of Ankole and the seat of the former king (Posnansky, 1975; Steinhart, 2007), failed and there are no khat plantations near Mbarara. In the 1960s khat was imported to the town from Goma in eastern Congo, while currently daily supplies arrive from both Kasenge and from Kabarole District near Fort Portal.

KIGEZI

The Kigezi region lies to south and west of Mbarara. It is a region of steep hills and deep ravines and the beautiful Lake Bunyonyi, which has become popular a tourist attraction for European and North American backpackers (Hodd & Roche, 2002). Part of the beauty of Bunyonyi is the steep terraced fields on the slopes above the lake. These terraces prevent soil erosion and allow a larger population to get a livelihood from agriculture. Robert, a farmer of the Kiga ethnic group living in the remote mountains near the provincial town of Kabale in southwest Uganda, owes his move to khat production to a Yemeni businessman. In 1986 Robert used to bring gifts of wild khat leaves to his friend, an Arab shopkeeper in Kabale. Before this he did not know about the effects of khat-chewing, as it is not part of his Kiga culture. Gradually, Robert started selling wild khat to other people. Then Ali asked for seedlings from Robert in order to start a big plantation. This gave Robert an idea and he took seedlings from his wild trees and started his own plantation of about fifty trees (Anderson et al., 2007). When Ali, a Yemeni resident in Kabale, decided to plant khat, he asked people to bring seedlings from the wild. He learned about taking care of his trees when he was a student in Masaka and there were khat farms nearby at Lyontondwe. Robert was the local man who brought khat to Ali (Anderson et al., 2007).

Lake Bunyonyi, a few miles to the south of Kabale, is the area of Fred's operation. An enterprising young man from the town of Kabale, Fred employs several people to harvest wild khat from the hills overlooking Lake Bunyonyi. He has also planted his own small plot of khat and buys from other local small-scale khat farmers. But they cannot meet local demand this way, and khat is brought to Kabale daily from Kampala.

Further north, but still in the Kigezi region, much of the district was forested as little as twenty years ago. To the west of the town of Rukingiri were large forests, where khat grew wild. Ahmed Khamisi, a second generation Yemeni born in Rukingiri, recalls cycling out of town to pick wild khat in his youth. Most of the forest has been cleared and planted with plantains in large plots that cover entire precipitous hillsides by farmers moving from the south of Kigezi in search of new land. These farmers say that they are also starting to plant tea, with the inducement from a large tea company and a new tea-processing factory where they can sell their leaves that had been erected in 2008. In the newly cleared fields and even within homesteads, the stumps and mutilated trunks of khat trees remain. Some of the trees are still alive, but local people do not touch them, as they have no interest in selling or consuming khat. A local leader, when I visited in 2008, told me that khat is illegal and they are afraid to exploit it. However, they do not obstruct the harvesters who come from Rukingiri and small trading centers.

Karamoja

Karamoja is a poor and underdeveloped region inhabited by the pastoralist Karimojong people. At the turn of the twentieth century, when British colonial officials and European missionaries were much involved in the affairs of the Buganda kingdom, Karamoja remained beyond their remit. A British army relief column, led by James Macdonald, passed through Karamoja in 1897 en route to Sudan (Muhereza & Otim, 2002, p. 114). There was no more government contact for the next fifteen years. Meanwhile, outsiders to the area were interested in Karamjoa only as a source of ivory and slaves: "Whereas there were no economic reasons for the colonials to be in Karamoja, non-official interest in trade in ivory by Arab, Greek, Abyssinian, Swahili and some British ivory traders continued to flourish. Over time Abyssinian traders established themselves in the region and large caravans were camped in what is now known as Dodoth county and were trading in both ivory and slaves" (Muhereza & Otim, 2002).

The traders involved in Karamoja introduced guns to the region by 1910 (Mkutu, 2007, p. 51), and since then, Karamoja has been plagued with violent cattle rustling of animals owned by rival Karimojong clans and neighboring pastoralist groups in Sudan and Kenya (Eaton, 2008; Mkutu, 2007). As recently as 2005, the Karimojong were reported to be trading arms across the border to Kenya and Sudan, with khat a part of this cross-border business, as Mkutu reports: "Interviews indicated that businessmen were involved in transporting arms and miraa (khat) from Kotido district in Uganda to Kachiliba town, West Pokot, in Kenya" (Mkutu, 2007, p. 61).

In a footnote, Mkutu adds that this information was collected through interviews in both Karamoja and West Pokot and by telephone and e-mail communication. He adds that he observed Karimojong warriors chewing khat in Namalu and Kangole in Karamoja (Mkutu, 2007, p. 61).

Khat consumption, although popular in the region, is not part of a Karimojong tradition of leisure or ritual. According to Muhereza and Otim, tobacco snuff and not khat is the key ritual gift in seeking blessings from elders (Muhereza & Otim, 2002, p. 142).

Both Somali and Yemeni traders settled in the Karamoja region, as was outlined in Chapter 1. In this lawless region, from the start of the twentieth century, Yemenis and Somalis were confined to trading centers and small towns such as Moroto. The extraction of khat from the wild would have depended on good relationships with local people, who had already some knowledge of where to find khat.

Eggeling noted that khat was indigenous to Karamoja but did not list any Karimojong name for the tree (Eggeling, 1951, pp. 78–79). Within Karamoja, khat is harvested from Mount Kadam and from Mount Nepak for commercial sale. In 2009, wondering whether it was possible that khat had been introduced to Karamoja by Abyssinian traders or by Yemeni or Somali travelers arriving in the area from Ethiopia or Kenya, I asked a group of khat traders in the trading center of Namalu, near Mount Kadam, where wild khat is harvested and about local names for khat.

Although all the men I talked to were Karimojong, nobody present knew of a local general name for khat. They told me it was called *emiraa* or *emurungi*. Both words are virtually identical to the Kenyan names for khat, miraa and murungi, and the latter is very similar to mairungi, the Ugandan common name for khat. A catalog of Kenyan food plants lists a number of local Kenyan names for khat including miraa and murungi and also includes *emairungi*, the name used by the Teso, neighbors of the Karimajong (Maunda, 1999, p. 87). The Namalu group said that they could not remember any specific Karimojong names for khat used by people living high on the mountains where khat trees grow. But, they added, there are lots of names for the different varieties of khat on Mount Kadam, including *nacupai*, *moroaullduk*, *nachgeliti*, *kaikuu*, *nayena*, *napuyak*, and *tenei*, which are all derived from the places the trees grow. The Kenyan sounding generic names are consistent with the history of the area, as the people on Mount Kadam came originally from Kenya. An elder explained to me that khat from Mount Kadam is harvested by the Kadam clan living on the mountain, who are originally from West Pokot in Kenya, and that they speak a Kalenjin language. The man added that, these days, long-stemmed khat from Mount Kadam is bought up by Somalis who smuggle it into Juba in South Sudan. This type of khat with woody stems and leaves, unlike khat produced in Buganda, keeps well on the journey north. Indeed, a Somali trader I had encountered a few months earlier at a truck stop in northern Uganda was carrying *namalu* khat to Juba. Once in South Sudan, it would become contraband with a sale price of $10.

In May 2009 I visited the trading center of Iriri on a busy market day that found government soldiers of the Uganda People's Defence Force rubbing shoulders with Karimojong cattle herders and petty traders. The soldiers made the scene feel like a military occupation. They were present because of the ongoing insecurity in the region that includes widespread cattle rustling by armed rival clans (Mkutu, 2007). I met some khat traders selling bundles of khat to passengers in passing buses that I had first interviewed in 2004 (Anderson et al., 2007). Later, I had posted photographs I had taken of them to the Catholic mission in Iriri. Now they told me that they had received the photographs. Consequently, they were happy to help me again and introduced me to a local leader who they thought would be knowledgeable about the history of khat harvesting in the area. Sakaya Langale, a retired teacher, was seated under a large neem tree surrounded by several skinny dogs and various men of different ages. He was friendly and informative and told me that

> the Karimojong Tapeth people who live on Mount Napak, [which towers above Iriri], have used khat for a long time, probably about eighty years. The Tapeth are a branch of Lotome subclan. The Tapeth were weak people who could not resist the enemy and had to climb the mountain to escape. There are two groups of Tapeth living on Mount Napak and Mount Moroto. In the past, Iriri was a grazing area for most Karimojong clans. The Karamoja region was a [British colonial] government Protected Area because it was more backward than other places. Then in World War II, Iriri developed into an area where animals were quarantined in order to control the spread of cattle diseases. People sold their animals to traders. A man called Smith had a warrant to buy animals. The animals were taken to the British base in Aden to feed the troops. The livestock purchased in Iriri were herded to the town of Soroti and then put on a train to Kampala and then another train to the port of Mombasa. From there they were sent by sea north to Aden.
>
> About forty years ago people migrated and settled in Iriri after the mission was established in 1958. Groups of Somalis and Arabs also

> came to the Iriri and the Tapeth found a market to sell khat to the Somalis. The Somalis and Arabs had heard that Iriri khat was the best, even "better than Meru khat in Kenya." Now the khat growing on Mount Napak is being destroyed by overharvesting and by drought. Nobody is planting new trees and nobody has thought of cultivating khat in small holdings. Iriri khat is therefore dying out. The residents of Iriri chew khat from Namalu. They harvest it from Mount Kadam where they are related to the Pokot.

These interviews with Karimajong elders indicate that, sometime after World War II, Somalis started purchasing khat from the Karimojong who, in turn, had acquired supplies harvested by the Tapeth and Kadam peoples. Neither of these groups constitute core Karimojong clans, an apartness hinted at by Sakaya Langale during his interview. The people on Mount Kadam are related to the West Pokot, while the Tapeth have only recently become Karimojong. According to Muhereza and Otim, "The Tapeth as a group were distinct from the rest of the Karimojong. In the past they were known to be primarily cultivators living on top of Mount Moroto. They spoke a different language from Ngakarimojong and had different norms and beliefs from those of the Karimojong. . . . Today they are part of the cattle-keeping groups of the Karimojong and they also take part in some Karimojong cultural practices like initiation and rainmaking ceremonies" (Muhereza & Otim, 2002, p. 124).

THE WEST

Kabarole

Large-scale khat production, using local, wild stock, failed in Ankole, Kigezi, and Mbale. In Karamoja the tough climatic and social conditions have ensured that production remains small scale. But as recounted in Chapter 2, the action of the Yemeni hunter who took a wild seedling from the wilderness of Karamoja or somewhere near that region led to the successful khat industry centered on the district of Kararole. In the early 1930s Sulyman Ali settled in Fort Portal and was given land by the *Omukama* (king) of Toro. Toro is one of the kingdoms of the Great Lakes region. In 1876 it fell under the control of the Bunyoro kingdom but by the late nineteenth century was part of the territory controlled by the British (Hodd & Roche, 2002; Medard, 2007). In order to further Lugard's plans for the control of western Uganda, as the kingdom of Buganda, Fort Portal was established by the British in 1893. In the 1930s Fort Portal was expanding: "In the 1930s Europeans and Indians came to set up large tea estates, and shops and residential premises were built" (Hodd & Roche, 2002, p. 164).

Sulyman Ali built his house on the junction of the road leading to Hakibale and Busoro subcounties and employed Toro farmers as porters in his skins and hides business. Rajabu Byarufu was a leading Toro Muslim and a policeman in the employ of the British. He took khat from Sulyman Ali's garden and planted it on his farm. For forty years, the khat remained a very minor crop, while tea production in the area was actively being promoted by the British agricultural officers, particularly from the 1950s (Aluka & Hakiza, 2001).

These days most tea in Kaborole is grown on large estates, including those of the Toro-Mityana Tea Company. Small-scale tea producers, known as outgrowers sell their leaves to the Uganda Tea Growers Corporation (UTGC), which was established in 1966 under the Ministry of Agriculture (Aluka & Hakiza, 2001, p. 439). Nationally, tea is "the third most important traditional export crop" in Uganda after coffee and cotton (Aluka & Hakiza, 2001, p. 440). While tea might be an important national export crop, in Kabarole, khat production is a local industry that supports, at a conservative estimate, hundreds of small holders. Abdullah, a prominent khat farmer, estimates that there are 1,500 farms producing khat in Kabarole. These farmers produce khat that looks like tea bushes: low on the ground and monocropped in neat fields, so the crop resembles a bright green carpet.

Arua

The idea of growing khat commercially spread from Kabarole to Arua, capital of the West Nile region in the extreme northwest (Leopold, 2005). Because it is a national research center, the Entebbe Botanical Gardens was the unlikely venue for the passing on of information about the profits to be had from khat farming. I met Hassan Drattibi, a businessman from Arua and member of the Lugbara ethnic group in Arua in 2007.

According to Hassan, it was his brother, Simei, who introduced khat to Arua. Simei was working as a gardener in the Botanical Gardens in 1962, just on the cusp of national independence. A Toro coworker from Fort Portal told Simei to take the khat seedlings from the Botanical Gardens and plant them at home. Just after independence, Simei took three plants to Arua, where his mother tended them. By the 1960s Simei had a few customers, mostly Yemenis and Somalis. A Mr. Alwi, now deceased, was a big customer. Hassan explained that Arua was particularly "wild" from 1979 when Idi Amin, "a son of the West Nile region" (i.e., indigenous to the region), was ousted from power. Many people from Arua went into exile in Zaire and Sudan. Hassan went to Nairobi and returned from exile in 1982. In the early 1980s they used to harvest their khat in Arua and walk eighteen miles into Zaire to sell to Somalis and Arabs. They were competing with khat from Goma, which is southwest of Arua in Zaire. A particularly good customer, according to Hassan, was a Yemeni who was a brother to the owner of a big bus company, Nile Coaches.

Perhaps a hundred or more farmers around Arua and to the north of the town in Maracha District now grow khat. The khat is monocropped and allowed to grow to a height of one to two meters. But khat is not the main cash crop in the area. Leopold (2005, p. 37), in his monograph of West Nile, mentions local khat production in or near Arua but, like many people in Uganda, incorrectly believes it to be an illicit drug: "The drugs trade in Arua involves locally grown illicit substances such as cannabis (in Uganda this is often confusingly referred to as "opium") and khat (known locally as *mairungi*)" (Leopold, 2005, p. 41).

Writing of the farmers living within "the orbit of Arua town," Leopold also mentions tobacco: "Many of them grow a few cash crops, such as vegetables for sale in the market or tobacco, which is by far the main crop, grown by small farmers on plots of 0.5 to 3.0 acres, and bought by the British-American Tobacco Co. (BAT), which until 1996 had a monopoly" (Leopold, 2005, p. 37).

Tobacco ranks fourth in the league table of Uganda cash crops, and Onzima and Birikunzira (2001, p. 501) have nothing but praise for the leaf: "Tobacco earns revenue to the government in the form of taxes of more than 6.5 million US dollars annually. It provides employment to over 750,000 Ugandans. About 10,000 ha of land is under cultivation of tobacco. Total cash flow earned as revenue within Uganda is more than 9.0 million US Dollars annually" (Onzima & Birikunzira, 2001, p. 501).

In 1928 British American Tobacco Company (BAT) built a cigarette factory in Jinja, in southeastern Uganda, far from Arua (Onzima & Birikunzira, 2001, p. 500). However, this period marked the start of the promotion of tobacco growing in northern and northwestern districts of Uganda. Harvested tobacco leaves are cured in situ, and in 1944, the Department of Agriculture introduced flue-curing, which is carried out in brick, stone, mud, and wattle barns (Onzima & Birikunzira, 2001, p. 515) to Arua District. This process requires wood for burning, "only 6.5 kilos of wood per kilogram of tobacco," according to Onzima and Birikunzira (2001, p. 515). However, sufficient wood is used that BAT and other tobacco producers encourage the planting of eucalyptus as a source of wood fuel, in Arua and elsewhere in areas with a tobacco production industry.

CONCLUSION

While coffee was, and is, the main "official" cash crop in Buganda, and tea the crop promoted by officials in western Uganda, tobacco was the cash crop considered suitable for northern Uganda (Onzima & Birikunzira, 2001). Cash crop production in Uganda was driven by British colonial policies throughout the first half of the twentieth century (Carswell, 2007; Richards et al., 1973). During the second half of the century, khat also became an important cash crop in many areas. Commercial khat did not take off in all areas where it was available in the wild or was introduced as a crop. The four main production areas are also regions where cash crops of legal, culturally acceptable, stimulant drugs (coffee, tea, and tobacco; Goodman et al., 2007) have been, or are, an important part of the local economy. Hence, khat farmers succeeded in Butambala and Kasenge in the coffee belt of Buganda and in Kabarole District in the kingdom of Toro, where tea production was promoted. In West Nile, a region troubled by violence, tobacco was the cash crop of choice, but khat farming was also taken up by scores of small farmers, using stock brought from the British botanical research station at Entebbe.

Chapter 5

Altitude and Attitude

Khat (*Catha edulis*) grows best at altitudes of between 5,000 and 6,500 feet above sea level. It is found growing wild in many mountainous regions of Africa and Asia. Oral histories collected in Uganda indicate that khat grew in hilly areas across Uganda and western Kenya, in south Sudan and in eastern Congo. Botanists believe that the origins of Catha edulis to be in Ethiopia or Yemen, both countries with centuries-long histories of khat consumption. Khat was "discovered" for the Western world by the Danish plant hunter Pehr Forsskal during his expedition to Arabia in 1763. He named the plant *catha* after the local Arabic name, qat. "The '*Catha*' here was his original coinage of the Arabic term into nomenclatural Latin; '*edulis*' signified that the leaves were consumed. . . . Today *Catha* refers to one of about forty genera in the celastraceae family. It appears to have evolved from *Catha spinosa*, a wild diploid variety in Ethiopia that is propagated naturally from seeds. *Catha edulis* is a triploid which is cultivated from shoots rather than seed" (Varisco, 2004, p. 103).

All cultivated khat is derived from Catha edulis in conditions that also favor coffee trees: "Khat shrubs thrive best at elevations ranging from 5,000 to 6,500 feet above sea level, with an average temperature of 65°F and 85°F, good drainage and freedom from frost. Interestingly, this ideal khat ecology is also the optimum condition for the cultivation of coffee" (Gebissa, 2004, p. 15).

However, the ideal khat and coffee ecological zone includes areas as diverse as the Yemeni Highlands where there are no permanent rivers, only *wadis* that remain dry most of the year and the lush agricultural regions of Buganda where rain falls in abundance. The main khat-producing countries are Yemen, Ethiopia, and Kenya, all of which have regions with centuries-long traditions of khat use.

YEMEN

According to Varisco, Yemeni khat consumption and production dates back to the late fourteenth or early fifteenth centuries (Varisco, 2004, p. 106). Agriculture in Yemen was once an "environmentally-sensitive, largely subsistence-based" system (Milich & Al-Sabbry, 1995), and khat was grown on a fairly small scale: "Given the food needs of the population, production of qat trees was rather limited in the past even though it was an important cash crop in some areas" (Varisco, 2004, p. 103).

Both rain-fed and irrigated khat have been grown in the northern Yemeni Highlands since the sixteenth century. As production increased the ecological balance in Yemen has been disturbed. From the late 1970s the increased use of tube wells enabled the spread of khat production but at the price of environmental sustainability. Hence, Varisco reports, "By the end of the end of the 1970s unchecked drilling of tube wells and widespread use of diesel pumps greatly increased the use of irrigated land, often leading to rapid drawdown rates of limited aquifers. Geographers and ethnographers who worked in North Yemen during the late 1970s and early 1980s report dramatic increases in qat production, primarily because of the unchecked construction of wells" (Varisco, 2004, p. 103).

Milich and Al-Sabbry (1995) argue that such an increased use of water from underground aquifers is a rational choice for individual farmers who seek to maximize their earnings from khat, which is by far the most profitable cash crop. These farmers were not defying government guidelines on water management. On the contrary, "One estimate suggests that 80 to 90 percent of new wells in the Highlands are used for qat production (Varisco, 1986). Farmers have been provided with subsidized pumps instead of education in appropriate water-conserving techniques, leading to the installation of wells without regard to future consequences" (Milich & Al-Sabbry, 1995, p. 6).

Milich and Al-Sabbry also report problems with decreasing soil fertility leading to declining crop yields of food crops grown alongside khat. Sorghum, the main staple food of the Yemeni Highlands, is being replaced with khat. Sorghum stalks are a fodder for animals and this resource therefore lost, leading to fewer animals and less organic fertilizer (Milich & Al-Sabbry, 1995, p. 6).

Coffee rivals khat as a longstanding Yemeni crop and is used the world over as a mild psychotropic substance. A Yemeni export cash crop since the Western world took up coffee drinking in the seventeenth century (Matthee, 1995), coffee production has been in decline for a over a century, and traditional Mocha coffee has been unable to compete with plantation-grown coffee in newer production areas across the world (Varisco, 2004, p. 114). Yet, in the 1970s, expanding Yemeni khat production was viewed with displeasure and considered the main cause of the destruction of coffee trees. Kennedy, however, disputes the common claim that khat and coffee grow best in identical conditions and therefore compete. He notes that in Yemen, coffee requires more careful placement on hillsides, while khat is hardy and can be planted on more marginal land that is less suitable for coffee or arable production (Kennedy, 1987). During fieldwork in the 1970s, Kennedy found no evidence of coffee trees being ripped out so that khat plantations could be expanded. Nevertheless, khat is commonly blamed for coffee's demise: "Development planners over the past three decades in Yemen have almost always viewed qat as an obstacle to the introduction of cash crops with market value outside Yemen. Indeed, the upsurge of qat production in the 1970s was directly blamed for the decline in coffee production" (Varisco, 2004, p. 114).

ETHIOPIA

Across the Red Sea from Yemen, khat appears to be directly competing with coffee production. As coffee revenues decline, khat is of increasing importance as an export crop. Ethiopian khat production appears to be less environmentally harmful than the Yemeni situation as reported by Milich and Al-Sabbry (1995). Indeed, two Ethiopian researchers, Gebissa (2004, 2008) and Hailu (2005, 2007) are upbeat about khat.

Khat production in the Eastern Highlands or Harerge, a region in Ethiopia, dates back at least eight hundred years (Gebissa, 2004, p. 3). Production and consumption were originally limited to Muslims to the extent that "the spread of *tchat* [khat] was at first heavily and jealously guarded by Muslims" (Almedom & Abraham, 1994, p. 249; emphasis in original). However, early in the twentieth century, Oromo farmers in Harerge started small-scale, commercial khat production. After World War II, there was an expansion of the land given over to khat, and "between 1954 and 1961, the size of arable land devoted to khat production in Harerge more than doubled, from 2,996 to 7,009 hectares" (Gebissa, 2008, p. 793). The area of land in Harerge devoted to coffee fell as khat production increased: "Khat's main rival cash crop, coffee, which occupied 6.6% of area under cultivation in 1975, dropped to 32,643 hectares or 4.4% in 1983. By the early 1980s, khat had overtaken coffee as a cash crop of choice and was planted on land previously used for growing coffee and food crops" (Gebissa, 2008, p. 793).

This shift from coffee to khat was a wise move, as national "earning from coffee dropped 2.1 billion *birr* [the Ethiopian currency] to 1.9 billion *birr* in 2004" (Hailu, 2007, p. 1). The price of coffee on the world market was also falling: "Its price per pound declined from US$123.4 in 1995 to US$26.9 in 2002. Earnings from pulses and cereals have also declined while those from fruits and vegetables remained low" (Hailu, 2007, p. 1).

Gebissa reports that incomes from khat have increased the well-being and food security of farmers in the Eastern Highlands, who are faring better than nonkhat producers in terms of income, diet, and self-sufficiency (Gebissa, 2008, p. 790). Unlike Yemen, khat has been integrated into mixed farming systems in ways that appear to be sustainable, in that land, water, and soil resources are not degraded by the cultivation of khat trees: "By the early 1990s khat had become part of a diversified cropping system that fit well both into the environment and the agricultural cycle of small-farm households without being too demanding on labor" (Gebissa, 2008, p. 795).

Hailu adds to the praise of khat as a suitable crop for small-scale farmers: "The plant has many advantages: it is resistant to many crop diseases, grows in marginal land, requires low labour inputs and can produce up to four harvests a year. Thus, its net return per acre is often greater than that from coffee. While khat accounts for only 13 per cent of total cultivated land, it contributes 30–50 per cent of farmers' total cash income per year" (Hailu, 2007, p. 1).

In the Oromia region that includes Harerge, khat production has been increasing throughout the twentieth century. From 2001 to 2002 the Oromia region produced 451 million kilograms of khat. However, in recent decades, farmers in other Ethiopian regions have also taken up khat production. Since the 1990s, Southern Region, particularly in Sidama and Gurage zones, production has increased. Government figures indicate that in 2001 to 2002 the Region produced 206 million kilograms of khat (Anderson et al., 2007, p. 24). In Southern Region, like much of Ethiopia where the crops are rain fed, the land is drought prone, and food shortages have occurred in some areas. According to Anderson et al., in Southern Region in recent years, "the food production gap is about 8 billion kg of wheat annually, which is satisfied by purchases from other regions and by food aid" (Anderson et al., 2007, p. 28).

Khat farmers in the region work without the benefit of agricultural extension services and in the face of official disapproval. However, their independent attitude appears to be paying off. Anderson et al. note that in Southern Region, "a meagre 0.0009 per cent of the total agricultural land covered with khat fell under the government's agricultural extension programme. However, farmers in Sidama clearly identified their improved living standards with khat farming, while non-khat farmers in Sidama and Gedeo are still in receipt of food aid following the collapse of coffee prices. Like their fellows in Oromia, farmers here use khat proceeds to purchase foodstuffs and consumer goods" (Anderson et al., 2007, p. 29).

In northern Ethiopia in the Amhara region, which is not a traditional khat-consumption area, farmers have also started planting khat to supply the nearby demand emanating from Addis Ababa. This is still a minor production area compared to Oromia or Southern Region. In Amhara, as in other areas, not only of Ethiopia, but also Yemen and Uganda, khat is replacing coffee: "Recent shifts towards khat cultivation here are mainly due to coffee diseases which have had a very detrimental effect on production in this area, coupled with adverse price fluctuations. Traditional crops such as corn, wheat and *teff* are also being replaced by khat" (Anderson et al., 2007, p. 30).

Another factor influencing the switch to khat is the recent fall in food prices that resulted from a government program to raise food production (Klein et al., 2009). Ethiopian farmers found that that khat prices rose, while the price of the main cash crop, coffee, fell, along with returns on food crops. Khat has a number of other advantages: "In addition to price stability, khat is attractive to farmers because it can be planted all year round, in a variety of soils and usually on terraced hillsides and marginal land. In Ethiopia it is pest resistant, requires minimal inputs, produces a range of secondary benefits (wood for fuel and construction, medicine), and does not compete with food crops" (Klein et al., 2009).

KENYA

Both wild and cultivated khat are available to consumers in Kenya (Anderson et al., 2007). However, the main khat production area lies in north Meru District in the Nyambene Hills that face north toward the arid plains of northern Kenya. Here, like Ethiopia and Yemen, coffee was the major cash crop but failed to bring prosperity.

From as early as 1900, the Igembe and Tigania clans of the Meru people of Nyambene were growing khat, or miraa, as it is commonly known as in Kenya, for sale to an ever widening geographical market (Goldsmith, 1994). In Yemen and Ethiopia, where coffee trees have been removed to make room for khat, there was a choice to be made between these cash crops. By contract, in the 1980s under Kenyan law, it was illegal to uproot coffee trees (Goldsmith, 1994, p. 117). Goldsmith reports that many small holders in the Nyambene Hills defied the law and openly planted food crops on coffee fields (Goldsmith, 1994, p. 118). Goldsmith reports that "the vitality of commercial miraa production contrasted with the decline of the small-scale coffee industry as thousands of small holders farmers were saddled with a crop they not only could not legally uproot or replace, but were bound by Kenyan law to maintain as a monocrop on their farms" (Goldsmith, 1994, p. 117).

As coffee production in the Eastern Highlands of Kenya faltered, miraa production thrived. It was a locally managed crop, grown without agricultural extension or state encouragement or approval. "Miraa cultivation in Meru is confined to a very small section of the Nyambenes, approximately fifty square kilometres, although cultivation is now expanding beyond this core area and even to other part of the district. In contrast to coffee, tea and pyrethrum, cotton, and many other crops produced for the market, miraa is a purely indigenously developed and marketed cash crop" (Goldsmith, 1994, pp. 94–95).

Mixed farming is a key feature of the Nyambene agricultural system (Anderson et al., 2007; Carrier, 2007). The area is intensively farmed with a wide range of food and cash crops that include coffee, pyrethrum, and macadamia nuts, and khat is intercropped with these (Carrier, 2004) in an ecologically sound system of permaculture that allows intensive but sustainable cultivation (Goldsmith, 1994). Tea fared better than coffee as a smallholder cash crop and fitted into the overall system. Hence, in the Nyambenes tea plantations have been planted under khat trees that provide shade (Carrier, 2005, p. 47).

UGANDA: KHAT BECOMES MAIRUNGI

Ethiopia, Yemen, and Kenya are the three leading global khat-producing countries. According to Odenwald,

> Today, the main producing countries are Ethiopia, Yemen and Kenya, where the production, trade and use of khat are not restricted. Ethiopia is considered to be the world's biggest producer, with khat being the country's second largest export product in 1999 (FAO, 2001). In

> Yemen, the area under khat production has expanded dramatically, and the khat sector now produces 10% of the GDP (Ward, 2000; World Bank, 2005). Also in Kenya, the economic importance of khat is considered great, with remarkable monopoly-like trading structures linked to Somalia, its main export destination (Maitai, 1996). The khat sector today feeds millions of farmers and people involved in its trade. (Odenwald, 2007, p. 11)

Ugandan khat production is also considerable. Until publication of *The Khat Controversy* (Anderson et al., 2007), the Ugandan khat industry appears to have been undocumented. Yet the Ugandan khat production cannot be far behind the big three producers. Considered the "khat frontier" (Anderson et al., 2007; Klein et al., 2009), Uganda has actually had a growing khat industry for the past twenty years. Production expanded when Museveni and his National Resistance Army (NRA) took to power in 1986. The NRA brought peace to the south of the country, notably to Buganda, where khat production flourished, particularly in Butambala and Kasenge. In the western kingdom of Toro, khat production in Kabarole District also took off on a commercial basis, while in the extreme northwest of the country, around Arua, khat was planted alongside tobacco. In addition to these main production areas, khat is cultivated in small plots or extracted from the wild by hundreds of enterprising men operating in local khat markets. Thousands of Ugandan men from all ethnic backgrounds, both Muslim and Christian, are engaged in khat production in a range of ecological settings. There are no Ugandan figures on khat acreage or on the volume or value of daily or annual khat sales. Both khat production and its marketing are highly decentralized, making it impossible to measure the extent of the industry.

The appearance of most Ugandan khat differs from that of most commercially produced khat in Yemen, Ethiopia, and Kenya. Yemeni and Ethiopian khat is sold in the form of leafy twigs (Gabissa, 2004; Weir, 1985). The leaves are chewed and the twigs discarded. Kenyan khat from the Nyambene Hills is also presented in the form of leafy twigs, but it is the tender stems that are consumed, while the leaves may be discarded (Carrier, 2007). In Uganda, only khat from Karamoja is similar in appearance to the Nyambene types. Most Ugandan khat is sold as loose leaves already detached from twigs. This Ugandan-style khat resembles *makokaa*, a Kenyan variety of khat grown near the town of Embu in the central highlands and sold in local towns (Anderson et al., 2007). Makokaa production is a minor aspect of the Kenyan khat industry, and Ugandan khat has an appearance that is distinct from the main types on sale in East Africa and, indeed, globally.

As in other countries where khat has become popular, in Uganda there is a plethora of names for the different varieties of khat on sale. These are all known under the generic name of mairungi. Just as khat is commonly known as miraa or murungi in Kenya, as chat in Ethiopia, and as qat in Yemen, the local Ugandan name, mairungi, is widely recognized in Uganda. The term khat, derived from the Somali version of qat or chat, has become the accepted standard spelling of the plant Catha edulis in the academic literature (Anderson et al., 2007). Khat has even made an appearance in a crossword of a Ugandan national newspaper: "22Across, Mairungi (3)" (Complex Crossword, *New Vision*, May 8, 2008).

The answer is qat, the celebrated "flower of paradise" of Yemen (Kennedy, 1987). The appearance of the clue "mairungi" in a crossword featured in the leading Ugandan daily newspaper heralds the arrival of khat on the national scene. However, a rival newspaper, the *Daily Monitor*, appears to be confused about the difference between marijuana and mairungi. In September 2007 it ran a small column where responses to the question "Should marijuana, which brings in a lot of money in Mpigi, remain an illegal crop?" were sent in the form of short message service (SMS) cell phone text messages by readers. Mpigi District is in Butambala, a major khat production area. Most of the responses were, unsurprisingly, about marijuana. However, one anonymous reply was published despite the warning on the column that "only SMS with names shall be published" (SMS Feedback, *Daily Monitor*, September 12, 2007). "You guys are mistaken because what is grown in Mpigi is mairungi not marijuana. Those two are different. Marijuana is locally known as njaga and it's smoked like tobacco while mairungi which is sold openly everywhere is chewed like mulondo [a cream colored root that is chewed for its taste and very mild 'buzz']. Anonymous" (SMS Feedback, *Daily Monitor*, September 12, 2007).

Another respondent did reply about mairungi, but called it marijuana: "I don't know the government's policy on marijuana but when I visited Moyo town recently, I discovered that this stuff is sold and chewed openly in the town centre. Agaba R. N" (SMS Feedback, *Daily Monitor*, September 12, 2007).

The *Daily Monitor* editors missed an opportunity for opening a discussion on khat and farmers' prosperity, and instead, four of the six responses were about cannabis use. Their confusion is only too common in Uganda, where the many people conflate khat and cannabis, talking about them as if they are one substance. The anonymous SMS response set the record straight, but the *Daily Monitor*'s error highlights that mairungi is only just emerging into the consciousness of the general population. Enterprising farmers, on the other hand, have realized that mairungi can indeed "bring in a lot of money," and in many parts of the country where there is sufficient altitude and other key growing conditions, new khat farms are springing up.

THE SOUTHWEST

Farmers planting khat exhibit both an individualistic attitude and an ability to learn from people from outside their own ethnic community. During fieldwork I encountered dozens of these men, each of whom had carved out a small local market for their khat. For example, near Muko trading center on the road to Kisoro in the extreme southwest of the country, a local man established a new khat farm. Silva is a Christian from Kiga ethnic group that intensively farm this part of Uganda (Carswell, 2007). Fred, the main khat trader from the town of Kabale, introduced me to Silva because he had been one of his major suppliers. Muko, where Silva lives, is a collection of not much more than several shops, a tiny café, and a church. Besides Silva's khat, the other farm produce on sale consists of tomatoes and chickens. Muko, however, is not entirely a backwater. Oil and other vital imports that have passed through the Kenyan port of Mombasa on the distant Indian Ocean travel along this route. Hence, although the area is remote from urban centers and the road is unpaved, this is a major trucking route to neighboring landlocked Rwanda and to the vast Democratic Republic of Congo (DRC). Other trucks and buses pass through Rwanda to Burundi. Silva's home and farm is situated on a steep hillside where the volcanic soil is gray. He is the only person in the area growing khat—so far. Silva tells me that he was taught about khat farming by a Somali man called Tawakal from Tororo in eastern Uganda near the Kenyan border. Back in the early 1990s, Tawakal started to supply khat to drivers at the Katuna border between Uganda and Rwanda. Then in about 1994 Tawakal supplied Silva with seedlings that had been harvested from the wild locally in southwest Uganda, taught him how to care for them, and how to harvest the leaves. After that, Silva ordered seedlings from Ethiopia. These were delivered by Ethiopian drivers en route to Rwanda, Burundi, or DRC. Later on Silva tried importing other seedlings from Kasenge, near Kampala, and found that they grew well. The Somali customers nicknamed the local type ***haluwa*** (a type of sweet in Swahili/Arabic), the khat of Ethiopian origin was called *nagasha*, and the third type grown from Kasenge seedlings was named kasenge. Now Silva sells all three types to the main retailer in Kabale rather than to the Tawakal, the Somali who set him up in business. Fred, is an enterprising young Kiga man based in Kabale. He has planted his own small plot of khat bushes and also employs several pickers to harvest wild khat from scattered trees growing high on the terraced slopes above Lake Bunyoni, just south of Kabale.

THE NORTH

Hundreds of miles away from Muko, on the outskirts of the town of Lira in midnorthern Uganda, a handful of farmers have been cultivating mairungi for decades and selling it locally. These men obtained their seedlings from other indigenous Ugandan sellers, and no Somalis or Yemenis were involved in their khat enterprises. Lira lies just outside the main conflict zone of the vicious war that was fought between Uganda government forces and the rebel group the Lord's Resistance Army (LRA). The LRA terrorized northern Uganda from the 1980s until 2007 when some stability was restored to the region. Peace talks were still continuing in late-2009, and many fear that the LRA could yet cause more trouble, as they are still operating in DRC. Cotton is the main cash crop around Lira, which is a bustling district capital with a multiethnic population. Lira lies within the Lango region, home to the Langi people. "The Langi are the ethnic group of Uganda's post-independence president, Milton Obote, and under him they enjoyed wealth as a region as well as ascendancy in the armies of his first (1962–71) and later (1980–85) regimes. The Langi have been subject to violent incursions since the 1970s by cattle raiders, random criminal groupings, armies and rebels" (Lautze, 2008, p. 416).

While Obote is remembered as a vicious tyrant in many parts of Uganda, in Lira a statue commemorates his life. The "Obote" I spoke to not only shares a name with the former president but also political affiliation to the Uganda People's Congress (UPC) and is a local councilor. In 2008 I found Tom Obote at home in his large compound on the edge of Lira. He tells me that he inherited the mairungi trees growing in his compound from his father who had got the seedlings from a Lugbara man from Arua. As we speak, three mairungi traders from Lira harvest khat leaves and put them in clear plastic bags. They charge 3,500 Ugandan shillings (approximately $1.50) per bag, which will be retailed in six smaller bags for a total of about $2.50. Obote said that he and the traders negotiate the price together.

In the dry season the price goes from 3,500 shillings to 5,000 shillings ($1.75–$2.50. In the dry season they try to irrigate, using mains water. But this is not a satisfactory solution as there is a shortage of water in Lira and often the water only comes at night. There is also a problem with fungus, according to Obote. Every week or two, he sprays a fungicide made for tomatoes and an insecticide.

A few kilometers outside Lira, Okello also cultivates mairungi for the local market. Indeed, he takes his harvested leaves to sell in his kiosk in Lira, where eight varieties of sachets of alcoholic spirits, many of them flavored, are also sold. The khat he sells in his kiosk comes from seedlings taken from Karamoja region, to the east of Lira. In 1988 Okello sent a Karimojong man to bring seedlings from near Moroto, he tells me. Okello explains the choice of supply of seedlings by reference to the "happy goat" story, in which a Karimojong goat herder notices that the goats have become frisky after chewing mairungi leaves. Once Okello's plants started yielding khat, he first sold them to Somali truckers, but now the market has diversified and people from many ethnic backgrounds buy mairungi. He sprays the crop regularly with pesticides and harvests them once a week.

MAIRUNGI PRODUCTION

Silva, Fred, Obote, and Okello have all had to learn how to cultivate mairungi "on the job." They are cultivating khat that is a mixture of wild stock (from the hills of southwest Uganda and from Karamoja) and seedlings introduced directly from Ethiopia (from Kenya via Kasenge and from the Entebbe Botanical Gardens via Arua). With no national or even localized traditions of khat production and no government support, mairungi producers have developed varied modes of production, which sometimes mimic and sometimes depart from the practice common in older areas in Yemen, Ethiopia, and Kenya.

Ugandan farmers have learned to cultivate mairungi by applying general agricultural knowledge and by sharing information. For mairungi, there is no traditional body of farming knowledge and nobody outside the khat industry from whom to get expert advice. Yet, by applying their own knowledge, most Ugandan farmers who have tried to grow khat have succeeded. Robert Chambers, in his classic book *Rural Development: Putting Last First*, celebrates local knowledge and regards it as sometimes superior to that of academically trained outsiders (Chambers, 1983). "Rural people's knowledge is often superior to that if outsiders. Examples can be found in mixed cropping, knowledge of the environment, abilities to observe and discriminate, and results of rural people's experiments" (Chambers, 1983, p. 75).

LAND USE AND SOIL FERTILITY

In Ethiopia and Yemen khat has been planted on land previously used for coffee and food crop production (Gebissa, 2008; Milich & Al-Sabbry, 1995; Varisco, 2004). In Yemen such practices have set in motion a process by which the soil is degraded: the best land is reserved for khat, sorghum yields have declined resulting in less fodder for animals, and the availability of organic fertilizers has also declined (Milich & Al-Sabbry, 1995, p. 6). Milich and Al-Sabbry conclude that Yemeni khat farmers, although acting rationally, are "mining the soil resource" of the country (1995, p. 6). In Ethiopia, too, there are similar concerns. Gebissa, although pointing out that khat production increases food security for peasant farmers, recognizes that if the trend for planting more khat continues, there will be increasing stress on land and water resources: "If this trend continues, national food production would diminish, since it is always the best, most productive lands that are converted to khat orchards. The country would be forced to spend ever larger amounts of hard currency on food imports just to maintain the status quo, exacerbating the already fragile food condition of the country" (Gebissa, 2008, p. 797).

By contrast, in the Nyambene Hills of Kenya, khat has been cultivated in an intercropping system that does not degrade the soil. In addition, khat is not planted on land with the best soils (Carrier, 2007; Goldsmith, 1994).

In Uganda, the most common system for growing khat that farmers have adopted is one of intercropping. Farms in Buganda usually intercrop small khat trees with bananas, coffee, and food crops, such as beans and maize. Low soil fertility is not reported to be a problem. On the contrary, many farmers told me that khat grows best in poor soils. Indeed, the superior nature of khat from Kasenge, where the soil is not particularly good, over the khat produced in neighboring Butambala, is often attributed to the superior soil of the latter area. Farmers are also adamant that they should not use chemical fertilizer because it is not good for khat. They do sometimes apply organic fertilizer in the form of mulched weeds or cow dung. This practice is applied by khat farmers across Uganda from the Arua in the northwest to Mbale in the southeast. Farmers have applied their overall local agricultural knowledge to khat cultivation, and also share information among themselves. Soil degradation by khat plantations does not appear to be a problem for future generations of Ugandans, provided the current practices of intercropping and the application organic fertilizers continue.

WEEDING

As a perennial tree or bush, khat does not require annual planting, and therefore, its cultivation is relatively light on labor (Gebissa, 2008; Goldsmith, 1994; Hailu, 2008; Varisco, 2004). Indeed, in areas of Uganda where khat is intercropped with coffee, bananas, and other crops, there is little need for weeding at all. Organic waste, such as leaves and banana fronds are left to rot on the ground where they fall, keeping down weeds and providing nourishment for the soil. The vast majority of farmers use family labor to do any necessary weeding of the fields planted with khat. However, on a few large plantations of up to ten acres, the farm owners employ outside labor to weed the crop.

The Byarufu family in Karabole District in western Uganda are one of the biggest producers of khat in the country. Their crop, in the form of monocropped, low bushes that resemble tea bushes, is planted in a large field covering several acres. Weeding of this valuable crop is carried on a seasonal basis by migrant laborers, mostly men from the Kiga ethnic group. These workers are housed in dormitory-style "quarters" provided by their employer. The Byafuru family spokesman, Ahmed, said that he considered his own ethnic group, the Toro people who are native to Kabarole, too lazy to employ, while Kiga people are hard working. Other prosperous but smaller khat farms in Kabarole, however, employ local labor for weeding, including Toro people, often women who have fallen on hard times. Local officials and farmers alike report that AIDS had affected Kabarole badly and that there are many struggling female-headed households in the area. Many people laboring on big khat farms cultivate their own small plots of mairungi. These provide poor farmers with "kerosene, sugar, and candles," in the words of Ahmed Byarufu.

PESTICIDES

Ugandan khat producers have no qualms about using pesticides, and the practice appears to be virtually universal. The sight of men walking in khat-production areas wearing gum boots and with plastic canisters of pesticides strapped to their backs is common. Across the country on thousands of mairungi farms, the spraying of plants occurs at least one a month and often more frequently than that. For example, the

Byarufu family sprays their mairungi bushes every twenty-one days, otherwise "caterpillars eat the leaves." As the area is blessed with frequent rainfall, it is expected that harvesting specific bushes in rotation leads to the washing away of residue by the rain. This may not always happen, however, and the sprayings every three weeks are too much for discerning consumers. Mahmoud, a trader who buys khat regularly from the Byarufu family, complained that *byarufu* mairungi sometimes had a bad taste due to the over use of pesticides. Mahmoud could have avoided the chemical residue on his khat by washing it before use. But this is not the usual practice, and the idea of washing the leaves does not even occur to consumers, who like to follow the same rituals in their chewing habits.

In some areas of Uganda, notably in and around the Mabira Forest, the fungal disease, coffee wilt (Trachomycosis; Musoli et al., 2001, p. 414), is a serious threat to the health of khat plants. One farmer complained about coffee production, saying "coffee dries up and get diseases and the payment for sale of berries is only twice a year." In this area, khat is grown as a small tree intercropped with coffee, bananas, and other crops. Farmers in the Mabira Forest and elsewhere report that vanilla prices have collapsed and that farming vanilla is a waste of time, money, and effort. Farmers report that first their coffee trees and khat are affected unless the crop is sprayed twice a month, otherwise the leaves will wilt and fall. Coffee trees have already been badly affected by coffee wilt disease: they first wilt and turn inward, becoming dry before falling (Musoli et al., 2001, p. 414). There was a brief attempt by the Ugandan government program, the National Agricultural Advisory Service (NAADS), to introduce vanilla as a cash crop (NAADS, 2003).

Care of khat, including spraying, can lead to a highly prosperous enterprise, even in areas where other farmers have given up khat production because their plants died from disease. For example, Vincent planted one and a half acres of khat on his farm to the east of the Mabira Forest, near the main highway to the town of Jinja. It was his wife's idea to import seedlings from Kasenge, an area producing premium khat, and not her home area, Butambla, also an established khat production area. The seedlings were planted in 1987, shortly after Museveni came to power. Vincent buys grass from his neighbors to use as mulch for the trees, he irrigates in the dry season, and he applies pesticides at least monthly. He spends 200,000 shillings (approximately $100) on chemicals and water per round of spraying. This outlay has helped to make Vincent prosperous: he now has three wives and a motorcycle. Yet, a few minute's walk from Vincent's farm, another family of khat producers complained that some of their trees died at the same time as the coffee wilt disease became a serious problem.

Pests are also a particular problem for khat producers in the northern West Nile region. One farmer reported spraying his khat as much as twice a week to "keep it fresh." Farmers in this area considered the dry season the worst time for pests, and many reported increased frequency of spraying during this period. Of course, during the dry season, there is less likelihood that rain will wash away chemical residue.

The type of pesticides used varies, with some farmers desperately trying out new brands. As one farmer in Arua commented, "We started using Ambush type, but now there are many types we use." I encountered another farmer in the area spraying his khat with foul-smelling Cypercle and with another stronger type in reserve. He picked up from my questioning that spraying might be problematic but remained adamant that it was necessary, saying that the trees that had not been sprayed recently had suffered from disease.

Brands such as Ambush and Roket, an Indian manufactured product containing profenofos and cypermethrin, are very popular, as are pesticides marketed for the protection of tomato plants. Farmers appear to have little technical knowledge about the chemical composition of the pesticides they buy. With no extension or agricultural service for khat, the choice of product is a matter of word of mouth and trial and error. Although voicing many concerns about the spread of khat consumption, Ugandan officials are silent about pesticides on khat and appear to have no knowledge of the practice. Internationally, however, the issue of the use of pesticides on khat trees and bushes is attracting concern and condemnation, as the use of chemical treatment on khat appears to be spreading.

In the Nyambene Hills of Kenya spraying appears to not be the general practice. Goldsmith, writing about the situation in the early 1990s, reports that farmers know how to treat diseases without resort to chemicals: "Miraa, like most indigenous cultivars is disease resistant. The scourge of *uura* (Aspirilla melea), . . . is especially a problem for valuable *mbaine* [old] trees. This bacterial disease affects many forest species as well as bananas tea, mwenjela, and other components of the indigenous agroforestry system, and is most common in formerly forested areas. The only chemical treatment for infected trees is the application of methyl bromide, a chemical used for sterilizing greenhouse soil so toxic that the sale of it to local farmers is out of the question" (Goldsmith, 1994, p. 124).

It may be that the Nyambene Hills have a microclimate that suits khat perfectly, as in nearby, hotter areas, khat trees were reported to be prone to fungal disease (Carrier, 2003, p. 50). Nevertheless, there is evidence a decade after Goldsmith's fieldwork of pesticide spraying in the Nyambene Hills, although Carrier still doubts that most trees are in the region are sprayed with chemicals (Carrier, 2003). Farmers in the Nyambenes report that that their trees are "hardy enough to resist many blights that affect other trees" (Carrier, 2003, p. 50). Carrier notes that the Nyambene khat traders' association, Nyamita, urges farmers not to spray any chemicals on their khat trees (Carrier, 2003, pp. 211–212). However, the very fact that some traders have taken to declaring their khat chemical-free (Carrier, 2003, p. 49) rather than allaying concerns raises suspicion that much Nyambene khat is indeed sprayed.

Chemical spraying is also becoming more common in parts of Ethiopia and Yemen. For example, "Farmers in Gurage zone have recently taken to spraying insecticides to exterminate a worm which attacks their khat and depreciates its yield and value. However, this innovation has caused outrage among consumers as many have complained of stomach aches and a rather 'strange euphoric effect' that they are inclined to attribute to the chemicals. After a spate of similar complaints in the early 1980s in Yemen, producers there retreated from the use of pesticides and fungicides for fear of contaminating the khat (Kennedy 1987)" (Anderson et al., 2007, p. 28).

Although it is asserted that "khat is relatively strong and resistant to disease and insect attack" (Anderson et al., 2007, p. 22), pesticides are causing concern internationally. Washing khat before consumption is not normal practice in Uganda, Ethiopia, London, or anywhere in the world. The fear is that residual chemicals are being consumed along with the khat leaves, causing illness and physical damage. Yemeni khat producers have embraced the practice of spraying their trees with pesticides, particularly dimethoate (Milich & Al-Sabbry, 1995, p. 6). The results of ingesting dimethoate can be can be dire, according to Milich and Al-Sabbry (1995): "Dimethoate is easily absorbed through the skin, and it is unlikely that precautions against exposure are taken the pesticide's applicators or casual passersby. Acute toxicity can cause convulsions and respiratory failure (Arizona Poison Control Center, Tuscon, pers. Comm. With authors, Jan. 1995). A growing concern in Yemen is that pesticides are being applied to qat shortly before harvest. While the chemical breaks down readily when exposed to water, Yemen is, after all, a country with very distinct dry seasons; the probability that dimethoate is not rainwashed from the leaves is therefore quite high" (Milich & Al-Sabbry, 1995, pp. 6–7).

A UK government report reviewing the medical and social effects of khat bases its discussion of residue dimethoate on khat leaves on a study by Date et al. (2004):

> Residue pesticide on khat leaves is a cause of concern for khat consumers. A study in Yemen has addressed this problem. The investigators reported that khat production and use of pesticides have increased in recent years. Two sources of khat were identified that had significantly different levels of the pesticide dimethoate on the leaves. There was a difference in adverse health effects depending on which source the khat came from; with more complaints of weakness, runny nose and congestion from the source with the higher level of residue pesticides.
>
> The report noted that although there were measures in place to regulate the use of pesticides in Yemen, many farmers were not compliant. Public information in Yemen advises chewers to wash khat before use. Although a causal relationship cannot be demonstrated, the association between residual pesticides and adverse health effects warrants consideration and future attention. (ACMD, 2005, pp. 24–25)

In the United Kingdom, Yemeni khat has gained a bad reputation with regard to residue chemicals, particularly dichlorodiphenyl trichloroethane, the synthetic pesticide more commonly known as DDT. UK customs officials wear gloves when making checks of imported khat to confirm that there are no illicit drugs packed in with the legal khat: "As they open boxes they wear plastic gloves to protect themselves from the DDT that has been found on some consignments, particularly those from Yemen. The presence of so toxic a chemical is worrying, especially as many khat chewers are entirely unaware that the harmful residues of pesticides used to protect the trees may be found on the leaves they will put in their mouths" (Anderson et al., 2007, pp. 168).

Irrigation and Seasonality

Khat is an adaptable tree that grows on marginal land and in semiarid areas. However, irrigation of the crop during the dry season can increase yields. For example, some Ethiopia farmers have installed irrigation systems that enable them to increase khat yields from twice to four times a year (Anderson et al., 2007, pp. 24). In Ethiopia, however, expanding khat production may lead to "stress to the finite water resources" (Gebissa, 2008, p. 796), while in Yemen, "water is being squandered" due to demand for tube wells to irrigate khat (Milich & Al-Sabbry, 1995, p. 6).

The situation in Kenya and Uganda, where rainfall is more abundant, is different, and in those countries mechanized irrigation is not used except by a handful of farmers. Yet, in Uganda, some enterprising farmers have tried experimenting with irrigating their mairungi crop during the dry season.

Ben's parents died of AIDS, and he is now in charge of the family farm and responsible for his siblings' care, including school and college fees. This enterprising young farmer in the Mabira Forest set up a system of pipes leading from a stream running through his land to individual khat trees. A small generator provides power to pump water directly to the roots of his khat trees. Before he set up this system, they used to pay contractors to truck in water in jerricans, and then they hand-watered the crops. The irrigation system has enabled Ben to maintain the same level of output and return all year round. Ben harvests his crop weekly: in the dry season, the yield is five large plastic bags of khat with each bag fetching 15,000 Uganda shillings (approximately $7.50); in the wet season, the weekly yield is fifteen bags, sold for 5,000 Uganda shillings (approximately $2.50) each.

In most cases, where Ugandan farmers do irrigate, the process involves nothing more than people hand-watering using buckets filled with water from streams or, where farms are located near urban centers, from taps. But most farmers do not bother with irrigation, and many report that they actually make more money during the dry season when the supply of khat decreases and the price shoots up.

In Ethiopia, too, Gabissa found that by the 1980s, farmers had started irrigating their khat, attracted by the prices rises in the dry season: "Farmers optimized their return, especially during dry seasons when khat prices usually rose to ten times the rainy season values. The use of irrigation intensified khat production by extending harvest periods and increasing yields per unit" (Gebissa, 2004, p. 145).

In eastern Ethiopia, irrigation was worthwhile as the leaves could be harvested more often, perhaps as much as four times year (Anderson et al., 2007, p. 24). In Uganda, while there is variation across khat growing regions and even between individual farms, khat trees and bushes typically yield leaves for harvesting between six and ten times annually. Frequent returns are due, not only to rainfall, but also to the form in which khat is harvested. In Yemen, Ethiopia and Kenya khat is typically harvested as twigs topped off with tender leaves. In Uganda, apart from khat harvested from the wild in the Karamoja region, leaves are plucked from the bushes or trees, making the wait for the plant to put out and grow new leaf-bearing shoots unnecessary.

HARVESTING

The Ugandan khat industry is decentralized and unregulated, and variation in the mode of production and marketing is wide. The arrangements for harvesting khat, even within the same producer region, differ from one farm and from one mountainside to another.

I estimate that over 95 percent of khat consumed in Uganda comes from leaves cultivated by farmers. But, although forests are dwindling, some khat is still collected from tress growing in the wild. In Karamoja, expert harvesters traverse the steep mountainsides and bring fresh supplies to wholesalers in the trading centers of Namalu and Iriri. These men and boys live in an unforgiving environment in a region remote from the services and structures of contemporary Uganda. Their existence is similar to that of harvesters of wild khat in the Chyulu Hills of southern Kenya, who live in the hills where they "poach" khat from a forest reserve, only descending to the plains to sell the leaves they have gleaned to wholesalers (Anderson et al., 2007, p. 94).

The harvesting of wild khat has been somewhat tamed in the southwest of Uganda. Fred, who buys khat from farmers and also has planted his own crop to supply the market in the town of Kabale, has also arranged a regular supply of khat growing on hillsides. He reports that he used to employ young boys as harvesters, but he now has a team of about eight adults, including himself. They walk the hillsides, harvesting from trees known to them, which they have cut so they sprout again quickly and to make the harvesting easier. Similarly, north of Kabale, near the town of Rukingiri, khat traders simply travel to areas that were recently forested but are now turned over to agricultural production, and they pluck leaves from the khat tees that have escaped being felled. In this area, farmers are not interested in khat, as they report that they believe it an illegal crop. They leave harvesting to the townspeople and simply ignore the potentially valuable khat growing around them.

These farmers in Kabale are less adventurous than the many thousands of Ugandan khat farmers who harvest their crops daily, weekly, or monthly. Larger producers usually harvest a different section of their khat plantation daily, while smaller producers settle for weekly or monthly harvesting. Some smallholders harvest khat themselves and sell it to wholesalers with whom they have a prior arrangement.

A common, alternative arrangement is for the traders to come to the farms, pick the khat themselves, and then pay the farmer on the spot.

More prosperous producers, however, employ local labor as harvesters, paying a few cents for each plastic bag filled. Typically, women and children work as harvesters. In Kabarole District the issue of child labor in khat production has resulted in an informal pledge from the farmers that they will only employ children during school vacations.

At Buwola Primary School in the Mabira Forest, which I visited in 2007 with a local leader and prominent khat producer, Issac, the teachers are reluctant to condemn khat outright as they are aware that it brings much income to the area. However, they do comment that they forbid chewing khat in class! Yet, once Issac moves out of earshot, they say they are concerned that children, particularly boys, stay away from school to harvest khat, and that there are more girls than boys in class, which is unusual for Uganda. School dropout rates are high in the area, and the teachers are not impressed by the claims of khat producers that "khat educates our children." The teachers insist that high educational attainment, such as a university education, is for a tiny minority, and that most khat farmers are not interested in education. The children are high earners, they explain: harvesters are paid about 2,000 shillings ($1) per bag of khat picked and can earn up to 10,000 shillings ($5) a day, which they use to buy nice clothes and soda. This money is not handed over to their parents, who may believe that their truanting children are actually in school.

The same situation pertains in the Nyambene Hills, where children routinely work in the khat industry (Carrier, 2007). A UN report on the practice cites the concerns of agricultural extension workers: "Child labour is widely used in miraa production. Agricultural extension workers report that young boys are employed to climb the trees to harvest the stems and that children do the bulk of the sorting into bundles—their small nimble fingers working quicker and more delicately than those of adult workers. The extensive use of child labour in the miraa industry is given as the explanation for the very low school enrolment in Nyambene district" (UNODC, 1999, p. 77).

ATTITUDE

Khat farmers in Uganda and elsewhere have in common a certain attitude: they are independent and not afraid to experiment. Quality khat, they found, does not favor rich soils, so that leaves from Kasenge are considered better than those grown in Butambala where the land is more fertile. Other lessons, derived from trial and error and passed on by word of mouth, include combating the problem of pests with chemical pesticides and the management of the dry season in some areas. Each of the Ugandan major khat production areas varies: the khat plantations look different, the names of the khat are different, and the organization of the production process varies. This is hardly surprising as families of many ethnic groups farm khat across much of the country.

Chapter 6

Wholesale Risks

Western explorers found both coffee and khat being consumed in Yemen and Ethiopia. Both substances are stimulants with a bitter taste, and, therefore, it might be expected that coffee and khat would have an equal chance in making the transition from a locally consumed plant product to becoming an internationally traded commodity. Yet it is coffee and not khat that became a global commodity and a vital part of social and commercial life in the seventeenth century:

> Coffee was sold in Venice in 1640. In France, Marseille had its first acquaintance with coffee in 1644 and Paris soon followed suit. The first European coffee-house opened in Venice in 1645.
>
> Simultaneously, coffee began to be imported via the Maritime trade. The Dutch, whose trade records from Mokha [Yemen] mention coffee beans in 1616, were the first Europeans to include coffee in their commercial activity. (Matthee, 1995, p. 27)

From the sixteenth century until the present day, coffee drinking continues to spread all over the world, while khat only became a minor global commodity during the last two decades (Anderson et al., 2007). What held back the spread of khat lies, not in its bitterness, but within the substance itself. Consumers and traders of khat have known for centuries that its leaves and stems must be consumed while still fresh if chewing them is to have a pleasurable psychotropic effect. If chewed more than a day after being picked, khat starts to lose potency. From 1887 until the 1970s researchers believed a substance they named cathine to be the main active ingredient (Gebissa, 2004). In the 1970s an unstable alkaloid, cathinone, was discovered. Since cathinone is approximately ten times stronger than cathine and is largely responsible for the stimulating effects produced by khat chewing, the reason for the short shelf life khat consumers reported finally understood by chemists.

Transport

As cathinone starts to break down rapidly in leaves and stems once twigs are cut from the live plant, efficient transportation systems are vital to an expanding khat trade. Therefore, as has been noted by all who write about the khat trade (Anderson et al., 2007; Carrier, 2007; Gebissa, 2004; Goldsmith, 1994; Kennedy, 1987), the volatile nature of cathinone defines the khat trade. For centuries, consumption was confined to the parts of Yemen, Ethiopia, and Kenya that could be easily reached on foot or mounted on donkey or camels. This volatility of khat is well known to producers and consumers, and rapid transportation has been key to the geographical spread of markets. Carrier (2005b) examines the urgency of the trade and transport of Kenyan khat that is linked to the economic necessity of fresh supplies reaching the market quickly. He notes that "to be involved in the miraa trade therefore requires operating in a highly compressed timescale, and the frenetic activity of traders and transporters bears this out" (Carrier, 2005b, p. 539). Khat is transported from the Nyambene Hills of Kenya in specially customized Toyota pickup trucks that rush khat directly to domestic consumers or to Wilson Airport in Nairobi for air freighting to remote parts of Kenya and to Somalia. Other supplies are delivered to the Eastleigh area of the city where they are repackaged in cardboard boxes for export to Europe, along with green beans and other vegetables (Anderson et al., 2007).

In his monograph, *Leaf of Allah*, Gebissa (2004) traces the spread of khat consumption within Ethiopia and to countries such as Somalia and Djibouti in the Horn of Africa, to the development of modern transportation by road and rail. The Harerge region is the traditional heartland of Ethiopian khat production and consumption, and this continued to be the case into the twentieth century. However, after the completion of a railroad that passed through the region from the capital, Addis Ababa, to the new French colonial port of Djibouti on the Red Sea khat was transported by rail (Gebissa, 2004). Hence, as Gebissa describes, "It was only after the Addis Ababa-Djibouti railroad reached Dire Dawa that small amounts of fresh khat began to be exported by rail to Djibouti, and thence by dhow to Aden. More khat could have been exported from Harer at this time to meet growing demand in the French and British colonies. The potential was not fully realized owing to the absence of a faster means of delivering khat from the production sites to the railhead in Dire Dawa" (Gebissa, 2004, pp. 53–54).

Dire Dawa has now developed into a major wholesale market for khat and a collection point for municipal tax revenue, with 60 percent of the city's income coming from khat (Anderson et al., 2007, p. 37).

TRADING KHAT IN UGANDA

In Uganda, where khat production is spread across the country, the trade of the plant's leaves is more localized and more recent than in either Kenya or Ethiopia. Just twenty-five years ago, when around the time that President Yoweri Museveni and his National Resistance Movement (NRM) came to power and order was restored to many parts of the country, the khat market was small and dominated by traders of Yemeni or Somali origins. Now wholesalers and retailers are drawn from a range of ethnic backgrounds with varying educational levels. Many are women. Like the farmers with whom they deal, the traders who get khat from the farm gate to deliver to consumers exhibit certain key attitudes: they must be entrepreneurial and not afraid of government authority and they must be adaptable and able to move fast.

Ugandan khat is transported to retail markets on motorbikes, in sedan cars, and minibus taxis, with suppliers, wholesalers, and retailers negotiating terms for delivery and payment. The business is completely decentralized and unregulated and each khat-producing area has developed different arrangements for wholesaling, transporting, and retailing the leaves. Arrangements for payment of suppliers also vary and are based entirely on trust. Prices are negotiated between farmers and wholesalers and between wholesalers and retailers, with the locus of the power to set prices varying from area to area but resting mostly with the wholesalers. In some areas farmers sell their own stock directly to local consumers, while in other places retailers visit farms and pick their own supplies, paying the farmer on the spot. Unlike the Nyambene region of Kenya, in most Uganda areas there is no system of sale or return (Anderson et al., 2007). The traders operate in a risky business environment, one where the police operating as if khat were illegal may seize your stock or even imprison you, where stock may be spoiled if it does not arrive at the market in good time, where unsold stock usually cannot be returned to the supplier, and where your business rivals may do all they can to sabotage you. On the other hand, lucky and resourceful traders can grow prosperous in the khat trade.

The daily commercial needs of rural areas and of travelers in Uganda are served by trading centers, which comprise a few dozen shops and kiosks selling basic supplies. Apart from in the north of the country, such as on the road to Kitgum, most of these trading centers also sell mairungi. In remote places, such as Kitgum in the extreme north of the country, only about twenty bundles arrive on the bus from Kampala daily. Kitgum is far from khat farms, without Yemeni or Somali residents and any tradition of mairungi consumption, but some people working in the transport business want, and get, khat. Khat is sold in all towns in Uganda: in small towns the consumers number in the hundreds, and in bigger towns thousands of people consume khat daily.

A review of all commercial khat outlets would be tedious in the extreme. But in the following sections, the supply system of khat to four major urban centers—Kampala, Gulu, Mbarara, and Jinja—are described.

KAMPALA

The capital of Uganda, Kampala, is the biggest market for khat. However, from the 1930s until the 1980s, small amounts were sufficient to satisfy the demand of Yemenis and Somalis based in Kisenyi, a low-lying, downtown area adjacent to the Nakivubo Channel, where non-Ganda, or "strangers," as the local people describe them, congregated to set up home and do business. The Saad family, which was led by successful businessmen of Yemeni origin, owned parts of Kisenyi. Still in Kisenyi but on higher ground, Somalis from Kenya and those discharged from the King's African Rifles (KAR) congregated in an area nicknamed "Little Mogadishu." To satisfy the needs of this handful of Somali and Yemen men, supplies of khat were imported from the Nyambene Hills of Kenya in the 1960s.

Abdulahi, an ethnic Somali whose father migrated to Uganda from Ethiopia and a long-term resident of Kisenyi, recalls the khat trade after Uganda's independence during the first period that Milton Obote was in office in the 1960s. At this time Abdulahi had an import license that enabled him to source khat from Kenya. When I spoke to him in 2007, he recalled that the customs officials treated khat like cabbages and taxed a customs duty levy of ten shillings per *bunda* (a wholesale package comprising ten retail sizes bundles; Anderson et al., 2007). Meru traders also brought khat from the Nyambene Hills to Kampala by rail from Nairobi at this time. It was in the 1970s, and a decade later, during the second regime of Milton Obote, popularly known in Uganda as "Obote II," that Abdulahi started trading Ugandan-grown khat. Abdulahi traded with khat farmers from the village of Kabasanda, where the founder of khat in that area, Sheikh Semakula, was based. Traders and farmers in both Butambala and the area of Kasenge recall that Somalis used to come daily from Kampala to buy wholesale supplies of khat and then returned to Kampala to retail it. Gradually, local, indigenous Ugandans took the initiative and the wholesale trade largely passed from Somali hands.

Originally from Tanzania and probably best described as a "Swahili," Mama Juma, another Kisenyi-based, veteran mairungi seller also recalls that khat used to be imported from Kenya in the 1970s. Then another supply route of khat harvested from the wild in Karamoja was established. Mama Juma and other veteran khat traders in Kisenyi also recall the second-generation Yemeni Nasher brothers and their friend Thabit as actively involved in the khat trade.

A strong tie between Kampala-based Somalis and the khat farmers in Butambala had been established since the 1940s. Somali traders also brought supplies from Kabasanda in Butambala during the 1960s and 1970s. Personal business links between individual farmers and traders were important, so that Abdulahi, for example, recalls his "friend" Simon who supplied khat. However, from the 1970s on, the area of Kasenge, about a thirty-minute drive south of Kampala, started replacing Kabasanda in Butambala as the producer of premium khat. It was not just that Kasenge was more accessible than Mpigi, which is situated more than one hour's drive from the city, but that the quality of the Kasenge khat is considered superior to the types produced in Kabasanda.

Denis Kasuga, who produces premium khat in Kasenge, which is branded as *kasuga*, got into the khat business through contacts with Somalis from Kisenyi. Denis's family owned land in Kasenge, but they were not full time farmers: his father worked as a finance officer in the East African Development Bank and his mother was a nurse in a city council hospital in Kisenyi. According to Denis, a Somali gave his mother a khat seedling and later came to see how the precious plant was faring. This was a typical pattern reported by many older farmers in the area: Somalis came to Kasenge and taught locals to cultivate and harvest khat.

As the demand for khat has grown since the 1980s, the number of farms producing it and the number of traders have kept pace. The type of people entering the business has also widened to include women and men from many ethnic backgrounds.

There are now perhaps five hundred farms growing khat in Kasenge. Farmers either sell the crop, unharvested in the field, or harvest it themselves or employ local people to pick khat. As I found in 2004 when I first visited Kasenge, arriving daily on foot and on mopeds at muddy spaces on the roadside, young men and women dressed in their city clothes deal directly with the farmers (Anderson et al., 2007). The situation remained unchanged in 2009. Wholesale and retail traders travel daily to the area, usually public transport on motorcycle taxis or shared minibuses. These traders make a good living but are far from wealthy people. Each farmer brokers deals with individual traders concerning price, with sellers of high quality khat able to negotiate a better deal.

Some of the wholesalers who brave the mud or dust of the farms take the stock they have just purchased a few kilometers to the central wholesale depot located at Kesenge trading center on the main, marram road to Kampala. At the depot wholesalers and retailers from Kampala, mostly young Ganda women, trade with wholesalers who live in the local area and broker sales between the farmers and people from the city. Perhaps five hundred people use the depot daily (Anderson et al., 2007).

Leaving Kasenge in August 2007, our car is flagged down by transport agents looking for a small cash "commission" for taking a young khat trader, Harriet, to Kampala. We see that Harriet, who we have not met before, is carrying two large carrier bags of khat and we agree to take her and give the tout his commission. After introducing ourselves and a brief explanation that I am researching khat, Harriet proves willing to talk and explains that she has just paid 35,000 shillings ($17) for her stock, which is destined for sale in Arua Park, the major lorry and bus depot for the West Nile region in the extreme northwest of Uganda. Harriet says that she expects to get 60,000 ($30) shillings from the sale of the khat she is carrying. But this is not pure profit as she has to pay about $2 for transport to and from Kasenge daily, and she has to pay 40,000 shillings ($20) for "rent" every three months for her pitch on the sidewalk near Arua Park, the Kampala bus station where transport to the north of the country sets out. Harriet has been in the business about a year, since she separated from her husband. She claims that she does not chew khat. Refusing payment for the lift, we drop her at the busy bus park, and she starts selling immediately to nearby bus passengers. A year or so later I meet Harriet again. She still trades in Arua Park, but now she chews as she sells.

Harriet is typical of the enterprising women making a living retailing khat. Women, particularly those who are single, divorced, or proclaim themselves widows, commonly make a basic living by retailing khat not only in Kampala but also across the country in Somali-dominated parts of Kenya and in the Horn of Africa (Anderson et al., 2007; Beckerleg, 2008).

In Kampala, khat is sold openly from pavement stalls and kiosks in Kisenyi and Arua Park and a host of other discrete outlets scattered across the Ugandan capital. In Kisenyi, now a sprawling slum area where metal recyclers are concentrated, khat consumption and trade is centered on some scruffy shops and cafés owned by the Saad family and located opposite the Nakivubo Stadium. Retailers selling their wares from wooden or cardboard boxes pay local business owners a monthly fee of 15,000 shillings ($7.50) to sit outside their shops and cafés. They are being pushed out by the redevelopment of Kisenyi, as parts of the area are demolished and the scrap dealers and welding workshops evicted, being replaced with shops and a bus depot. Despite this redevelopment, for the time being at least, the Kampala city council usually tolerates the khat trade but does not collect trading license revenue. Only in the run up to the British Commonwealth Heads of Government Meeting in 2007, according to Mama Juma, did council officials harass traders, curtailing the number of hours they could operate in an apparent attempt to clean up the city before the anticipated arrival of Queen Elizabeth II in Kampala. Usually, however, khat is on sale in Kisenyi for twenty-four hours a day. Daily from midmorning, scores of retailers sell the *kasenge* and *kabasanda*, types of khat (Klein & Beckerleg, 2007). Business peaks in the afternoon and early evening with new supplies arriving from Kasenge and Kabasanda.

Some customers pay in as little as 500 shillings for khat, the same amount of money that the sensationalist *Red Pepper* newspaper reports is required to enable prolonged sexual performance! Hence, under the heading, "Sex and Mairungi," the subheading read, "With mairungi of only Sh500 you can romp [have sexual intercourse, in *Red Pepper* parlance] for four hours non-stop" (*Red Pepper*, July 13, 2008). Consumers may well debate the veracity of the *Red Pepper* claim, but in fact most people in Kampala actually pay more than 500 shillings for khat at each purchase. A survey carried out in late 2004 revealed a higher level of expenditure on khat in Kampala and western Uganda (Anderson et al., 2007, p. 133). Kampala chewers were more likely to be weekend chewers but tended to be bigger spenders when they did consume khat. There were also gender differences in relation to daily expenditure: "When khat expenditure is analysed in relation to gender, the data show that women spend less on khat than men. For men, a spend of USh3,000 (approx. £1) is the most common outlay, while for women a spend of USh1,000 is more common" (Anderson et al., 2007, p. 137).

People who buy kabasanda may be able to spend less than consumers of kasenge. Indeed, in the former county of Butambala, at Kabasanda and Mirembe in Mpigi District, the trade by wholesalers and retailers supplying khat to Kampala is less buoyant than in Kasenge. In this area, where there is an oversupply of khat of indifferent quality, seasonal price fluctuations exceed those experienced in Kasenge. During the last three decades, hundreds of farmers planted khat in Butambala. Some of these farmers' business is not doing well. For example, Athuman farms khat planted by his father in 1984 from seedlings taken from Sheikh Semakula's farm. The wholesale buyers who come from Kisenyi determine the price. During the wet season, when supplies are abundant but the quality of the leaves falls because they are too watery, the price fetched for a large plastic basin of khat sometimes fall as low as 300 shillings (less than $0.10). In the dry season the maximum price obtained for the same measure is 10,000 shillings ($5). Athuman complained that it was a buyer's market, and that although the price fell immediately after the rains started, rising prices in the dry season were slow to be offered by dealers. Typically, dealers pay Athuman and his mother every three days. Nevertheless, this family still considers khat a better cash crop than coffee or vanilla.

Along the road from Athuman's farm, near Mirembe trading center, Mohammed is doing better than Athuman. He has about four acres of land where he grows khat, which he planted in 1986, and is using the profits from sales to buy more land in the area. Mohammed used to take khat himself to Kisenyi and is a well-known face there. Now, however, traders come daily to purchase his supplies. His khat is considered to be of high quality and the price per frosh, or banana leaf package (approximately half-meter square) varies. It can be as high a 10,000 shillings, but in November 2007 it was selling at half that price. Although some farmers reported negotiating the price of khat they supply, many said that it was a buyer's market and that they had no producers' organization or association by which they could set prices. Most farmers in Butambala take what traders offer. For their part, the traders, having obtained wholesale supplies at the farm gate, enter into another set of negotiations with retailers or directly with consumers.

The innovative ways that khat dealers cope with market fluctuations was brought into focus in January 2008 when a severe gasoline shortage led to a short-term fuel crisis across East Africa (Anderson & Lochery, 2008; Lonsdale, 2008). Following the disputed results of the December 2007 general election in Kenya, violent protests caused the disruption of road and rail transportation from the Indian Ocean port of Mombasa via Nairobi and western Kenya into Uganda. As Uganda is dependent upon oil supplies from this route, shortages in gasoline and diesel occurred, and in early January the prices at the pumps rocketed from about 2,400 shillings per liter to 8,000 shillings ($4) a liter. In Kasenge khat prices did not rise, and it was the traders who had to bear the increased transport costs. At this time the price of khat was, in any case, relatively high because it was the dry season. Wholesalers responded to the fuel crisis by buying smaller amounts and then selling reduced portions at the normal price. One trader selling kasenge khat commented, "We've reduced the size of the frosh, and if the customer complains we just put in a couple of leaves from Kabasanda." Often the customers did not recognize that they had been given inferior leaves as an extra, and the retailers were doing good business passing off khat on sale as kasenge.

A discussion with a group of about ten consumers in Kisenyi confirmed that they were aware that the portions sold were smaller than normal but had not noticed any drop in quality. At this time, the khat market in Kisenyi was jammed with people trying to buy personal supplies. Unruly lines formed and consumers even tried buying partly used supplies from other consumers. A man might sell his khat for double the price he purchased it and then try to replace what he just sold by buying more from the retailer. The retailer may declare her supply to be "sold out," but she has just "a bit put aside," which she then sells for double the price a couple of hours before. Overall, retailers attempted to exploit the shortage so that prices were rising steadily through the afternoon. But this was a risky strategy: if the price rose too high for the consumer and compared to fellow retailers, a greedy trader could be left with unsold stock, which can be sold when it's a day old but at a much lower price.

GULU

Khat from Kasenge and Kabasanda is also sent daily to the north of Uganda with most going to Gulu, the largest town in the north. One supplier is Jacob, a farmer in Kasenge.

Jacob trained as a structural engineer but now earns his living as a khat and coffee farmer. Although his mother warned him that khat was not a respectable crop, he went ahead and planted seedlings in 2000. He has not been disappointed as he can make up to 1.2 million shillings ($600) per month from his trees. Although the price he gets for a kilo of coffee beans has risen from 200 shillings to 1,000 shillings ($0.10–$0.50), he still gets about ten times the return on his khat compared to coffee. The mixed farming he practices is good for the khat trees, slowing the rate that they dry out. In the dry season Jacob employs people to hand-water the khat from jerry cans of swamp water supplied from a pickup truck. Every ten days a wholesaler brings his group of pickers to harvest khat. The price paid for the crop is negotiable and varies from 300,000 shillings to 500,000 shillings ($150–250), depending on whether it is the wet or dry season.

One of the wholesalers who regularly buys Jacob's crop of the trees is Godfrey. Tipped off by Jacob concerning the timing of the next picking, I return early the following morning. I find Godfrey sitting with two other men folding fresh khat leaves into small banana leaf packages. Behind them on the sloping field are eight women picking khat. The women bring the leaves to the men, who continue packing at a brisk pace. The packages are put in cardboard boxes, which are then labeled "Gulu," "Kitgum," and "Tororo," which is a town near the Kenyan border. Once several boxes have been filled, they are transported immediately by motorcycle by one of Godfrey's assistants to the bus station in Kampala where northbound buses set out. In stark contrast to the openness of Jacob, Godfrey declares that is he unwilling to talk to me about money and is evasive about the volume of his business. He views my visit as a possible harbinger of "trouble" from the authorities. Somewhat assured that I am not sent by the government to investigate the khat trade and that I am just a foreign researcher, he tells me that he has been trading in khat for about six years. He used to sell in Kisenyi but now sends all the stock he buys out of Kampala. He adds that the trade to the north has been going on for many years but was better during the war with the LRA, which lasted for twenty years but had just ended. "Soldiers and contractors are bored and like chewing khat and will pay high prices for it." Now, in peacetime, people have got a taste for khat, especially in big towns like Gulu, so the trade continues.

Although it is not mentioned in any guide books and there are no signboards or hanging banana leaves as in Kenya and Ethiopia, khat is not hard to find anywhere in Uganda. Gulu lies four hundred kilometers due north of Kampala, and khat is sold at the truck stops and trading centers all along the road. Inquiries about where to buy khat from market traders led me to a man selling some kabasanda in a trading center about one hundred kilometers south of Gulu. He gave directions to a café called the Republic Hotel in Gulu where khat can be purchased daily. Once in Gulu, it was a matter of finding the bus park; from there I started to look out for the Republic Hotel and found it in the next street. Wrappers of BigG chewing gum, a popular accompaniment to khat, and some wilted khat leaves littered the ground outside the café. It was about midday and some young men of local Acholi and Nubi ethnic groups, together with several Somali itinerant perfume sellers, were hanging around on the veranda of the café, awaiting delivery. Two hours later three young men had set up shop and were doing a brisk trade in the khat that had recently arrived on the bus, possibly sent by Godfrey from Jacob's farm. Kasenge and kabasanda types of khat arrive in Gulu on buses from Kampala throughout the afternoon. Supplies are delivered in cardboard boxes, containing prepacked small frosh of the type Godfrey was packing, to the various retailers.

Hashim, a former khat dealer and now a customer, was sitting on the veranda of the Republic Hotel. These days he works in the public transport business, operating a passenger service between Gulu and Juba in South Sudan. Of the people there at the Republic Hotel, he was the person who was most inclined to answer questions and give out information. He told me that apart from the Republic Hotel, there were two venues in Gulu where khat is sold, and he agreed to take me to them.

The second venue, still in the center of the commercial district of Gulu, was nearby and was comprised of a wooden counter and bench for customers placed in the shade against the side of a half-built house. Hashim introduced us to the seller, Robert, a young man wearing youth-fashion baggy orange clothes and dark glasses. While I was talking to Robert, his boss came along to check on the trade. The check entailed going through the bookkeeping, laid out in school exercise books. The boss did not seem to be worried by our presence, so I continued to sit on the bench and talk to Robert's customers. Once Robert was free to talk, he told me that he was paid a daily salary of 4,000 shillings ($2). He had made a loss yesterday, which was the reason for the discussion with his boss. The system at this venue and across Gulu is for supplies to arrive in "dribs and drabs" throughout the afternoon and early evening on the buses from Kampala. Each batch may be sold out almost immediately, and it is difficult to know what is *bareh* (left over from the day before). As kasenge sells for 1,500 shillings and kabasanda for 1,000 shillings, there is a temptation and suspicion among my informants that kabasanda is often passed off as kasenge.

The third venue Hashim showed me was on a Kampala road, at a place called Cerelendo. This was much busier than the second venue.

There was a shop selling general supplies next to a couple of cement steps and a wooden bench, next to it was an open space with a mat. Immediately behind the general store was a structure where mechanics' tools and spare parts were stored. We found four male traders on the steps of the shop and seated on the mat selling khat out of cardboard boxes. They were chewing in a group with several male consumers. One vendor, Khamisi, was prepared to provide estimates of the volume of the khat trade in Gulu: in 2008 there were thirteen khat retailers in Gulu, each earning a profit of 500 shillings ($0.25) per frosh sold. One trader sitting next to Khamisi said he usually sold sixty frosh per day. From observation and discussion, it appears likely that most retailers sell between sixty to one hundred frosh per day. These estimates indicate that between 780 and 1,300 frosh containing portions of khat leaves are sold daily in Gulu.

MBARARA

In the 1970s khat from Kenya was not only sent to Kampala but also Kasese and Mbarara in the west of the country where Yemenis had settled and wanted to use the substance on a daily basis. Several Yemeni men recall how in the 1970s khat arrived in Kasese in refrigerated milk vans, which had the primary purpose of supplying the senior staff at the copper mines at Kilembe just outside Kasese. These days, however, all the khat reaching Kasese and most of the supply to Mbarara comes from farms situated to the north of the town of Fort Portal in Kabarole District.

There are over a thousand farms growing khat in Kabarole District, according to the estimates of a leading producer. A few farmers take their own produce to nearby Fort Portal to sell but most harvest the crop and await collection and payment by traders who travel to the area daily. Local buyers who traded in Fort Portal or other places nearby were purchasing not more than ten to twenty frosh each. Once they take out transportation costs of 3,000 shillings ($1.50), they were left with a small profit.

In July 2007, on the large Byarufu farm where premium khat has been produced for over twenty years, the price of a medium-sized, banana leaf–wrapped bundle, or frosh, was 2,000 shillings ($2). This same frosh fetched 2,500 shillings in nearby Fort Portal; 5,000 shillings in Kasese, about sixty miles south of the farm; and 7,500 shillings ($3.75) another ninety-four miles south in Mbarara.

Since 2007, the trade has been complicated by a local bylaw banning khat in Bushenyi, a district en route to Mbarara. In addition to this barrier to the smooth supply chain, the traders are in vicious competition with each other and sometimes the business turns nasty. For example, in February 2008 I was in Kabarole District en route to interview a local official. At a junction dividing the main, marram road from a lesser road that branches west and leads to the Byarufu farm, I spotted a car and about eight to ten men, several with motorcycles, awaiting khat supplies from the nearly farms. We recognized Mercy, an ambitious Kasese-based khat trader standing near the car and stopped. She was packing frosh into sacks assisted by her boyfriend, the driver and owner of the car. I was surprised that Mercy declined to greet me, but the boyfriend, Amouti, was quite chatty. He explained that some of the stock they were packing was for Kasese and some was to be sent onto Mbarara. They had trouble because the police in Bushenyi District had put up roadblocks to search for khat. He explained that to evade police attention, he had started switching cars, but they were sometimes caught because somebody was tipping off the police. Suddenly, Mercy jumped on the back of a motorcycle and the driver roared off quickly. Meanwhile her boyfriend turned the car round so that it was pointing in the direction of Fort Portal. The motorcycle quickly returned, and Mercy got in the car. Just then another motorcycle passed us on its way to Fort Portal. The car driven by Amouti and with Mercy in the passenger seat roared to life, passing the moving motorbike and stopped in front of it, forcing the driver to brake abruptly. Mercy jumped out of the car holding a jerry can and poured its contents over a full sack tied to the back of the motorbike, shouting angrily as she did so. Kerosene from the jerrican damaged the contents of the sack, rendering all the khat it contained worthless. A lot of angry shouting between the driver of the motorcycle and Mercy, backed up by Amouti, followed. Next, Amouti got a machete out of the truck of the car and waved it about wildly. After a few minutes of furious altercation that threatened to turn physically violent, the motorcycle rider drove off with the contaminated khat still on board. Shortly afterward Mercy and Amouti drove away, leaving the other traders to explain to me what was going on.

Andrew, a leading khat trader based in Mbarara, was the driver of the motorcycle, they said. Andrew had tipped off the police in Bushenyi (where a bylaw outlawed khat) about the movements of Mercy and several other traders, which had been the cause of their difficulties there. Control of the lucrative Mbarara market was at stake, and Andrew was prepared to play dirty. The use of kerosene to destroy the khat he was carrying was a direct retaliation. Later in Kasese, another trader, Mama Salim, was able to shed more light on the incident. She explained that the dispute between Andrew and Mercy went back to last Christmas. At that time Mercy was sharing a vehicle with another trader. As it was the Christmas holiday period, demand for khat was high, and the car was jammed full of supplies. Andrew went to the police and told them when the car would be passing and how to identify it. After they were caught in a roadblock, Mercy had to pay off the police. "Andrew is bad," commented Mama Salim, adding that he controls the rural market all along the road from Fort Portal to Mbarara. Her final comment on the subject was that "these days, people leave the trade because of police harassment. It is too expensive to pay off the police. A 100,000 shillings [$50] payment is a typical amount."

Mercy also lives in Kasese and, some time after the incident with the kerosene, I went to find her. She was living in a couple of rooms in an Indian-built block designed so that multiple occupants were housed in rooms opening onto a central courtyard. A few months before, I had come here to see khat being sold by another trader. Mercy is a new resident and, although it was early afternoon, a prime time for sales, there were no khat customers in sight. This time, Mercy was not concentrating on executing her well-planned revenge, and I was welcomed into the small living room that was jammed with two armchairs and a cabinet full of plates. On the wall were various posters and calendars, including one showing pictures of "Kenya's post-election violence" that had occurred recently (Lonsdale, 2008). There was also a sign hanging on the wall warning against "trusting friends." Mercy's boyfriend, Amouti, was dozing off on a chair, paying no attention to a woman who was trying to sell Chinese medicine "that cures everything" to Mercy. Seeing that there would be no business to be had, the woman departed. All was quiet in the early afternoon heat, and Mercy said that "only a few high class customers come here." Although Amouti has business interests elsewhere and a home of his own in Kasese, every morning he gets up before dawn and drives Mercy to Kabarole. He sees khat as a risky business and does not want to get further involved. Mercy, however, is in the khat business in earnest. Her living arrangements indicate that she makes a decent living but is far from wealthy.

Mama Salim and her husband used to sell khat in Kasese from a shop on the main street, which sold little else except the accompaniments of khat, such as BigG chewing gum and cigarettes. She recalls how in 1993 they started trading in khat, which subsequently built the substantial house she now inhabits with the profits and sent their children to college. Now that many people have entered the trade, profits have fallen because of the increased competition. Mama Salim was widowed in 2007 and shortly after decided to reenter the khat trade. In 2008 she would travel in the early morning from Kasese to the farms at Kabarole, return south with fresh stock to Mbarara, and in the early evening return again to sleep in Kasese, a daily round trip of about three hundred miles.

In Mbarara, Mama Salim rented a former butcher shop situated around the corner from the main khat market near the bus depot. She justified her business decision in terms of decorum and respectability, commenting that the other shops, besides the main trade in khat, sell cannabis and alcohol. In her shop she said did not even allow people to smoke cigarettes because she dislikes the smoke. The reality of the business style does not entirely match Mama Salim's claims, however. Mama Salim sits on the floor on a mat that lies on top of some flattened cardboard. Sacks and black plastic bags of khat surround her. She has a large green Muslim-style cloth covering her head and upper body. She takes money from customers and puts it in her black handbag. Opposite Mama Salim is a bench. A disabled man, probably a polio victim, is sitting on the bench chewing khat. Behind the counter is another woman dressed in an unusual outfit: a wide cotton skirt made of white and maroon bands and a white blouse with a cloth in same design as the skirt covering her head and shoulders. She acts as Mama Salim's assistant, selling BigG chewing gum and making coffee and tea for the customers. At the back of the shop is a partitioned-off section where three men have set up a chewing session. Besides khat, soda, milk, water, BigG, and peanuts are placed on the floor ready for consumption during the chewing session. There is a steady trickle of customers, all male and mostly young. They squat on their haunches as Mama Salim opens up three frosh for them to choose. Most take a half portion of *bisanga* or *byarufu* types. A full frosh retails at 3,000 shillings ($1.50). But *bode* is much cheaper. Most customers pay 1,000 to 1,500 shillings ($0.50–$0.75) for their khat, which is then taken out of its banana leaf coverings and placed in the light plastic bags that were officially banned in 2007 but are used with impunity throughout the country by traders in all types of goods. Indeed, Mama Salim says the plastic bags are now sold openly and there is no restriction. Most customers stuff the bag containing their khat in their jeans pockets and leave.

Mama Salim is competing with about fifty other retailers operating in the buoyant Mbarara khat market. Just around the corner is a row of about fifteen small shops, numbered but not named, where khat is sold. Each day supplies from Kabarole and from Kasenge via Kampala arrive at about two o'clock p.m. Retails and keen consumers await deliveries anxiously. For example, on one weekday in May 2008, I observed the following scene: There were a few people hanging around—young men in jeans and street gear—several Rasta but only one woman who the others said was mad. Yet she is a khat trader. Some traders were already there and others were trickling in; the women from shop 102 came and greeted me. They tell me that the price has not fallen much as there is not much rain. Several consumers could not wait and bought leftover khat from the previous day (bareh) and settled down in one of the shops to chew. I checked several of the shops to see what else they sold besides khat. One was selling only coffee beans in banana leaf sachets, another was quite well stocked with general goods and with alcohol, condoms, and cigarettes; Shop 102 was completely empty. At 1:50 p.m. a sedan car pulled up and two full sacks and several partly filled sacks of khat were off loaded and taken into one of the shops. From there, the traders took the supplies they had ordered: up to a sack each to their shops or away to other, more distant venues. One man said that he was sending khat to Rukingiri, some seventy-five miles from there. The peanut sellers arrived in time to sell to customers who prefer peanuts to BigG as an accompaniment when chewing khat. In the well-stocked shop the accounts were being done: one man had an exercise book and a pile of cash, while a couple of women and a man were discussing the accounts with him in the local language, Ruankole. Shop 102 was the busiest, doing a brisk trade, but not as busy as the last time I visited on a weekend. The customers were all men, mostly in their twenties, but a few appeared no older than about fifteen years of age.

JINJA

In contrast to the highly competitive Kabarole-Mbarara trade, the town of Jinja, situated on Lake Victoria at the source of the mighty River Nile, boasts Uganda's most highly organized khat market (Anderson et al., 2007). In 2004 a Somali-owned shop known as Master Coffee was "the hub of khat distribution and retailing for Jinja and the surrounding districts" (Anderson et al., 2007, p. 128). In 2007 to make way for redevelopment, the Master Coffee building was demolished, a common practice in urban Uganda, where old buildings are perceived to be a blight rather than a cultural blessing. Despite the demise of Master Coffee, the supply of khat to Jinja from the Mabira Forest plantations continues in much the same way. From midmorning each day large, black plastic bags containing wholesale portions of khat known as frosh and carried by farmers and traders begin to arrive in Jinja. They are delivered directly to retailers at their pitches near the bus station. The two main types of khat are on sale in Jinja are *mabira* and the superior Mabira-grown kasenge, which is harvested from seedlings from the Kasenge area.

The Mabira supplies are sold by members of a trade organization, registered with the local municipal council. In 2004, Mama Fatouma, a Kenyan-born Somali, was the "chairman" of the trade association (Beckerleg, 2008), but by 2007 she had retired from the business and a male, indigenous Ugandan taken over the leadership of the khat traders. In Jinja the khat business is a closed shop, and only association members can sell the leaves. The association also decides who can sell and allocates pitches. Most retailers are men, but there are also some women sellers. The payment system for retailers to agents and wholesalers varies, with some paying up-front and others on a weekly basis.

The trade in Jinja is generally orderly and usually peaceful because the farmers and traders have united in a khat traders' association and successfully negotiated rights to sell khat in specific areas of the town. Yet it is near Jinja that a khat trader was murdered in 2007, according to local people. Many active in the local khat business say he was killed by a rival trader. Hence, even here, competition between traders is fierce and possibly deadly.

TRUST AND RISK

Many khat wholesalers and retailers come and go in the Ugandan marketplace. They compete with each other daily in an unregulated market to get a highly perishable commodity to consumers. They face the same challenges as khat traders operating in different settings. For example, Weir writes of the situation in Yemen where khat is bought while still on the tree: "The key factors which determine the character of the qat trade and which act as constraints on the development of large-scale capitalist enterprises dominated by big merchants are the high perishability of the product and the impossibility of predicting the state of the market. Qat must be sold within one or two days of picking or its leaves wilt and its value can drop to well below the price paid on tree" (Weir, 1985b).

Hence, khat traders risk losing their capital and their livelihoods if they miscalculate the volume and unit price of the khat they have to sell.

Some Ugandan traders face additional problems and have been forced out of business by police harassment, an issue discussed at length in Chapter 8. Although getting and staying rich through the khat trade is not easy, a minority do succeed and become well off. However, for the majority, the khat business is a way of making ends meet.

Over the past twenty years, Yemenis and Somalis have lost control of the khat trade, which has been taken over by men and women from diverse backgrounds that do not include a khat-using dimension. Given the diversity of the traders, trust between individuals drawn from many ethnic and social backgrounds is important but regularly breaks down in the face of business competition. Scholarly attention has turned to how trust is central to the maintenance of civil society and trading networks in a range of settings undergoing rapid social change (Fukuyama, 1995; Gellner, 2000; Landa, 1995; Seligman, 2000; Sztompka, 2000). The problems encountered by khat traders, outlined earlier, include snitching on each other to the police or authorities, criminal damage of stock, and possibly murder. The lack of trust in the Ugandan khat industry can be linked to the multiethnic nature of the business. The players in the case of the vicious competition of the supply of khat to Mbarara had nothing to bind them, and their common business interests pushed them apart. While the vast majority of khat farmers in Karabole District are of the Toro ethnic group, the traders are more diverse. Mercy is also a Christian Toro living in Kasese; Mama Salim, the widow of Tanzanian trader based in Kasese, is of Rwandan Tutsi origin and is a convert to Islam; Andrew is an Ankole Christian from Mbarara. Although Andrew and Mama Salim are associate members of a Kabarole khat farmers' association set up to promote the interests of the industry, they have no other bond and never meet socially. Trade associations, in any case, have their limitations: it was in Jinja where the traders are well organized and apparently united that rumors abound of a murder motivated by rivalry in the khat business.

In Kenya, the khat wholesale and retail trade is dominated by two ethnic groups: Meru members of the Igembe and Tigania clans who are also the main producers of khat and Somalis who control most of the export market and the trade in northern Kenya (Anderson et al., 2007). For the Meru traders, trust is an important aspect of the industry: "Through the operation of numerous personal business relationships that are based on trust, miraa is sent to cities, towns and villages throughout Kenya. Miraa passes through wholesale markets in Nairobi and Mombasa and into the hands of young Meru men who retail miraa far and wide" (Carrier, 2005a).

In many places in Kenya the Meru men work alongside traders from other ethnic groups with whom they may develop good business relationships. As the khat business has come to dominate economic life in the Igembe and Tigania areas, youth of these clans have little alternative but to become khat traders. The Meru have the advantage of being part of the ethnic-based network that links farmers, agents, wholesalers, and retailers (Anderson et al., 2007, p. 91). A typical Meru retailer runs a kiosk or small shop far from home, often sleeping on the floor of the business premises. Their aim is to acquire capital in order to move into khat wholesaling or to diversify into other business ventures (Goldsmith, 1994, p. 110).

Across Kenya the Meru traders are organized into welfare societies that help members with the cost of burials and medical fees. Mutual support also extends to the business arrangements. Hence, "traders provide for each other, and if one does not receive miraa one day, someone will share their consignment with him" (Goldsmith, 1994, p. 110). However, while ethnic-based mutual assistance is a key aspect of the Meru khat trade, the situation is different when it comes to working with Somalis. Carrier reports on the tensions between Meru and Somali dealers: "Somalis have much control over the international trade, exporting the commodity to Somalia and the diaspora in Europe and beyond. Somali control has created much tension, as some Meru see themselves as exploited by the Somali network: this tension was most evident in 1999, when a Tigania who had started to trade a little miraa died in London. Suspicion that he had been killed by Somalis jealous of their monopoly led to clashes between Meru and Somalis back in the Nyambenes and in Nairobi" (Carrier, 2005b, pp. 541–542).

The demand for Kenyan khat has risen in many cities across the world since the 1990s, when many Somalis fled the civil war in their country and settled in Europe and North America as refugees. Supplies for the Kenyan export market come from the Nyambene Hills, but the Meru have failed to make an impact on the export market of their product (Anderson et al., 2007).

THE UGANDAN EXPORT MARKET

Kenya and Ethiopia, with Yemen lagging behind, dominate the export market for khat (Anderson et al., 2007). Somali consumers prefer Kenyan khat from the Nyambene Hills to types from other countries. This type of khat, in the form of twigs, travels well. Although many Ugandan producers and traders say they would like to break into the lucrative export market, there is little demand outside the country for their product. Yet small amounts of khat are exported from Uganda to the neighboring countries of Rwanda, Democratic Republic of Congo (DRC), Sudan, and even to western Kenya.

Three types of Ugandan khat account for the export market, with kasenge taking the biggest share of the market. Kasenge khat leaves from south of Kampala are bagged up near the farm where they have been plucked, taken to Kampala, and dispatched by bus to Kigali, the capital of Rwanda (Anderson et al., 2007, pp. 129–130). Although khat was still tolerated by the police and customs officials in 2005, by 2008, khat was treated as an illicit substance and the trade turned into trafficking. Traders also report that small amounts of khat are sold in the no-man's land between Uganda and Rwanda to truck drivers en route to Kigali or further south to Burundi.

The second type of khat exported from Uganda is that grown in Arua and Maracha, in the West Nile region of the country. Khat from this area is sent into nearby eastern region of the DRC and to South Sudan. The authorities from South Sudan do all they can to stem this trade by searching buses at the border and arresting anybody found with khat. Godfrey, the trader encountered earlier in this chapter sending kasenge to Gulu, told me that the Sudan market was "not worth the risks." In any case, kasenge, which comprises loose, highly perishable leaves, is not the ideal type for a smuggling operation. It is khat from Karamoja, which resembles the twiggy miraa of the Nyambenes of Kenya, that is being smuggled into Juba in South Sudan, according to informants.

The Proliferation of Local Types and of Branding

Despite the efforts of Ugandan traders to open up legal or illegal export markets, Ugandan khat is overwhelmingly a homegrown and locally consumed commodity. Across Uganda, sacks of khat are transported along pot-holed highways and marram tracks from large and small plantations as well as forest areas daily. Each production area produces khat that is distinctive in appearance, in packaging, and, consumers say, in the effects produced by chewing it. As in other production countries, the market is differentiated and a myriad of khat types command different prices (Carrier, 2007; Gebissa, 2004; Kennedy, 1987).

In Kabarole District, *byarufu*, originally named after the family who produce it, is the top brand. The name originates from the khat planted by the founder of production in the area. Ahmed Byarufu leads the family business but has also given seedlings from his plantation to numerous neighbors who therefore also cultivate byarufu. Consumers may think they are getting byarufu from the original farm and retailers do not correct them. Few consumers can tell the difference and often feel the khat effects that they expect. Khat from the original field of the Byarufu is presented in banana leaf packages distinguished from other khat in the area by the signature mark in ballpoint pen of the Byarufu family. In Kasenge near Kampala, Denis Kasuga also signs his banana leaf–wrapped khat but complains that forgeries have started to appear on the market.

Each growing area produces several types of khat each with a different name, often simply the name of the producer or the area where the farm lies. Sometimes, however, new names occur in the marketplace. For example, in Mbarara a type of khat called *kanifa*, after a Kasese-based trader by the same name, is on sale. In the town of Lira, *gapco*, named after a farmer who grows khat near a Gapco filling station, is a known brand. The opposite process also occurs whereby there is less differentiation of product type as khat is sold farther from its origin. For example, in one place near the production area, three types of khat may be available, but if that khat is sent to more distant markets, the three types may all just be called after the place of origin, a phenomenon that is also a feature of the Yemeni khat market (Kennedy, 1987).

CONCLUSION

The perishability of khat has always made trade in the plant a risky business. Before motorized transport, khat was traded and consumed in and around the highland areas where it was grown alongside coffee. Coffee beans, which could be stored for long periods as they were transported across the world, became a worldwide consumer item while khat remained a largely unknown drug, made exotic by the writings of explorers such as Burton in 1856 and, more recently, Rushby (1999). The volatility of khat has enabled numerous small traders to earn a living, albeit a risky one. In Uganda, as control of the trade has slipped out of the hands of a few Yemenis and Somalis, the khat industry has developed into an unregulated and sometimes wild enterprise that people from all backgrounds enter. The numerous khat plantations scattered all over Uganda and the proliferation of types of khat is keeping pace with the spread of consumption. In the next chapter changing styles of khat consumption are considered. The Yemeni acme of khat ritual is contrasted to newer patterns of consumption in East Africa.

CHAPTER 7

STYLE AND SUBSTANCE

The efforts of thousands of Ugandan traders ensure that consumers across the country are able to buy khat daily. These consumers have taken up a pastime and given it a distinctly Ugandan orientation, for in Uganda, khat chewing has become a new leisure activity, which for many users involves multidrug use (Beckerleg, 2009b). In countries with a khat-chewing tradition, as well as in cities around the world where people from areas of popular khat consumption have migrated, the leaves and twigs of Catha edulis are consumed in very different ways. National styles encompass chewing for ritual, leisure, and work, but as khat use spreads and becomes a global phenomenon stripped of its traditional significance, consumption patterns are changing (Klein & Beckerleg, 2007).

YEMENI STYLE

The main model for the consumption of khat in Uganda derives from the classic Yemeni style of use: ritualized, even when used for leisure. In Yemen, chewing is scheduled for afternoons, after the consumption of a heavy meal (Kennedy, 1987). The setting for a group chew is, for the wealthy, the *muffraj*, a room specially designed for khat chewing. Large rooms at the top of multistoried houses were designed with chewing in mind. Windows provide a good view, often of spectacular mountains, while low cushions are arranged along the wall so as to direct the gaze of those seated to the view from the windows. Armrests, colorful rugs on the floor, large hookah pipes for smoking tobacco, and spittoons wherein an overlarge wad of khat can be discretely placed complete the scene (Kennedy, 1987, p. 84). The muffraj is designed to create a pleasant atmosphere conducive to an enjoyable khat chewing session. Writing of Yemen in the 1970s,

Kennedy has observed, "It is obvious to any visitor that the whole purpose of the muffraj is the creation of an environment facilitating pleasure, relaxation and human companionship. Even in the muffrajes of country Shaykhs, whose houses may be far from the road among mountain peaks, a traveller may find similar graceful and pleasurable rooms. This comfortable setting, which cannot help but remind one of storybook tales of oriental potentates, is the preferred environment for chewing qat" (Kennedy, 1987, p. 84).

Men usually bring their own bundle of khat and gather in such rooms every afternoon to chew as a group. Hence, Yemeni chewing is a collective experience, with up to one hundred men present (Varisco, 1986). At these gatherings, social distinctions are maintained and even reinforced in many ways, including the seating arrangements (Gerholm, 1977; Weir, 1985a). Prayers are sometimes said before chewing. The chewing sessions provide a forum for discussion, an opportunity for resolving differences, and the chance to lodge petitions. The etiquette of the chewing session and the desire for social respectability precludes excessive consumption as individuals do not want to be the last to leave or to be seen chewing too much (Klein & Beckerleg, 2007, p. 248). Social life is organized to fit in with khat chewing. For example, in the coastal Yemeni town of Zabid, "influential Zabidi men almost always chew qat in their own homes, hosting regular qat chewers daily. Those who wish a favour from the host, or support in a dispute, will attend his qat chew. Other men entertain on a specific day of the week when those who wish to show friendship or discuss business come to chew in the male entertaining space, the family *mabraz* [another name for the muffraj]" (Meneley, 1996, p. 49).

Thus, in Yemen, the ritualized use of khat for leisure is not solely a male activity. Women chew less often and in smaller amounts than men (Kennedy, 1987), but khat is an important part of their daily life and an opportunity to display generosity, by hosting chewing sessions and sharing khat, thereby reinforcing the social status of the giver. Women's gatherings focus as much on the social exchange as on the stimulating quality of khat (Klein & Beckerleg, 2007). Hence, Meneley describes a scene at a women's khat chewing session she attended in Zabid: "We began by rubbing the dust from the qat leaves with our fingers; Magda immediately cleaned a small bunch for me and wordlessly aimed it at my mouth. This kind of qat exchange is commonly performed between women who are affectively, socially, and, of course, spatially close. As is common for affluent hostesses, Jamaliya distributed a generous portion of qat to each of the chewing guests" (Meneley, 1996, pp. 28–29).

Kennedy (1987) argues that khat consumption is institutionalized in North Yemen, so that it is used to by people cementing business deals and marriage arrangements, settling local disputes, and planning political campaigns, all within the context of an Islamic society where many people pray the prescribed five daily prayers. Yet, in Yemen, Islamic scholars, while shying away from banning khat on the grounds that it is a drug and therefore forbidden, have never completely endorsed its use. The theological debate dates back to the fifteenth and sixteenth centuries and centered on the degree to which the plant can be considered an intoxicant. Although the religious debate persists in some circles, the liberal interpretation allowing khat chewing among Muslims has the upper hand (Klein & Beckerleg, 2007).

ETHIOPIAN STYLE

While Yemeni khat consumption has remained a secular ritual, associated with the demonstration of social status, networking, and the pursuit of pleasure, in eastern Ethiopia khat use has long been part of Islamic observances. In the Harerge region, "For centuries it has been a standard practice for those who participated in religious ceremonies held at the Muslim shrines in the province to spend long hours of the day and night chewing khat while reciting passages from the Holy Qur'an and praying to Allah" (Gebissa, 2004, p. 11). Some devout Muslims even consider khat holy, refer to it as the "flower of paradise," and often offer prayers before they begin to chew it (Almeddom & Abraham, 1994, pp. 249–258).

In the secular sphere, khat is chewed to facilitate business negotiations and to seal important and long-term contracts. It is reported from eastern Ethiopia that "the use of the leaves in dowry arrangements is evident in contemporary Harerge. When an Oromo couple enters into a *naqata*, an engagement, the groom's parents send *jarsaa* or representatives to negotiate the matter with the bride's family. The first act of this process is the presenting of *jimma naqata* or 'engagement-khat' to the woman's parents, who will signify their agreement through accepting the leaves" (Gebissa, 2004, p. 11).

Similarly, friends and relatives will "bring khat to a *taziyya*, a mourning, as a way of consoling the bereaved" (Gebissa, 2004, p. 10). However, secular patterns of use by traditional users in the Harerge appear to be very similar to those practiced in Yemen. Rushby (1999), recounting his khat-fuelled travels, describes visiting homes where men gathered in the afternoons in rooms set aside for chewing. They were usually seated on cushions on the floor, coffee was served as an accompaniment to khat, and incense sometimes wafted around the room. In the home of a prominent merchant, Rushby found that the sharing of khat accentuated differences in status. He describes the scene in the merchant's house as follows:

> Already seated with piles of qat in front of them were eight men, some along the back wall and some in the middle of the room on the bare floor. I greeted them and shock hands with each.
>
> "Ahlan wa sahlan!" said a venerable old man with a kindly face. "Come and sit here beside me."
>
> The man, I soon discovered, was sheikh Muhammed, sheikh being a title of respect from those who knew him. On his right was Ali, another goldsmith, and next to him in the corner, Omar Ibrahim. To his right were two more merchants. In front of these great personages sat the workers, servants and messengers . . .
>
> The first thing to do was to give the qat and a whisper from Abera told me to hand it to sheikh Muhammed. He laid it in front of him and rocking gently, began to recite the Fatiha, the first chapter of the Koran. The men assumed a kneeling position with palms upwards, quietly following his words.
>
> "In the name of God the compassionate and merciful. Praise be to God, lord of the universe."
>
> When this was over he took a small handful of sticks and threw them across to one of the men in front of him. This portion was then carried off to the women. Further small portions went to the other servants, workers and messengers. (Rushby, 1999, pp. 63–64)

THE IMITATORS

As khat use has spread from the classic khat-chewing sessions of the Yemen Highlands and eastern Ethiopia, it has spawned many imitations. In the first half of the twentieth century, Yemeni migrants were the main disseminators of khat-chewing cultures of consumption. Traditional chewing patterns also spread from the highlands to the coast, first to the Yemeni ports of Hodeida and Aden and then across the Red Sea to Djibouti and Hargeisa within the greater Somali region (Anderson et al., 2007; Gebissa, 2004; Kennedy, 1987). Gebissa (2004) dates the growth of popularity of khat chewing in ethnic Somali areas, such as the port of Hargeisa to the 1940s. Khat consumption was primarily an aid to work rather than as a leisure activity. "Truck drivers carrying goods and passengers to and from towns as far west as Jijiga [eastern Ethiopia], near the khat-producing

Harer highlands, began to rely on khat to stay awake during long trips and transported fresh sprigs on their return trip, thus making fresh khat readily available to town dwellers" (Gebissa, 2004, p. 81).

Local people at first imitated the mode of consumption of local Yemeni traders. The wealthy chewed at home, but others started using khat in cafés, which they called *mafrish* after the Yemeni room, the classic khat venue (Anderson et al., 2007; Gebissa, 2004). As Somali migrants have moved around the world, the mafrish has traveled with them. At least in places where khat is legal, such as in British towns, Somalis continue to chew at the mafrish, a venue where khat and nonalcoholic drinks are on sale and a fee for entry is sometimes levied (ACMD, 2004; Klein, 2008).

In Kenya, however, khat use moved outdoors. Yemeni migrants arriving in Mombasa and other port towns took up the use of khat from the Nyambene Hills:

> Slowly the people that the Yemenis lived among, the Swahili at the coast and people of all ethnic groups in the highlands, also started chewing khat. A khat sub-culture emerged with local names for khat such as murungi, veve, gomba and terms for describing different grades of khat and its effects. In the coastal town of Malindi, for instance, Yemeni street-corner coffee sellers had initially introduced miraa to their Swahili customers. By the 1980s, miraa chewing was part of the daily routine of many young Swahili men in the town of Malindi (Peake 1989). But in this new setting, consumption lacked the ritual and cultural finesse of Yemen. (Anderson et al., 2007, pp. 99–100)

At the Swahili coast many khat-chewing sessions are held outdoors, on the traditional cement or stone benches, or *baraza*, which are placed for men to meet and discuss the day's events (Ghaidan, 1975). The idea that, for the best effects, khat should be consumed in a closed room has been lost (Kennedy, 1987; Varisco, 2004). At these informal gatherings, khat is chewed with the typical accompaniments of BigG chewing gum, soda, and sometimes coffee. However, as khat has become popular among Kenyan youth of many backgrounds, the style of consumption bears less and less resemblance to Yemeni chewing sessions. Carrier describes group chewing sessions popular among Kenyan youth as follows: "These gatherings might take place in someone's house, in a café, under a tree, or even by the bus stage in the market. Miraa's use cuts across ethnic differences, with many participants of different ethnic backgrounds joining in the fun and sociability generated by the sharing of banter, soda, cigarettes, music, and whatever brand of miraa is deemed appropriate or affordable" (Carrier, 2005a, p. 213).

THE SUBSTANCE OF "KAYF"

Despite changes in consumption patterns, the long afternoon khat-chewing sessions, traditional to the Yemeni Highlands and to eastern Ethiopia, should be considered the ultimate khat experience. The scene and setting of the chewing session, an enclosed room with the accompaniments of hookah pipes, cigarettes, coffee, and even incense, enhance the experience, as does the ebb and flow of the conversation of participants. Zinberg (1984) has written on the importance of "setting" in enhancing the overall experience of a drug user. Khat is no exception, and the setting of the chewing session is an important part of the drug experience. Yet the setting is not all of the chewing experience. Khat is chewed for its particular effects, and these effects are the major reason for consumption. Western scholars and travelers often report that khat produces affects similar to drinking several cups of coffee, nothing more.

By placing large amounts of leaves or the plant's tender roots into their cheeks, the main psychoactive ingredients of khat, cathinone and cathine, are absorbed into the bloodstream. However, the process takes time: "Maximal plasma concentrations are reached 2 to 2.5 hours after the start of a session; for cathine, after 2.6 hours" (Odenwald, 2007, p. 10). After about two hours of chewing, the assembled group becomes noisy as animated conversation flows (Kennedy, 1987, p. 93). The stimulant effects are documented by Varisco, who describes the effects of participants in a classic Yemeni qat chew: "As the bitter juice descends into the stomach, a heightened sense of mental alertness begins within quarter of an hour. The result is stimulus to conceptualization and conversation, which can become animated or remain at a minimum, depending on the individuals present and the news of the day. After two hours a more reflective mood sets in, a state of euphoria or well being that is sometimes called *kayf*" (Varisco, 2004, p. 108).

According to Kennedy (1987), this experience of kayf is the goal of chewers. He describes the kayf experience as having six pleasurable dimensions: "contentment, ability to concentrate, increased flow of ideas, increased alertness, increased confidence, and increased friendliness" (1987, p. 115). It was the experience called kayf, which the Victorian explorer and great linguist Burton found untranslatable into English (Rushby, 1999, p. 67). The word denoting the kayf experience has many versions in a variety of languages. In Yemeni Arabic, Kennedy notes *taradi*, *mintashi*, *murtah*, meaning literally happiness, and *nashwa* (Kennedy, 1987, p. 111). It is a slightly changed version of the latter term, nashwa, which has made the journey to East Africa. In Kenya and Uganda the desired high from khat is often called nakhwa (Carrier, 2007), a Swahili Arabic loan word common along the Kenyan coast and among Swahili-speaking people of Yemeni descent. However, another term, *handas*, is a more popular rendering of the kayf feeling. Handas appears to be a slang word, originating among Somali language speakers. Use of the word handas is now part of the vocabulary of speakers of Sheng, the street talk of East African multiethnic youth. Hence, Carrier notes that in Kenya, the most popular term for the effects of khat is handas, which "appears to be sheng" (Carrier, 2003, p. 234). According to Carrier, a more specific Somali term for the khat high, or kayf, is markhan (Carrier, 2003, p. 234), a word I never heard used by Somalis or anybody else in Uganda.

The period, about two hours into the chewing session, is the time that people may "build castles in the air" or, in East Africa, "of spit" (Klein & Beckerleg, 2007). Clearly, conversation and ideas are important to participants of a khat-chewing session. However, Carrier's informants play down the effects of Kenyan khat, or miraa: "Chewers suggest that the social importance of miraa chewing sessions marks a clear difference: miraa consumers want not an intense 'high' but instead a convivial social gathering with fellow chewers. As one Somali told an American reporter when comparing miraa with other substances, '[t]he pleasures others are looking for, they won't find in khat.' For such a consumer, the pleasures of miraa lie more in company than in an altered state" (Carrier, 2008, p. 815).

Perhaps these Somali chewers had discarded many of the rituals of consumption and thus failed to achieve the full kayf, so sought after in Yemen, but it is more likely that they were trying to convince a potentially hostile American audience that khat is harmless. The evidence that Kennedy collected, by observations of others, and personal experience of khat use indicate that the substance needs the correct use and frame of mind for a pleasurable kayf to be achieved during the session. The kayf must be nurtured with good conversation conducted in the right setting. I have heard consumers in East Africa complain, and have experienced it myself, that an intrusive thought, word, or action during a chewing session destroyed the sense of nakhwa, as the khat high is often termed in East Africa, especially among Swahili speakers. Kennedy notes that many foreigners, trying khat for the first time, "feel no psycho-physiological effects at all" (Kennedy, 1987, p. 194) or do not notice that, for example, they have become more talkative after consuming khat. It takes experience to recognize and work with the cathinone and cathine once it has entered the bloodstream. One must learn how to chew khat. According to Kennedy, "Qat users seem to make partially unconscious choices regarding the optimum levels of the psychoactive substance for the sensation they want to achieve. Cultural use patterns, regulated somewhat by natural limitations upon amounts of active ingredients which can be ingested, enable Yemeni users to gauge and anticipate the effects on their systems fairly accurately. Each person learns to produce his own kayf, in terms of its intensity and duration" (Kennedy, 1987, p. 196).

The individual experience of kayf remains fragile, and once the extrovert, garrulous phase of a chewing session has passed, the whole session may turn nasty if the chewer is predisposed to depression or is hoping to escape problems with khat usage. Kennedy calls the reflective mood following the kayf "the 'introvert' phase" and describes it as a time when people withdraw and focus on their own "seething thoughts" (Kennedy, 1987, p. 114): "Whether the direction of the thought will be optimistic, pessimistic or objectively neutral, however, seems to depend upon variables of setting, chance conversation, physical condition, recent life events, personality factors, and the amount of qat chewed. The preoccupation can take any direction; the mood may be somber or optimistic according to circumstances" (Kennedy, 1987, p. 114).

Once the introvert phase has been reached it is not long before the khat session breaks up, and each participant quietly goes his or her own way into the dusk. Rushby describes his experience upon leaving the chewing session he attended with Sheikh Muhammed: "We said goodbye and I resisted Abera's wish to drink tej [local alcohol]. The qat was taking me down and I wanted to sit alone in the garden of the hotel. Sometimes it does that: brings weight upon you, a great sighing melancholy for something you cannot quite put a name to. Then your face becomes inert and emotionless as thought the nerves have been cut, but your thoughts drift on. The qat has stirred the mind and stilled the body until the moorings have slipped and the one has sailed free from the other" (Rushby, 1999, p. 67).

This is the time, after the chewing session has broken up but the effects still linger, that many khat consumers, even those living in strict Muslim areas, resort to the discrete use of various types of alcohol such as Ethiopian tej and Scotch whiskey: "Though alcohol is strictly prohibited in Yemen, some groups, and in particular the young men of more affluent families, rendezvous to drink at another house after a qat session. A bottle of Scotch whiskey is brought out and each man drinks several glasses filled with one-third whiskey and two-thirds water. It is believed that three such drinks are sufficient to counteract the effects of the qat; somber moods are dissipated permitting early sleep, allowing sexual activity, and stimulating an appetite for food" (Kennedy, 1987, p. 129).

OLD AND NEW UGANDAN STYLES

In Uganda a whole subculture around khat, with its own language, rules, and rituals of consumption, is emerging. Until recently Ugandan khat etiquette and language was borrowed from Yemeni and Somali conventions, ensuring that khat remained an alien and minority cultural phenomenon. One man of Yemeni descent described the chewing sessions hosted by his father in the 1970s: "The Arabs came to the house and he took out the chairs and put cushions on the floor, like a muffraj. They had a mada'a [hookah, shisha, or hubble-bubble pipe whereby tobacco smoke is filtered through water that bubbles as the smoker draws on the pipe]. They chewed their khat plain, without BigG chewing gum. My father used to write in a notebook while chewing—questions and points that had come up in discussion. He studied the notes afterwards. In the evening they drank milk and goat soup. It was men only; the women did not chew."

The sons of these migrants from Yemen chew in another way. Kassim, a second-generation Yemeni, lives in the center of the western town of Fort Portal. His family members are shopkeepers, but their business is geared to a daily routine of chewing. Every afternoon at about 3:30, a small group of men gather in Kassim's small sitting room. Each man has brought khat packed in small, clear plastic bags or in banana leaves. They sit in comfortable chairs and place their supplies on a coffee table. Kassim provides tap water, but other accompaniments to the khat are the responsibility of the individual group members. They bring cigarettes and BigG chewing gum. There is no television, but a radio is playing pop music. The session continues for five hours before the chewers start to disperse. The following day the routine is repeated and the conventions of the chewing session adhered to. Kassim tells me that he has recently banned one man from his session because he usually arrived with a bottle of whiskey and proceeded to drink it while chewing. Kassim explained that even after being told not to return with whiskey, the man had done just that, but when he put the bottle on the table, it shattered. As Muslims are forbidden alcohol or even to facilitate others' use of it, Kassim saw this as "God's work." But Kassim has also developed problems with excessive substance use: his khat consumption extends beyond the afternoon chew, so that he often chews alone in the morning.

Another man, a first-generation migrant from Hadhramawt now living in Kasese with whom I chewed one day in August 2007, had strong ideas about how khat should be consumed:

> It is important to have a heavy lunch first, and then to spit out the mairungi after a few hours, and not just continue chewing. Then if you do spit out, many people can eat, but others just drink milk. Khat can ruin your life if you chew every day with no plan for earning your living. Somalis chew in an undisciplined way. Now people all over Uganda have started chewing, but they do not do it properly. Mairungi has got a bad name. It happens that a young man who has been smoking cannabis and drinking alcohol is arrested. The police find a bag of mairungi in his pocket and blame his behavior on khat use.

As new patterns of consumption emerge, the locus of consumption has moved from the sitting rooms of wealthy Yemeni businessmen to video halls, alleys, and the "ghettos." Some men of Yemeni descent have started chewing in the style of the new consumers without ritual on street corners. For example, the eastern town of Jinja is a quiet and pretty place that allows licensed khat traders to operate and tolerates some public chewing. Jobless Corner is situated at a crossroads near the center of town. Frequenters of the corner sit on the steps of a 1930 art deco building that is typical to Jinja. There in the early afternoon, I find Salim, a man of Yemeni descent from a prosperous family, sitting with a couple of other men. He is chewing: taking khat leaves from the black plastic bag that also conceals a large sachet of waragi, local gin. An aspiring musician of Swahili-style tarab, Salim is jobless. He picks up some money for performing and by doing odd jobs for his family. When he has no money, his mother gives him 1,000 shillings ($0.50) to buy khat. After chewing, he usually rounds off the evening by smoking cannabis and drinking more spirits.

Among people of Yemeni descent, Ugandan khat use can be likened to consumption patterns in diaspora settings by Somali migrants. For example, a study of Somali chewers in London found that consumption had been "trans-planted to a foreign setting' and where 'previous roles and restraints' concerning levels and patterns of use might be less effective" (Griffiths et al., 1997, p. 283).

UGANDAN VENUES AND PATTERNS OF KHAT USE

Khat is chewed across Uganda by groups gathered in informal clubs such as the khat retail outlets, at video halls, and at home. These venues are what Carrier, writing on khat in Kenya, calls *majlis* (2007). In Uganda many khat consumers talk about the "ghetto," a term also coined by heroin users in Dar es Salaam (McCurdy, 2005), while disapproving Ugandan onlookers say that khat use is confined to the "slums." Certainly, the semipublic settings of khat shops, clubs, and video halls are usually situated in poor, if not notorious, urban areas. A newspaper report on the crime-ridden Katwe area of Kampala identified khat as a blight on this "slum" area:

> In Katwe, some of the video clubs, commonly known as *bibanda*, operate till after midnight. The *bibanda* harbour consumers of mairungi and opium [cannabis].
>
> The Member of Parliament for Makindye West, Hussein Kyanjo, attributed the high crime rate to unemployment, which "is unfortunately coupled with the slum nature of the area." (Businge, 2007, p. 10)

During the past twenty years, video clubs have sprung up over the country, and khat retailers often operate outside the entrances to these establishments. The young, mostly male moviegoers purchase khat and chew as they watch films, sometimes shown with a crude Luganda language voiceover that explains the action and translates some of the dialogue. Police officers and NGO workers have expressed disquiet concerning these operations in the morning when people should be working. Yet, as khat is rushed from the farms to the retail outlets each morning, it is not usually available for retail purchase until about midday. It is also widely alleged, by the police and local government officials, that moviegoing khat chewers consume alcohol and cannabis along with khat (Beckerleg, 2009, p. 45).

Overall, there is much variation in where and how khat is consumed in Uganda, but I have identified two main groups (Beckerleg, 2009): consumers who use khat alone, or *maqatna*, a term used by chewers of Yemeni origin and their associates to denote khat enthusiasts, and consumers who mix khat with consumption of alcohol, cannabis, or both. These people I call "mixers."

The Magatna

As a khat session takes several hours, if the full sequence of effects—from euphoria to quiet contemplation to speedy activity—is to be achieved, sufficient time to enjoy the chew is required. The maqatna follow the conventions of chewing that originated in Yemen and Ethiopia. Across the world from Yemen to Mombasa to London, khat is chewed with an accompaniment of soft drinks, tobacco, and tea or coffee by people sitting together for several hours. Kenyan khat is often consumed with BigG chewing gum, an innovation dating from the 1970s (Goldsmith, 1994). Additions of small amounts of the gum to the wad of khat in the cheek bind and sweeten the wad. Ugandan chewers, including Yemenis and Hadhramis, have adopted the use of BigG, which is imported from Kenya and sold by most khat retailers. Others consumers, notably Somalis, may use a small amount of groundnuts to soften the wad but often chew without any accompaniment (Beckerleg, 2009, p. 45). Although even the maqatna group has drifted far from the stylized chewing session of Yemen and Ethiopia, this group is defined by its refusal to mix khat with other drugs, although alcohol is often taken afterward to counteract the effects of the stimulant properties of khat.

Included among the maqatna group are people for whom khat use has no particular cultural importance but who nevertheless adhere to some self-imposed rules and routines. For example, in the northern town of Gulu, I met Boniface sitting on a bench provided by a khat retailer with a couple of other young men. At first, he tried to sell me his bead work, but when he met with no success, he remained chatty, as the khat he was chewing was already taking effect. Boniface is a university arts dropout who does handicraft for a living. He tells me that he chews daily and often but not always and drinks *waragi* gin afterward in order to sleep better. On weekdays he chews as he does his craftwork, while on weekends he chews but does not work. Boniface first saw khat while at boarding school and first tried it at college. He had decided to wait until he was eighteen before taking any drugs. Boniface finds that khat stimulates his creativity, but it is not useful when studying for examinations. He first started using khat when he went to buy it himself in Arua Park in Kampala and tried chewing alone.

Female maqatna are not usually found sitting at khat retail kiosks or at the informal clubs where men gather to chew. Most women in this group of dedicated chewers are Muslim, from the Somali, Yemeni, and Nubi communities, and chew at home because public consumption of khat, and even socializing with men in public, is not done by respectable women.

THE MIXERS

These khat consumers can be better described as multidrug users. Women from different ethnic backgrounds are included in this predominantly male mixer group. Some are sex workers and others independent traders and businesswomen whose conventional respectability has been compromised, both by their status as single women and by their drug use (Beckerleg, 2008). Both male and female mixers conform to the stereotypical view most Ugandans hold of khat consumers being uncontrolled drug users. Indeed, some mixers, for example an elderly Karimojong man whom I interviewed in the trading center of Iriri in 2009, are unashamed of mixing alcohol with khat:

> Muslims use *mairungi* to remove sorrows and at celebrations, but that is not the case for the Karamijong. Mairungi gives us strength to dig, especially during moonlight when it is cold. If you are watching for enemies it keeps you awake. Of course, people chew with alcohol, taking *waragi* or crude [home distilled spirits] as you are chewing. The negative part of mairungi is sex, as it affects performance, although for some people it is the opposite. Here [in Karamoja] we chew mostly with groundnuts or *simsim* [sesame]. Some people dip a stick into honey and add the honey to the wad to sweeten it. After spitting out, you clean your teeth, continue drinking, and have your supper. Some also smoke cannabis when or after chewing. People who don't chew with *waragi* may drink strong tea instead, but people around here cannot afford to buy soda. *Mairungi* chewing is good in company and also for personal reflection, but some people who chew get plans to go and steal. Some chewers become idle and do not go to the farm to dig. If they have no money to buy *mairungi* they think about stealing. Both *waragi* and *mairungi* are dangerous. *Mairungi* can also cause a hernia or destroy the teeth. It causes you to waste time; you can go somewhere where there is *mairungi* and forget about your family.

Although this man takes it for granted that khat is used with alcohol, he acknowledges the potential harm of both substances. Many more Ugandans, however, do not see alcohol as a drug that may cause harm to health and home. People talk about the dangers of khat use while ignoring the high rates of drinking in their midst. While the mixers are practicing a new mode of khat consumption that is increasingly fashionable among predominantly male, urban youth, the mixers appear to be the minority of Ugandan users.

CONSUMPTION SURVEYED

In order to find out more about the patterns of khat use in Uganda, 210 khat consumers were interviewed between February 2008 and March 2009. I used a convenience sample that recruited consumers chewing in venues, such as clubs, bars, roadsides, alleys, and at home. This research design ensured that all respondents were active consumers of khat and therefore qualified to answer questions on consumption of the substance. The purpose of the short questionnaire survey was the collection of data on reported behavior in relation to khat consumption in combination with other drugs, particularly alcohol. I interviewed some respondents, but most of the questionnaires were administered by Musa Almas, a multilingual Ugandan of Yemeni heritage, a long-term khat consumer who chewed "on the job" while recruiting respondents in a range of chewing venues. The questionnaires were translated from English to Swahili, a language spoken widely across East Africa. However, many of the questions were asked and answers given in languages spoken in the region where the interviews were held, for example, the language of the Toro Kingdom in and around Fort Portal, and in Kampala, Luganda, the language not only of the Ganda people but the major means of everyday communication in the city.

The men and women agreeing to complete questionnaires as they chewed encountered Musa Almas, a peer interviewer, a fellow khat consumer who was part of the khat scene. In this way, I hoped that evasive or dishonest answers would be minimized, and respondents admit to any multidrug use that they had been practicing, even if that use was illegal or socially stigmatizing. For the same reason respondents were not asked about religious affiliation, as asking a person who has just reported being a Muslim and then one minute later asking if they drank alcohol during or after chewing khat would be likely to cause embarrassment and possibly concealment of the truth. Of course, respondents who reported their ethnic group to be Arab, Somali, or Nubi were obviously Muslim. The reported ethnicity of the respondents is discussed in detail the next chapter. Among respondents from other ethnic groups, there were Christians, Muslims, and a few who said they did not belong to any religious group. A similar survey of khat users I conducted in Kampala and western Uganda during 2005 found that "the respondents were almost equally divided in terms of religion: 52% of respondents were Muslim; 43% were Christian, while the remainder reported that they had no religion or being pagan" (Beckerleg, 2006, p. 232).

Of the 210 interviews carried out between 2008 and 2009, 166 (79 percent) were with men and forty-four with women. Just over half (113) the interviews were conducted in different locations around Kampala, and seventy-three interviews took place in and around the western towns of Fort Portal, Kasese, and Mabarra. Other interviews were conducted in the towns of Bombo, Gulu, and Lira, and in various rural locations.

In terms of reported occupation and conforming to the stereotype many Ugandans hold of khat consumers, the biggest occupational group (sixty-four respondents or 31 percent of the total), worked in the transport sector as drivers or drivers' assistants (twenty-six), mechanics (eighteen), bus touts who direct passengers to public transport for a small commission (ten), vehicle cleaners operating from "car wash" informal enterprises located in swampy areas where there is running water (seven), and taxi drivers (three). A further twenty-six respondents (12 percent) reported working in the retail sector: some were prosperous shop owners, others their assistants or mobile street hawkers who walk many miles each day carrying their wares. Eleven (5 percent) respondents said they were unemployed, and nine respondents were students, either at secondary school or a university. The sample also included several khat sellers, policemen, two security guards, two intelligence agents who report on affairs of the local community, three people who gave their occupation as being "refugees," and another respondent described himself as a cannabis dealer.

Among the female respondents, there were ten who reported that they were housewives, six women said they were unemployed, and three more gave their occupation as sex workers. Other female occupations ranged from khat seller to journalist to teacher.

Capturing the varied forms of marriage, including polygamy and cohabitation, and the complications of multiple legal and cultural forms of separation and divorce was beyond the scope of the survey. Therefore, respondents were asked if they were "single" or "with a partner." Of the recorded responses, 51 percent reported that they were single, while 48 percent said they were living with a partner. Twenty-three percent of respondents reported that they had no children, while a further 65 percent had one to four children. Many people who reported being single also reported having children: in the case of women, it would be usual for them to be bringing up the children as a single parent, while men are expected to contribute to the upkeep of their children. However, no questions were asked to probe such complicated and emotionally fraught issues.

Due to the youth of the majority of respondents, it is not surprising that that 23 percent of respondents said they had no children. Fifty-two percent of people interviewed said they were between eighteen and twenty-nine years old, a further 35 percent were between the age of thirty and thirty-nine, and the remainder were forty years and above. The oldest respondent said that he was sixty-five years old.

In all, 67 percent of respondents had between seven and thirteen years of schooling, and among this group, 20 percent had completed the seven years of the Ugandan system of primary education. Twenty (10 percent) respondents reported having had no formal education at all.

Hence, these mostly urban chewers were typically young men with some education and making their way in the world through work as drivers, hawkers, shopkeepers, and mechanics. As such, they typify the majority of the population of Ugandan towns. The women, 20 percent of the sample, ran the social spectrum from wives who chewed discreetly at home to the shop assistants and petty traders to sex workers who were encountered in informal chewing clubs in the poorer parts of Kampala and other towns. Well over half (65 percent) of the khat consumers interviewed reported that they had chewed every day of the previous week. This finding is shown in Figure 7.1.

Of the survey respondents, 73 percent had adopted the Kenyan practice of chewing khat together with BigG chewing gum (Anderson et al., 2007; Goldsmith, 1994). However, 17 percent reported adding small amounts of peanuts to the wad of khat on the last occasion that they had chewed. Most of the remainder of respondents reported that they had chewed without any accompaniment to the actual wad of khat in their cheeks. Two respondents, however, had added sugar to the wad, while two more reported that they enjoyed adding to the bitterness by chewing khat with kola nuts. Kola nuts, although available from hawkers in Kampala and western Uganda, are not widely consumed in East Africa. They are far more popular in West Africa where they are important in life cycle rituals as well as everyday use (Lovejoy, 2007). The use of kola nuts by a two-khat consumer illustrates the willingness of this group to seek out new and interesting drug experiences that suit them. Indeed, one respondent reported using both kola nuts and cannabis mixed with khat.

Yet, according to the survey results, the mixers are in the minority, as is shown in Table 7.1.

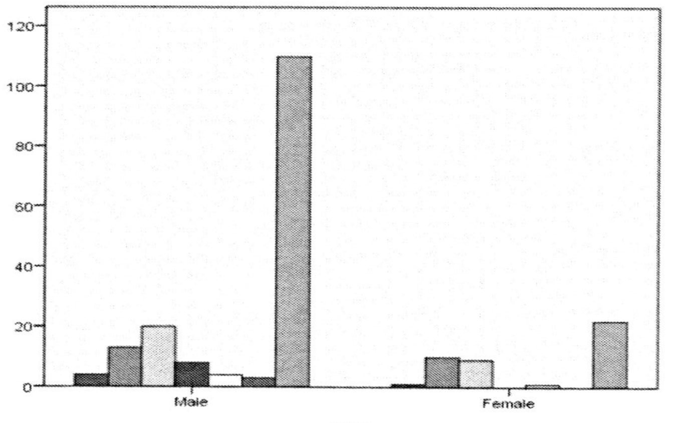

Figure 7.1 Number of days in the last week that 210 respondents chewed khat, by gender. "Other" equals cannabis and waragi.

Table 7.1 Other substances reported as used while chewing khat

Substance	Number of respondents	Percentage of respondents
Cigarettes	123	59
Beer	5	2
Waragi/spirits	10	5
Cannabis	14	7

These data indicate that, excluding tobacco, 17 percent of respondents chewed khat while also consuming either beer or alcoholic spirits, or while smoking cannabis. The situation with substance use after spitting out khat at the end of a chewing session is different. Table 7.2 shows the reported use of various substances after chewing khat.

The pattern of use of drugs and alcohol with khat is similar among men and women. However, men consuming alcohol preferred waragi gin over beer, while for women it was the other way round: they preferred beer over waragi, as is shown in Figure 7.2.

Almost half the respondents reported taking another drug after chewing. The use of alcohol in particular is considered to help the user sleep. However, respondents were asked how they had slept after their last use of khat, and their reported sleep patterns do not appear to be linked with additional substance use. Figure 7.3 shows the reported quality of sleep in relation to the use of various substances consumed after chewing khat.

"Other" in this chart refers to a cocktail of waragi-type spirits and cannabis and seemed least likely to help people sleep. Of course, such multidrug users may have also consumed more khat than other

Table 7.2 Reported use of substances after chewing khat

Substance	Number of respondents	Percentage of respondents
No substance	110	52
Beer	37	18
Waragi/spirits	35	17
Cannabis	14	7
Cannabis + waragi	12	6
Valium	1	0.5
Total	210	100

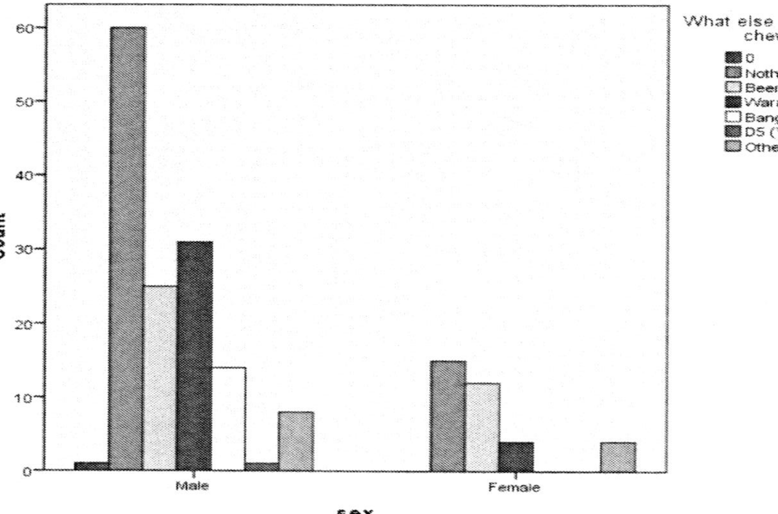

Figure 7.2 Substances used by 210 respondents after last consumption of khat, by gender. "Other" equals cannabis and waragi.

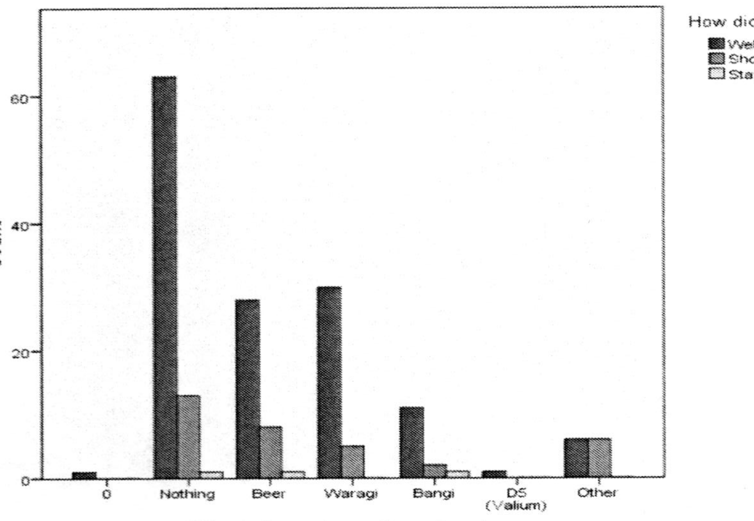

Figure 7.3 Reported quality of sleep of 210 respondents in relation to use of substances after last khat consumption

respondents, thereby making good sleep more elusive than in chewers of modest amounts.

Most of the respondents were interviewed while they were relaxing after work, typically in informal chewing clubs. However, 22 percent of respondents reported that they had chewed at work on last occasion they had consumed khat. Transport workers were the biggest group of consumers in the Ugandan survey, with 31 percent of respondents reporting that they work in this sector. However, it was mechanics and not drivers that were most likely to be chewing at work. Six of the eighteen mechanics (33 percent) reported last chewing khat while at work, while only two of the eighteen drivers interviewed reported chewing at work and were more likely to chew at clubs as a form of relaxation. As khat chewers often claim, and some evidence suggests (Kennedy, 1987), the drug is an aid to concentration. Mechanics carrying out repairs, which require analyzing the fault in the vehicle, may be assisted in their analyses by khat. Unsurprising, the other group that frequently chewed during work were the khat sellers, who often consume their stock with their customers.

KHAT AND WORK

In other settings, khat is used as an aid to work by a range of occupational groups. For example, in eastern Ethiopia khat use is woven into the daily work routine. Gebissa (2004) reports the following pattern among Oromo farmers in Harerge:

> A typical farmer commences the day by going to his *oyiru*, the family garden, to feed his animals and inspect the farm. Between eight and nine o'clock, he walks into his khat orchard and settles down with the other men of the family or the neighbourhood for the morning chew, the *igabana*, literally the "eye-opener." This session usually lasts about an hour. Only a small quantity of khat is chewed at this time for the purpose of it all is to achieve a quick *mirqaana*, the desired state of euphoria, for a burst of energy for the work ahead. . . . In the early afternoon, another chewing event starts, the *bartcha*, a popular and commonplace sight throughout the region. (Gebissa, 2004, p. 8)

In East Africa and in Yemen, farmers can benefit from the stimulating and appetite-suppressing attributes of khat when working in the fields. Like other substances, khat can be used in a variety of ways to achieve different effects. Newer khat consumers across East Africa tend to be urban youth (Carrier, 2007a; Gebissa, 2008), who either enjoy the stimulation of khat or need to keep awake and alert for long periods. Khat is popular among night watchmen and security guards, as Carrier reports: "Nightwatchmen throughout Kenya chew. In Isiolo, those on duty at the Catholic Mission are keen on miraa *kukaa macho* (Kiswahili: "to remain alert"). Even far from the Nyambenes, in areas not especially associated with miraa, nightwatchmen chew: around Lake Naivasha, watchmen on duty at tourist campsites use miraa pragmatically" (Carrier, 2003, p. 255).

As it causes insomnia, khat chewing keeps night watchmen and students studying late into the night awake (Carrier, 2003, pp. 255–256). However, in East Africa, khat is most closely associated with long-distance drivers, who chew to keep awake on long journeys and those working in long distance transport services. "Miraa use by drivers—of lorries, miraa pick-ups, passenger vehicles, and private cars—is one that raises some concerns. Whilst it is certainly helps some drivers remain alert, some consider that its effects lead to recklessness, and hence to accidents" (Carrier, 2003, pp. 255–256).

Given the widespread concerns about the safety of driving while chewing khat (Ihunwo, 2004, p. 471), some readers may be relieved to read that among the sample of drivers interviewed in Uganda, most were not chewing on the job. Nevertheless, wherever khat is consumed, it will attract criticism and concern. Indeed, despite new fashions of khat use both as a leisure activity and as an aid to gainful employment, khat has long been associated with laziness and incapacity to perform work. For example, the colonial authorities in Kenya and elsewhere observed khat use and were unimpressed. Carrier (2008) finds strong expression of this negative viewpoint in a letter sent by Malcolm Clark of the Native Civil Hospital in Wajir, Kenya, on May 12, 1939: "My experience is that people under the influence of kat live in a 'dream world' and lose all sense of realty. In large doses kat makes them excitable but not, in my experience, violent. . . . A kat addict gradually becomes a listless, lazy, 'good-for-nothing' person who lacks all energy and ambition. Kat addicts also lose sexual desire. In Somaliland, where it was worse than here, it was usual to dismiss any domestic servant found eating kat because of its bad effects on their work (KNA: DC/ISO/2/2/13)" (cited by Carrier, 2008, p. 809).

A more recent assessment of khat use comes in a study of three Ugandan occupational groups: students, transporters, and police officers. Reporting on a survey carried out in Mbarara on 181 respondents of whom 57 had chewed khat at some time, the authors comment that "in this study, the khat chewing habit has been established among students, law enforcement officials and transporters in south-western

Uganda. Our findings showed that substance abuse involving khat cuts across all ages. Youths and young adults between the ages of 16–25 years constituted the majority in khat consumption" (Ihunwo et al., 2004, p. 471).

The authors, who equate all khat use with abuse, could find no benefits of chewing the substance. On consumption by students, it was found that "the abuse of central nervous system (CNS) stimulants especially among students is for staying awake for prolonged periods and while preparing for important examinations as it is believed to sharpen the mind and senses. From this study, students did use khat to suppress sleep, but also for euphoria, confidence, increased sexual desire, increased alertness and to suppress hunger, in that order" (Ihunwo et al., 2004, p. 471).

The authors could find no evidence that use of khat improved academic performance in examinations and are equally dismissive of the reasons given by transporters and law enforcers for using khat: "Law enforcement officials used khat basically for euphoria, a good level of concentration, increased sexual desire, confidence and ability to socialise and communicate with others. Transporters used khat for increased alertness, confidence, euphoria and to suppress sleep. They correlate with Selassie and Gebre's findings that most of the reasons given for substance abuse were associated with the situation of the abuser" (Ihunwo et al., 2004, p. 471).

Thus, Ihunwo et al. (2004) equate all khat use with abuse and doubt the reported effects sought by consumers, such as students and transport workers who report that khat helps with work, to be beneficial. In 2005 in an earlier survey of Ugandan khat consumers, I asked respondents whether they thought khat affects work productivity. About half of the respondents agreed with the statement "khat lowers work productivity," while about half agreed with the statement or were uncertain as to whether it was true (Beckerleg, 2006, p. 234). Hence, the issue of work and khat can be controversial even among users.

Khat users who chew primarily as an aid to work will achieve different effects to those who chew in a leisurely manner in pursuit of the high called kayf in Yemen and handas in East Africa, but the type of drug high achieved also depends on which other substances are combined with khat.

VARYING THE HIGH

Ihunwo et al. (2004) also collected data on khat in relation to cigarette and *waragi* (refined gin) use among the fifty-seven khat consumers in their sample. They found that 57.9 percent of respondents who chewed khat also smoked tobacco, a finding very similar to the 59 percent of people who smoked while chewing khat in the survey I conducted. Furthermore, Ihunwo et al. calculated that "those who smoked cigarettes were twenty-eight times more likely to chew khat" (Ihunwo et al., 2004, p. 468). The levels of tobacco use by Ugandan khat chewers in the two surveys appear quite low, considering that many khat consumers claim that smoking enhances the chewing experience, and that in Yemen smoking the water pipe is an essential part of the khat session (Kennedy, 1987). In terms of public health, tobacco use should be of greater concern than khat, a substance that has relatively minor bad effects on the health of those who, even frequently, use it (Anderson et al., 2007; Kennedy, 1987).

The Mbarara study carried out by Ihunwo et al. found that 44.3 percent of the khat chewers interviewed also drank "alcoholic beverages such as refined gin (waragi) and local brews"; this amounted to a strong statistical association between khat and alcohol use. Respondents who drink alcohol are three times more likely to use khat compared to those who do not drink (Ihunwo et al., 2004, p. 471). These results compare with a total of 35 percent of the 210 respondents in my survey who reported using waragi or beer after khat use.

Yet, although according to the two survey results there is a strong association between alcohol and khat use in Uganda, the majority of khat consumers chewed without the addition of alcohol. The effects they achieve will be closer to the classic kayf of Yemen than the multidrug experiences of mixers who use cannabis or alcohol with khat. Yet, in Uganda, the chewing style of the majority, the maqatna group, has drifted far from the classic khat sessions enjoyed in Yemen and eastern Ethiopia. The effects experienced by khat users depend partly on the nature of the substance or substances consumed and, partly, on their expectations of certain feelings, their mood at the time of chewing and of others in the company they share, and where they chew and drink and smoke (Kennedy, 1987; Zinberg, 1984). The style of khat consumption adopted among Ugandan consumers is determined partly by desires to emphasis or to reject ethnic affiliation as a marker of identity, and ethnicity in relation to khat is the subject of the next chapter.

Chapter 8

Khat Consumption and Changing Ethnic Identities

Ethnic Identity in East Africa

Some anthropologists and historians have argued that in East Africa ethnicity and tribalism were products of European colonial ideologies and policies. Hence, Chabal and Daloz in their insightful analysis of African politics, *Africa Works*, write that "there is now ample evidence of what has been called the 'invention of ethnicity,' by which is meant the ways in which it was constructed and instrumentalized during the colonial period" (Chabal & Daloz, 1999, p. 57). In Africa, the "invention of modern ethnicity" occurred as part of the imposition of the colonial state. Anthropologists were employed by the colonial governments, and sometimes ethnographers were also district commissioners or held other colonial administrative posts. Dividing the people they encountered into discrete ethnic groups was an important part of the Western creation of conceptual and physical order through classification. For example, along the East African coast, since the eighth century there have been Muslims who spoke the Swahili language and had a distinct cultural style (Beckerleg, 2004). The people making up the Swahili have diverse origins and have long intermarried. Under British rule, different groups of people were classified and ranked as Arabs, Indians, or Africans and treated differently in terms of education, permitted area of residence, and even conditions of imprisonment (Mazrui & Shariff, 1994). The Swahili people were defined in various ways and classified by the British as "Arabs," and thus, as migrants to the coast rather than an indigenous African people. In the minds of Christian mission-educated East Africans, the Swahili were, and often still are, seen as slave traders. As ethnicity remains a key identity marker in Kenya, the debate about who the Swahili people are and if they actually exist still rages, but now some Swahili seek to become a "tribe" (Caplan, 2007), thereby taking on a defined ethnic identity similar to the nineteenth century European fixed notions of discrete ethncity.

From the 1960s, the period when most East African states gained independence, ethnic identities did not remain frozen and certainly did not melt away as an anachronism in the heat of nation building, as was expected and hoped at that time. Thus, although nation builders and modernizers in East Africa would have liked to consign ethnicity or "tribalism" to the past, ethnic identity remains a highly topical political issue. According to Chabal and Daloz (1999), "There is, of course, no denying the fundamental impact which colonialization had on the configuration and reconfiguration of ethnic identities, although it is quite clear that such an effect was distinct in every region and impinged differently on existing or imaginary 'tribal' perceptions."

Hence, although Chabal and Daloz acknowledge the role of the colonial enterprise in the "invention of ethnicity" in Africa, they also argue that this understanding of past processes should not detract from analyses of current notions of ethnicity: "The fact that some ethnic groups were more creatively invented during colonial rule than others does not in and of itself make them any less genuine, or legitimate, than others" (Chabal & Daloz, 1999, p. 57).

Each ethnic group imagines the country from their own unique perspective depending on how they fare in the modern nation state. The notion of "imagined communities" within the state has been applied by Arero in his analysis of the urban Borana in Kenya (Arero, 2007). "Kenya is made up of several communities that continue to imagine themselves to be members of the larger Kenyan community or nation. Each community imagines Kenya differently. Those communities that comprised the politically and economically powerful elites, such as the Kikuyu, Kalenjin, Luhya, Luo, Kamba and Meru, will have a different conception of the Kenyan nation from the marginal groups such as the Borana, Rendille or Somali of northern Kenya" (Arero, 2007, pp. 301–302).

Since the 1960s when East African countries gained independence from European powers, the working through of the practical consequences of the colonial "invented ethnicities" has resulted in much suffering. The ways that different ethnic groups have fared in terms of commanding power and privilege in East African nation states is a potent cause of dissatisfaction and political violence within the countries that make up East Africa. Ethnically related violence has marred Rwanda in the second half of the twentieth century, turning to the outright genocide of the Tutsi minority and moderate Hutu who refused to join in the killing (Taylor, 1999). Violence in Rwanda spilled over into the Democratic Republic of Congo (DRC); Tutsi and Hutu militiamen continued to cause great civilian suffering in the region. More recently, in Kenya the disputed results of the general election of December 2007 resulted in ethnic-based violence that left more than 1,000 people dead and 300,000 displaced (Anderson et al., 2008, p. 328). In Uganda, political violence in the form of several wars that had an ethnic dimension marred daily life from 1979. In 2009, although peace has been restored in the north of country, Joseph Kony, the leader of the Lord's Resistance Army is still kidnapping children and causing havoc in the neighboring countries of Central African Republic and the DRC.

In addition to ethnic-based violence occurring within countries, border disputes are still occurring over lines on maps drawn up in at the turn of the twentieth century (Meredith, 2005). Hence, the Eritrean and Ethiopian governments are sworn enemies; Ethiopia invaded Somalia in 2006 (Barnes & Hassan, 2007), while Eritrea has been the supporting Islamic insurgents that Ethiopia had tried to dislodge. As ordinary, and therefore mostly poor and powerless, people in East Africa try to make sense of the political scene, they adjust their ethnic identity to create a stronger, more positive group identity to suit the current trends and the location. As Reid and Dirir point out, "Identity is expressed in a myriad of ways, embodied and symbolised in a vast array of activities and institutions. Space, or physical territory, is a potent expression of identity; but territory is only past of the story and, in some cases, only a very small part. Identity is also commonly founded on particular interpretations of the part, at local as well as national level, and on the manipulation and interpretation of 'cultures'; it is linked to ideas about dislocation, and separation from ancestral pasts and homelands" (Reid & Dirar, 2007, p. 235).

Ethnic identity is expressed through language, dress, diet, occupation, and drug use, including khat consumption. Individuals also seek to change their ethnic identity or to renounce ethnicity as an essential part of their identities, with self-definition the main criterion for group membership. Such processes occur particularly among members of cultures that are disputed as ethnic groups, for example the Swahili (Caplan, 2007; Caplan & Topan, 2004; de Vere Allen, 1993) and the Nubi (Johnson, 2009; Leopold, 2005).

ETHNIC IDENTITY AND KHAT

In Uganda throughout the turmoil of political violence of the 1970s and 1980s, khat production and consumption spread. This was also a period where many people fled their home districts, resulting in a high degree of ethnic "scrambling" (Van Acker, 2000). In Uganda, small-scale khat producers, agents, and wholesales from many ethnic groups supply consumers from equally diverse backgrounds. The new khat consumers were drawn mostly from the urban centers and were from many different ethnic communities. The sample of 210 khat consumers interviewed in different locations in Uganda described in Chapter 6, was made up of people from khat-consuming cultures of longstanding as well as from ethnic groups with no khat tradition. The 210 men and women interviewed were from a wide range of ethnic groups (see Table 8.1).

As most interviews were carried out in Kampala, the Ganda capital as well as the national capital, and many more in Fort Portal, the seat of the Toro kingdom, or in Mbarara, the capital of Ankole, the predominance of these three groups among the khat users is unsurprising. Many respondents reported an ethnic or national affiliation to a minority group resident within Uganda, such being Rwandan, Kenyan, or Karimojong.

Table 8.1 Reported ethnic group/nationality of 210 khat consumers in Uganda

Ethnic group/nationality	Number of respondents	Percentage of respondents
Toro	34	16
Ganda	28	13
Ankole	22	10
Arab	15	7
Somali	15	7
Lugbara	13	6
Mixed race	12	6
Nubi	11	5
Konjo	10	5
Rwandan	6	3
Kenyan (Kikuyu, Maasai, and Nandi)	5	2
Karimojong	5	2
Others	34	16

Uganda is a country with speakers of thirty indigenous languages (Kawoya, 1985) and with varied forms of ethnic-based social organizations. The Ganda (Hanson, 2003), Toro, Nyoro, and Soga peoples are members of longstanding and extant kingdoms (Medard & Doyle, 2007). Ankole, too, was once a kingdom, while the Konjo are in the process of creating a new kingdom, or according to pretenders to the throne, resurrecting an old one (Stacey, 2003). By contrast, in the north of the country the Karimojong, Acholi, Langi, and Lugbara are divided into lineages and clans. Writing of the West Nile region, Leopold sums up the differences as follows: "Unlike the Bantu language-speaking kingdoms of southern Uganda, the traditional social units throughout this region were small-scale, kinship based 'segmentary' societies, of the kind represented for generations of social anthropologists by the work of E. E. Evans-Prichard on the Sudanese Nuer" (Leopold, 2005, pp. 5–6).

KHAT USE AS AN EXPRESSION OF NONETHNIC IDENTITY

From the 1930s onward, khat in Uganda was a marker of ethnic identity for immigrant Yemenis and Somalis. Seventy years later the situation is very different. Globalization and modernity have facilitated the spread of new drug cultures in Uganda as elsewhere and khat plays a vital role in forging social identities that are not based primarily on ethnicity or religion. Although ethnic identity may be a matter of life and death in times of war and civil disorder, it is less important to many urban dwellers who live and work in a multiethnic milieu. No consumer who was surveyed refused to answer the question concerning ethnicity or nationality. In many cases, respondents will have been proud to declare their heritage, but other consumers, including many of those surveyed, appear more interested in forging a new urban identity, delinked from ethnicity, including khat use. New khat consumers have taken up a habit that is not part of their culture but is closely associated by most Ugandans with Somalis and Arabs and therefore also with Islam.

Many of these new consumers mix khat with alcohol and cannabis, and such innovations in the mode of chewing have given Ugandan khat consumption a bad name and led to the labeling of consumers as "low-class people" and unemployed "idlers." A khat session takes up to six hours, time when young men are nonproductive (Beckerleg, 2009, p. 45). Unlike time spent drinking in bars and watching football, khat is not a socially accepted leisure pursuit. Rural chewers also congregate in informal meeting places, typically near a shop that sells alcohol, cigarettes, and BigG chewing gum. For example, during an afternoon visit to the khat farms of Kasenge in October 2007, I encountered a group of eleven men near a shop. Four of them were engrossed in a game of cards, several were chewing khat, another four of the men were smoking cannabis, and one was drunkenly waving a sachet of *waragi* around. They were conversing easily in Ganda language, which is the main *lingua franca* of central Uganda. These men live in an area where, although part of the Buganda kingdom, there has been considerable ethnic mixing. It was impossible, however, to tell from their physical appearance, dress, or manner what ethnic group or groups they represented.

Most Ugandan chewing sessions in informal clubs are not confined to one ethnic group; rather, the conviviality and group identity of khat chewers is enjoyed and ethnic differences played down. In Kampala, however, specialist clubs for khat chewers have appeared in recent years and are popular among Kenyans, Somalis, and Ethiopians. These clubs selling khat and sometimes alcohol provide comfortable seating and a pleasant atmosphere dedicated to chewing. Up to fifty chewers at a sitting gather in venues similar to those found in the neighboring countries of Ethiopia and Kenya. Although indigenous Ugandans and Ugandan Somalis also use these clubs, they function as a gathering place for Kampala residents and residents from neighboring Kenya and for refugees from Ethiopia and recently arrivals from Somalia. The chewers attending khat clubs in Kampala are following a trend toward youth, orientated, nontraditional consumption styles also observed in Ethiopia and Kenya.

STYLE VARIATION IN NATIONALITY AND ETHNICITY

Goldsmith has linked the popularity of khat in Kenya as a youth activity that crosses ethnic boundaries to the use of BigG chewing gum (Goldsmith, 1994, p. 136). In about 1975, according to Goldsmith, khat consumers discovered that they could counteract the bitter taste of khat by adding small pieces of chewing gum to the growing wad in their cheeks, and BigG, which is sugary but not sugarcoated or mint flavored, was found to be the best for this purpose. Most Kenyan chewers, apart from Somalis, use BigG. Before the advent of BigG, most consumers chewed without adding anything. But in Yemen some people would add a small amount of sugar or cloves (Kennedy, 1987). In Uganda, the earliest chewers were Yemenis and Somalis, who often chewed without accompaniment or with small pieces of peeled groundnuts added to the wad. Since the 1980s, however, BigG has become popular in Uganda, in line with the growing popularity of khat itself, as it crosses ethnic lines. Hence, in the survey of 210 khat consumers conducted in Uganda, 73 percent of respondents reported using BigG the last time they had chewed khat.

The popularity of BigG in Uganda and the type of venue for chewing chosen by the Ugandan consumers surveyed indicate that the dominant style of Ugandan khat use is similar to Kenyan consumption patterns. First in Kenya and now in Uganda, consumers from many different ethnic backgrounds have taken up khat and BigG, spurning the older styles of consumption still practiced in Yemen.

Across Kenya, where BigG is widely available, Somalis chew mostly without chewing gum. Hence, Somali khat chewers, be they in Nairobi or miles from the nearest town in a roadside hut, use certain accompaniments to increase the enjoyment of khat chewing. They drink tea or soda, but scorn the use of BigG chewing gum that is popular with consumers from other ethnic groups. However, some Somali consumers add one or two peanuts with the shell removed to their miraa wad to make it softer and to remove the bitterness. After consumption, the use of Valium to aid in sleep is reported to be a widespread problem in both urban and rural areas (Anderson et al., 2007; Beckerleg & Sheekh, 2005).

There were fifteen respondents the survey of 210 khat consumers interviewed in Ugandan who said they were Somali. Of these, ten reported at the last occasion of khat consumption to have chewed with peanuts, three reported using BigG, and two said they did not add anything to the wad.

Kenyans and Khat

Kenyans from most ethnic groups do not have a strong association with khat consumption. Only for the Tigania and Igemebe clans of the Meru people of Kenya is khat chewing a practice of centuries-old ritual significance (Carrier, 2007; Goldsmith, 1994). During the twentieth century in Kenya, khat became a "tradition" among Somalis and Swahili (Anderson et al., 2007; Beckerleg, 2004). However, for the Nandi, Kikuyu, and Maasai chewers included in the Ugandan survey of 210 consumers that I conducted, khat use is an expression of youth culture and possible contemporary Kenyan national identity but not an expression of ethnic identity. As Carrier (2005a) points out, "Today, many young men—and some young women—from all ethnic groups throughout Kenya have taken to miraa chewing, and miraa itself can be seen to fit together with other elements of a youth ethos that values qualities such as daring enterprise, dance and most validates items of consumption originating far from the Nyambene Hills [where it is grown]" (Carrier, 2005a, pp. 211–212).

Kenyan youth culture, like youth cultures in most settings, spurns mainstream values, and many middle class youth have joined poorer Kenyans in the pastime of khat chewing. According to Carrier, "Miraa consumption is associated with the likes of prostitutes and *matatu* (public mini-bus) touts: hardly the sort of people middle-class Kenyans would wish to emulate" (Carrier, 2008, p. 808). Figures on the changing volume of khat sales within Kenya are not available, but the spread of the plant to all ethnic communities and all locations within the country, no matter how remote (Anderson et al., 2007), is a cause of concern for many Kenyans of all ethnic backgrounds, including many Swahili leaders (Beckerleg, 2006).

Ethiopians and Khat

Three respondents in the survey of 210 khat users reported that they were "Ethiopian," and one of them gave his occupation as "refugee." The ethnicity of these three Ethiopian chewers resident in Kampala was not recorded. However, in contemporary Ethiopia, khat chewing is no longer an ethnic-related activity. The first consumers in Ethiopia were confined to the area around the city of Harer in eastern Ethiopia from at least the fourteenth century (Gebissa, 2004). Then in the early twentieth century, Oromo people started producing khat on a commercial scale, first to supply residents of Harer and then for a wider market. The farmers and others in the Oromiya region also started consuming the leaves in increasing numbers (Anderson et al., 2007; Gebissa, 2004). According to Gebissa,

> Despite the negative attitudes of non-chewers, the ambivalent policy of the Ethiopian government, and the dire warnings of the medical community, khat consumption has spread from Harerge to all parts of Ethiopia's Oromiya Regional State in the last three decades. A survey of secondary school students in Agaro, Western Oromiya, for instance, revealed a current khat chewing prevalence of sixty-five percent and that two thirds of the most frequent users were students between the ages of fifteen and twenty-two years (Adugna et al. 1994:162). A cross-sectional survey conducted in 2003 at Jimma University, located in a larger town about thirty miles to the west of Agaro, showed a lifetime

> and current prevalence of forty-six percent and thirty-nine percent, respectively. (Gebissa, 2008, p. 785)

The widespread popularity of khat use among all ethnic groups, across the country started about sixty years ago: "From the 1940s the civil service expanded, and with higher educational qualifications being demanded of officials through the 1950s and 1960s, there was a greater movement of professionals between the various regions of the country. At the same time the expansion in secondary and higher education has seen movement of students and teachers. These two factors have led to the introduction of chewing habits to previously khat-free regions" (Anderson et al., 2007, p. 66).

Khat has continued to be popular among students: "In the Amhara Region in the north, the conservative bastion of Ethiopia's Christian heartland where khat had traditionally been despised, khat consumption has become a ubiquitous pastime in the city of Bahir Dar and surrounding districts. A study on the incidence of khat chewing among college students in the Amhara region revealed a prevalence of twenty-seven percent lifetime chewing with forty-six percent reporting the onset of the habit during their senior year in secondary school (Kebede Y., 2002: 9–17)" (Gebissa, 2008, p. 785).

The recent growth of khat consumption in Ethiopia is considerable. In 1980 to 1981, 116,376 tons of khat was consumed in the domestic market; by 2000 to 2001 the amount consumed had jumped to 208,332 tons, a 79 percent increase in twenty years (Anderson et al., 2007, p. 67). Khat use has become a mainstream activity among Ethiopian youth for whom it has no value as a marker of ethnicity identity and is indeed a long despised substance by the Amhara people. Gebissa reports that "in Ethiopia, khat gained notoriety among anti-drug elements earlier this century. Many of the critics were Christian rulers and settlers from central and northern Ethiopia who established their suzerainty over the local Muslim Oromo, Somali, and Hareri peoples in the late nineteenth century. For the Christian rulers of the Oromo inhabitants of Harerge, khat consumption was a mark of apostasy. In 1916, Lij Iyasu, Emperor Menelik's designated successor, was deposed for indulging in khat chewing with Muslims and thus converting to Islam during one of his visits to Harer in the early 1910s" (Gebissa, 2008, p. 790).

Rwandans and Khat

Six of the 210 khat consumers surveyed reported that they were of *Banyarwandan* (Rwandan) ethnicity. Their responses do not make clear whether they are Rwandan citizens or Ugandan citizens whose ancestors had migrated from Rwanda to settle in Uganda. Their responses also conceal their actual ethnic affiliation of either Hutu or Tutsi. Since the Rwandan genocide of 1994, when up to a million Tutsi and "moderate" Hutu was slaughtered by the majority Hutu, it is forbidden in Rwanda to mention ethnic origins; everybody is supposed to be Rwandan first and only (Meredith, 2005; Taylor, 1999). Even in Uganda, the terms "Hutu" and "Tutsi" are rarely used, and both groups are usually described as "Banyarwanda." The killing in 1994 was ended by the Uganda-based, Tutsi-dominated Rwanda Patriotic Front that is still in power in Rwanda.

Rwanda has no tradition of khat consumption and only a very small number of consumers, comprising mostly of migrants. Until recently, the Rwandan police and customs officials mostly turned a blind eye to small scale imports of *kasenge* type khat brought from Kampala by traders traveling on public buses (Anderson et al., 2007). However, by 2007 when I visited the Rwandan capital, Kigali, khat was being traded clandestinely as a de facto illicit drug rather than in the semiopen fashion, like it was only two years earlier. My previously unpublished notes on my visit recorded the attempts of our small Ugandan group to buy khat in Kigali.

> Much has changed here since my last visit two years ago. Khat has become contraband, like cannabis. Ramadan, a Ugandan who works with Khalid, a mechanic of Yemeni origin, agreed to help us purchase khat. Ramadan says that the police leave Arabs and Somalis alone and even Ugandans to some extent. What they do not want is Rwandans consuming khat. We first drove to the industrial area where UN food aid warehouses are situated, alongside Somali cafés that meet the needs of the UN drivers, many of whom are ethnic Somalis. In the cafés, Ramadan was told that the khat had not yet arrived from Kampala. Next, we drove to the main bus station, where buses from Uganda and elsewhere arrive. Ramadan left me in the car and went to look for contacts. He returned after about ten minutes with a young woman called Janet, who, judging by her appearance, was probably a Tutsi. She got in the car and produced two small *frosh*, portions, of khat. These were opened to reveal two wilted portions of *kasenge*. Ramadan rejected these as *bareh* (old stock from yesterday). Janet, having failed to make a sale of yesterday's leftovers, agreed to give Ramadan the

> cell phone of another khat seller, Amina. Ramadan duly called Amina and arranged to meet her on the forecourt of a nearby gas station. Amina was known to Ramadan, and indeed to me, as the sister of Layla, the khat trader that I had encountered in 2005. Layla and Amina are Ugandans of mixed heritage and claim that their Yemeni grandfather was a pioneer of khat production in Uganda. By 2007, Amina had moved on to Brussels in Belgium where she worked in various menial jobs. Meanwhile, her sister, Layla had taken over the khat importation and retailing business in Kigali. Upon arrival at the gas station, there was no sign of Layla. When called again on her cell phone, she explained that she was at a nearby lodging but would be along shortly. Layla arrived dressed in skirt and blouse and wearing a Muslim-style headscarf. She was clutching a large paper bag and accompanied by another woman who looked scared. The two women got in the car and we drove off to Layla's home. As we drove, she opened the paper bag and allowed Ramadan to purchase fresh *kasenge* khat. Layla explained that over the past year or so, she had been arrested and locked up eight times for dealing khat. They disguised the khat, which comes from a specific farm in Kasenge, as fruit. They used different bus companies to carry this disguised cargo, as if any one company realized what the supplies really were, they would refuse to carry it. The operation supplied about fifty customers during the week and more during weekends. Since khat was made illegal, Layla said, her customer base had gone down. Most of her customers were Ugandans, not Rwandans.

Foreigners, such as the dealers we encountered, are the main consumers of khat smuggled into Rwanda. There is little demand for khat among indigenous Rwandans and no cultural connection to its use. The Rwandans surveyed in Uganda, regardless of their ethnic affiliation, country of birth, or personal circumstances, are part of the Ugandan and wider East African trend of khat chewing as a nonethnic, mostly urban leisure pursuit.

The Ugandan Vocabulary of Khat

Although khat consumption in Uganda has become a popular, multiethnic pastime, the words spoken to talk about the substance and its use employ a vocabulary that derives largely from the Somali language and from Yemeni Arabic. Even though khat producers, traders, and hardcore consumers may speak different languages, when it comes to talking about khat there is a basic vocabulary that is used across the country. I have already introduced some of these words in describing trade and consumption patterns and now will examine the vocabulary of khat in Ugandan in relation to ethnicity and identity.

The word *Maqatna*, used by khat enthusiasts of Yemeni heritage and by those in contact with the Yemeni community is interesting. Qat is the Yemeni Arabic term for khat and is the correct form of the word "khat," the internationally recognized term for *Catha edulis*, being a bad transliteration of qat (Kennedy, 1987). According to Gebissa, "qat" predates the Ethiopian Amharic form "chat," thus pointing to a possible Yemeni origin for khat (Gebissa, 2004, p. 14). Ugandans with a Yemeni connection have taken the original Arabic word qat and put a Swahili prefix "ma" in front of it. In the Swahili language, one noun class that includes occupational groups denotes the plural of the word with "ma." For example, a craftsperson is a *fundi*, while two or more craftspeople are called *mafundi* (Johnson, 1979). The "na" suffix means "with" and has a general connotation of connection (Johnson, 1979, p. 326). So "maqatna" could be translated as "we with khat." Talking with khat consumers across Uganda, I found, however, that many did not recognize the term *maqatna*. Their ignorance of this term is an indication off their status as recent consumers with no cultural tradition of khat consumption to inform their chewing style.

Khazzan is also Yemeni Arabic and means, literally, "to store." In Yemen the verb is also used to denote khat chewing (Kennedy, 1987). Maqatna tend to "khazzan" khat, while newer consumers do not understand the term and speak of "eating" khat.

Other khat-related terms are derived from Ugandan languages. Thus, a common term for a glut of khat, when supplies are plentiful and prices fall, is *kibbo*, literally a basket in Luganda, the language of the Ganda people. Khat itself goes by a number of names in Uganda. Most consumers use the generic term mairungi, which is a Bantu word similar to murungi, a term used by Swahili and Kamba speakers in Kenya for khat. Some Ugandans, mostly in the east of the country near the border with Kenya, talk of khat as miraa, which is the most widely used term for the substance in Kenya. In some areas, such as southwest Uganda, consumers just call khat "leaves" in their local language. There are other names for khat trees in Uganda, but these are known only to farmers, pastoralists, and forestry officials and not to the bulk of consumers.

From Fort Portal in the west of Uganda to the Mabira Forest in the East, khat producers and traders deal in *frosh*. A frosh is an imprecise measure, either a large plastic carrier bag full of khat or a banana leaf package of the leaves. The term is not used in Kenya, where the producers in the Nyambene Hills devised a metric system based on counting rather than weighing twigs so that khat is sold in *kilo* packages (Goldsmith, 1994). The subdivisions of a kilo of Kenyan miraa are known at the coast as *durba*, a Swahili term derived from Arabic. In Uganda, where most khat comes in the form of packages of loose leaves, this terminology is not commonly used. Rather, people speak of large wholesale frosh and small retail ones. It is hard to identify the origin of this word. Traders assume it was introduced by the Yemenis and it is therefore an Arabic or possibly a Swahili word. It is probably a corruption of the Swahili word *frasila*, meaning a measure of weight of thirty-five pounds, which according to *Madan's Standard Swahili-English Dictionary*, may be derived from an Arabic term *far sila*, meaning a full basket (Johnson, 1979).

Sometimes the problem for *maqatna* consumers seeking a good high is obtaining a supply of fresh khat. "Bareh," or *Barehe* in an alternative spelling of the word, is a Somali word used across most of Kenya and across Uganda to denote khat that is a day old from the time of picking. Bareh khat is not only wilted but also has less cathinone content, the main ingredient causing the *handas* high. According to Carrier, "barehe" means "slept" in Somali language (Carrier, 2005b, p. 545). Traders may try to pass off khat as fresh, but discerning Ugandan consumers of all ethnic backgrounds and speaking a wide range of languages will complain that old-looking khat is bareh and either move off or negotiate a discount.

Each production area produces khat of different grades that are named differently. The names usually denote an area or the grower and sometimes the trader. However, around Fort Portal there is also a vocabulary, known only to maqatna, for the way that khat is harvested. There, a portion of khat where the harvester has preselected only tender leaves, which can all be used without the consumers checking or sorting the portion, is called by the English word *grade*. By contrast, *karanja* denotes poor quality khat with a mix of coarse and tender leaves that the consumer must sort in order to find the ones fit for consumption. The word karanja is used by maqatna and appears to originate with Ugandan Yemenis who spoke Swahili. The term karanja may derive from a beef stew dish of the same name sold in Kenyan cafés, particularly at the Swahili coast. As well as denoting poor quality khat, the word karanja is also used to describe the effects of chewing. So karanja also denotes the bad dreams caused by consuming karanja khat and a term denoting khat that produces no high or handas.

Handas is the mostly widely used term for the khat high used by Ugandan maqatna. Handas is not mentioned by Kennedy (1987) as one the alternative terms for *kayf* used in Yemen. In Uganda and in Kenya, handas is a far more popular way of describing a khat high than *nakhwa*, a Swahili word derived from Arabic, in popular usage at the Kenya coast. Most Ugandan khat chewers, and not just the maqatna connoisseurs, recognize and use this word, which is closely associated with Somalis but does not appear to be an actual word in that language. My own suggestion is that handas could be derived from an Arabic word, *hanaddis*, meaning "dark nights" (Cowan, 1976, p. 210).

Ugandan "Arab" Identity and Khat

Discussion of the vocabulary of khat illustrates the strong cultural influence of Yemenis in Uganda on matters relating to the khat trade and to modes of consumption of the drug. In the survey of 210 consumers that I conducted, Yemenis were overrepresented. Fifteen respondents reported an "Arab" ethnic identity. Within Uganda in general, and in settings where khat is chewed, most people labeling themselves "Arab" are of Yemeni descent, while a few have Omani origins. Many of these "Arabs" would have been counted as "Swahili," and may have considered themselves "Swahili" if they were living in Kenya (Beckerleg, 2004; Mazrui & Shariff, 1994).

In the survey of khat consumers, twelve respondents reported being of mixed race, or in Swahili, "chotara." Any of these respondents could have identified themselves with the ethnic identity of their father, or if they did not know their father, their mother. These "chotara" respondents may have wanted to play down the importance of ethnic identity and align themselves with the new nonethnic orientation of khat consumption. It is probable that many of the twelve respondents were of partial Yemeni ancestry but that they identified with the "chotara" label. For second- and third-generation Yemenis, cultural and linguistic integration into Ugandan cultures and retaining Arab identity are problematic. On one hand, their appearance and (faux) Swahili cultural orientation marks them as separate from the majority of Ugandans, who have no Asian origins. On the other hand, the language they speak and their cultural traits, including food and dress, originate among the Swahili of the East African coast. In East Africa their Arab identity is expressed through the medium of Swahili culture and language. But, as the existence of a Swahili people is itself contested in East Africa, they have adopted a cultural identity that is highly problematic (Caplan, 2007). Many Kenyans do not "see" Swahili but only "Arabs." Similarly, Ugandan Yemenis do not perceive themselves, nor are considered by others, to be Swahili. However, if

Ugandan Yemenis de-emphasize their Arabness or their Swahiliness, they are able to forge their own identities of their own choice, to some extent. Maternal networks can be emphasized and an indigenous Uganda ethnic identity claimed. Yet the "chotoara" label can never be completely erased. Life in Uganda is about fitting in and "creating a place for ourselves as best we can," as one man of Yemeni paternal descent put it.

Khat chewing in Uganda is closely associated with "Arabs" who migrated from Yemen. Those coming from the north of the country brought a khat tradition with them, while arrivals from Hadhramawt in south Yemen rapidly adopted the habit and claimed khat as part of their cultural heritage. One migrant from Hadhramawt described his khat use to me as part of the range of Swahili cultural attributes that he took on when he arrived in Mombasa in the 1970s, before moving onto Uganda. According to another Yemeni informant, Saleh, an elderly man long settled in the town of Fort Portal, "There is no khat grown in Hadhramawt. If seen you were seen chewing there it is equated with being a drunk. I started chewing in Uganda when a northerner taught me. Hadhramis took up chewing in East Africa because they were young men who wanted to try everything."

Another Hadhrami man, a daily consumer, explained that fifty years ago, khat was not part of the culture or even available in Hadhramawt; the nearest place where it was sold was Aden and later on in the port of Mukalla.

In East Africa migrants from Yemen have redefined the significance of khat chewing to include people from Hadhramawt, who adopted chewing as part of their ethnic identity and because they liked it. In north Yemen, according to Varisco, khat chewing is an important marker of national identity, marking Yemenis apart from other Arabs in the region. The identity of Yemen as a nation was defined by the outcome of a civil war in 1962 and the deposal of a traditional ruler and by the unification in 1990 of North Yemen with South Yemen of which Hadhramawt is large region. "The emergence of Yemeni identify, first in the north after 1962 and then expanded sense after unification of the north and south in 1990 has necessitated an ongoing refining of traditional status and tribal categories. I argue that the chewing of qat has served as a powerful identity marker both to affirm the value of Yemen's rich cultural heritage and individual self worth in a climate where Yemen was continually being disparaged by Westerners and fellow Arabs alike" (Varisco, 2004, p. 111).

Kennedy, on the other hand, argues that such an explanation of "group identity needs," for the popularity of khat in Yemen is "one dimensional" and argues that Yemenis chew because the practice has become institutionalized and there is no other form of entertainment available (Kennedy, 1987, p. 235). He also dismisses Weir's (1985) analysis of Yemeni khat chewing as a form of conspicuous consumption that creates prestige and reinforces hierarchy as only one reason among many for Yemenis to continue chewing khat in large numbers. "Prestige emulation and nationalistic identity feelings are often important aspects of complex motivations which also include powerful rewards of communitas and general ego enhancement, along with pressures towards conformity. All these motivations are reinforced by the lack of alternative institutions, as Yemenis frequently explain to the visitor. However, when all psycho-social explanations have been given, it is important to remember that the chemical effects of this drug still remain one of the most important reasons why the people of Yemen chew qat" (Kennedy, 1987, p. 235).

Kennedy's assertion that people chew khat for the effects is an important reminder that drug use is often a matter of availability and personal preference, and for many people, not an expression of ethnic identity. However, for Yemenis in Uganda, khat use does seem to be a cultural cement and a identity marker uniting Arabs from north Yemen, Hadhramawt, and even Oman.

Somali Identity and Khat Consumption

Ethnic Somalis are a small minority group in Uganda, and, like Arab khat consumers, overrepresented in the survey of 210 chewers. A total of fifteen respondents reported their ethnic group as "Somali," and one of these reported his occupation as "refugee."

Leaders of the well-established Ugandan Somali community, with historic links to Somaliland and the British army in the form of the King's African Rifles (KAR), refute cultural connections to khat use. In particular the younger Uganda Somalis typically claim that they are not interested in chewing, and that most of the Somalis chewers around Kampala are recent refugees from the ongoing conflict in Somalia. Rashid, a young Ugandan Somali lawyer referred me to Sheikh Abdul, chairman of the Somali Elders and Imam of the mosque located in the Somali dominated part of Mengo in central Kampala. The mosque is a large and modern building in a compound with ample space for car parking and an attached school. When I visited in February 2009, I found Sheikh Abdul seated behind a desk in a large, comfortable office with two other men. The Sheikh looked distinguished: a late middle-aged man with a big white beard and a good knowledge of the English language. Although I had come without an appointment, Sheikh Abdul agreed to talk to me immediately. He confirmed what the lawyer Rashid had already told me: that he often preached against khat in the mosque. He said that he tells the congregation the following: "khat is food for animals"; "socially, khat is not good"; a chewer "won't keep his family because chewing is too time consuming"; economically, "khat is bad because men use the family budget to buy khat"; a chewer can "stay twenty-four hours without eating or sleeping, something you could not do without drugs"; "anything which intoxicates [as khat does] is forbidden." The final point in the case against khat is that "spiritually khat is not good because you will fail to pray five times a day if you chew." He explained to me that his preaching that khat is "haram" (forbidden to Muslims) is his own interpretation of the proscription on intoxicants, and that there is no fixed Muslim line in Uganda on khat. I asked if he was Ugandan, and he replied that he was not but did not volunteer any information on his nationality. However, the Sheikh was adamant that khat is not part of Somali culture, whether in Somalia, Somaliland, or Uganda, rather "it's a habit."

The leaders of the Ugandan Somalis seek to distance Somali culture from khat. Nevertheless, at the very least, there can be no doubt that khat chewing is a very popular habit, and that many Somalis living in different settings also claim that it is part of their culture. Khat consumption as an expression of Somali ethnic identity is complex, partly because there are several distinct groups of people that can be described an ethnic Somali. Worldwide, Somalis are probably the major consumers of khat. Although widespread Somali khat use dates only from the twentieth century, many Somalis living in Europe or North America now claim khat use as a key signifier of their cultural identity. In diaspora settings, such as the United Kingdom, where khat is legal, Somalis chew khat in the *mafrish*, a term and setting derived from the traditional Yemeni *muffraj* described in the previous chapter. Recent refugees from Somalia have also set up mafrish-style chewing venues. In Kampala, near the mosque where Sheihk Abdul is Imam, several cafés where Somalis and other chewers sit during long afternoons for chewing sessions have sprung up. These venues are clearly visible to passersby and are a new phenomenon, even in parts of Kampala where Somalis and Ethiopians congregate. These small mafrish-type venues are distinct from the bigger more organized clubs favored by Kenyans, Ethiopians, and Ugandans precisely because they are so visible. The small chewing clubs scattered around Kisenyi, where maqatna gather, are also tucked away from the public gaze. The refugees from Somalia who patronize these establishments have brought khat to the streets of Uganda.

By contrast, the residents of Nakivale camp, near the border of Tanzania, are certainly tucked away from mainstream Ugandan life. The camp is nearly a two-hour drive from Mbarara to Isingiro District, near Lake Naki Vale. The land en route to the camp is dominated initially by Ankole people and then by Hutu farmers who have moved out from the camp to farm. The camp is managed by the United Nations High Commission for Refugees (UNHCR) and the German aid agency, GTZ (Deutsche Gesellschaft fur Technische Zusamenarbeit). In 2008 there was a wide range of people in the camp: Ethiopians, Eritreans, Somalis, Tutsi from DRC, Hutu from Rwanda, and Kenyans, recent arrivals from the election violence of January of that year. Entering the camp, the visitor sees a trading center, then lines of tented warehouses for the food aid—a maize ration is given to everybody. There were also several large churches, but I could see no mosques, although a Muslim in our small group said he saw a couple of small ones and heard the *muezzin* calling the faithful to prayers. The road through the sprawling camp was sandy and wound its way through hedged compounds constructed of mud and sticks. There was no visible security in the form of police or UN officials, and, in stark contrast to Daadab camp in Kenya where hundreds of thousands of Somalis languish (Anderson et al., 2007; Beckerleg & Sheekh, 2005), a good atmosphere prevailed. The big difference in atmosphere between the two camps seems to be that people are free to come and go from Nakivale, while in the Kenyan camps such as Daadab, residents are forbidden to leave the camp and move into Kenya.

Amir, a young Rwandan Tutsi man born in the camp and now a Muslim convert and khat trader based in Mbarara, was my guide to Nakevale and its khat-chewing culture. Amir first took me to meet a Tutsi family that had fled the fighting in the DRC about two years earlier. The family explained how they were given corrugate roofing material by the camp authorities and then built their own house; they lived off food aid and appeared to be completely dependent on camp assistance. This family had not taken up khat chewing, a pastime mostly confined to the Somalis in the camp. Residents of the camp are segregated into quarters by ethnic and national origin. However, we moved freely between the Tutsi, Ethiopian, and Somali areas. After leaving the Tutsi family, we went to the Somali area and found Amir's "people." A teenage boy, who is the youth chairman of the Somali community, accompanied us to the Ethiopian area to a small *hoteli* for a lunch of traditional *engera* bread and peppery sauce, followed by coffee served in Haile Salassie flag-decorated cups. Apart from our group, there were also Eritreans present at the hoteli, which was run by Ethiopian, Amhara supporters of Haile Salassie. The hoteli owner was a musician who has been in the camp for decades. He does not chew khat and says that, among the Ethiopians, only young people who are "undisciplined" chew.

After lunch, we walked back along the narrow, hedge-lined lanes to the Somali area. There is a "main street," a sandy thoroughfare with mud built and thatched shops and hotelis. Along this road, khat sellers were seated on mats in the shade or were selling khat from the shops. Both men and women were visible on the busy street, but the majority of the ten or so khat sellers were male, as were the vast majority of customers. One man I spoke to was doing a steady trade. He said he sold about eighty portions per day, each at a price of 2,000 shillings (about $1). Once out of earshot of my informant, Amir told me that the man used to be the bodyguard of the warlord Farah Aideed. Amir reckoned that the refugees were a mixture of "fighters" and ordinary people caught up in the war and that there were various factions and many clans present.

All the khat sold in Nakivale is kasenge, presented in small frosh of clear plastic bags. The residents of Nakivale have rejected the khat grown in Kabarole District, which is the most popular type consumed in Mbarara. They prefer kasenge because, they say, it is stronger than khat from Kabarole. According to Amir, who supplies the entire camp, twelve boxes of one hundred frosh of kasenge khat each are sent to the camp daily (i.e., 1,200 portions). They arrive in Mbarara on a Gateway bus in the middle of the night, and then he offloads and puts in a "special hire" taxi to arrive in the camp in the early morning.

A tall, elderly man greeted us and said he was Amir's "father" and that Amir was the main supplier of khat in the camp. The man added that he sells about 100 to 150 frosh from his shop. Most people do not use BigG when chewing khat, but he does sell it. He gave us a soda from his stock. As I sipped my warm Coca Cola, a small group of young men gathered around me in the shop, asking what I was doing and voicing opinions on khat. The consensus was that khat is haram, that hardly any women chew, while most men do on a daily basis, some mixing khat with cannabis and Valium. They explained that the camp authorities do not encourage khat use, but neither do they try to regulate it. Some people buy khat on credit, based on surety of their maize ration. They chew at home or in "clubs." The elderly chairman agreed with me when I said that khat is not part of Somali culture and only something taken up since the 1970s.

One of the men from the shop, who introduced himself as Abdi K., agreed to take me to meet groups of consumers chewing in their clubs. He is a translator for the UNHCR, assisting them to communicate with the Somalis in the camp, he said. We found about twenty-five Somali men of all ages seated in a circle around the walls of a roomy thatched hut seated on clay benches that lined the room's walls. Virtually all the men present were chewing, some had cups of sweet black tea besides them, others water, and one or two of them had purchased bottles of soda. Most were chewing khat without BigG. After Abdi K. introduced me, the discussion quickly turned to the bad points of khat: that it's a waste of time and money and causes people to take out credit based on their ration.

After I took my leave of the group, we went to a smaller chewing venue, which also sold coffee and food. I spoke to four Somali men who were chewing. Introductions were made, and any awkwardness eased when one of them men said he knew me from Kisenyi in Kampala. This time the conversation was different. The group claimed that chewing was part of their Somali culture, an opinion that I challenged, saying it was a recent pastime adopted by Somalis who did not even grow khat. After some more animated discussion, they agreed that what I said was probably correct. By this point in the discussion, Abdi K. was speaking out against khat and saying that he bought his daily supply but did not want to start chewing it! They asked questions about the health effects of long-term chewing, which I answered to the best of my ability. Eventually, I told them that I had not come to ruin their handas high, bought some khat, and departed for Mbarara.

ETHNICITY AND DRUG USE

For centuries East African khat consumption was confined to ethnic groups living near production areas in Ethiopia and Kenya. The unstable nature of its main ingredient, cathinone, delayed the spread of khat use within and beyond the region for centuries. While coffee originally from Ethiopia and Yemen lost its status as a mild stimulant drug and became a beverage enjoyed almost everywhere in the world, khat languished. Muslims in Ethiopia, and to a lesser extent in Somalia (Martin, 1976), used khat as part of their Islamic observances. It was also a drug used for leisure by Yemenis, in ritual by some, not all, Meru people in Kenya, by the Oromo of Ethiopia and by the related Borana pastoralists of northern Kenya (Arero, personal communication). The nature of cathinone, combined with the bitter taste and unsightly manner of consumption of khat have combined to put a brake on the spread of khat use worldwide. Other substances, notably tobacco and coca, have made the transition from a being a plant substance used by indigenous groups in the Americas to being processed into legal cigarettes and illegal cocaine that have largely lost its association with a particular culture (Goodman et al., 2007; Porter & Teich, 1995). Khat, by contrast, is now available in many parts of the world but is consumed almost exclusively by people with origins in East Africa or Yemen (Anderson et al., 2007). In East Africa, khat use is still associated with specific ethnic groups but also increasingly with urban youth who seek to deemphasize their ethnic identity. They chew against a political backdrop of ongoing, ethnic-based power struggles and a pervading East African culture of patronage based on ethnicity.

Chapter 9

"Idle and Disorderly"

Whether Ugandan leaders and policy makers like it not, khat has arrived in Uganda. For some academics and for administrators working at the district level, khat chewing remains an alien, non-Ugandan practice, with even the *Catha edulis* plant considered an interloper. Botanists at Makerere University were unsure whether *Catha edulis* was indigenous to Uganda or a plant imported from elsewhere in East Africa by Somalis. Although such an origin of wild khat is a possibility, the linguistic evidence that many Ugandan languages having a name for khat suggests the plant is indigenous to Uganda (Eggeling, 1951). With khat use considered an unwelcome Somali or Arab innovation, the Bantu name for khat, *mairungi*, is considered an alien term rather than a local name. Mairungi is also commonly confused with cannabis, which many Ugandans, including district-level police officers, call "opium." Indeed, most Ugandans, including academics, police officials, and government officials, know little about khat but are wary of, or hostile to, it.

Ugandan Khat chewers are part of the growing numbers of hedonists who have adopted a form of recreation that defies mainstream values. Khat is not a socially accepted leisure pursuit in the way that drinking in bars and watching football is. A khat session takes up to six hours, time when young men and women are nonproductive. Many chewers work in the informal sector in jobs that that demand no formal qualifications. Khat chewers washing cars do a good day's work but are still widely considered "idlers." By chewing khat, consumers are taking up a reviled and misunderstood habit and further subverting it by chewing as they drink alcohol and smoke cannabis. During their leisure time, khat chewers are "idle" in the "slums," branded as dropouts and violent criminals by their local leaders.

The growth of khat consumption is not confined to urban areas. Although for older farmers khat is a cash crop to be sold and exported from their area, attitudes to khat are changing and young male farmers have started chewing, thereby taking on a new identity as khat users and also as consumers of leisure. The sight of young men languishing in towns and rural trading centers chewing khat and, it is automatically assumed, smoking cannabis and swigging sachets of waragi causes disquiet among observers. Young men, many of whom are well educated but have failed to find work in the formal sector, have defiantly taken on the identity of "idlers," who leaders fear will threaten social order. Yet the "problem" is not khat use per se but increasing multidrug use. Politicians, health workers, and police officials may be right to be alarmed about escalating multidrugs but mistaken in designating khat as the main enemy of social order.

Khat and the Law

The legal status of khat varies across the world and the drug is subject to frequent review and revision by the governments, often acting on the advice of the World Health Organization (WHO) and the UN Office on Drugs and Crime. Khat is a legal substance in Yemen, Ethiopia, Djibouti, Kenya, and Uganda but is illegal in Tanzania and Rwanda. It is legal in UK and the Netherlands but an illicit substance in the United States and Canada (Beckerleg, 2008; Klein, 2005). In 1936 a League of Nations advisory committee on khat report set the trend for prevarication by stating that there was "no proof one way or the other of its specific negative effects" (Gebissa, 2004, p. 18). WHO reviews in the 1950s, 1970s, and 1980s found that there was insufficient medical evidence of harm. The Advisory Council on the Misuse of Drugs undertook a major review of khat in the United Kingdom and recommended that the substance remain legal, but doubts persist among policy makers in the United Kingdom and elsewhere (Anderson & Carrier, 2006; Klein & Beckerleg, 2007; Klein, Beckerleg, & Hailu, 2009).

Ordinances

Within East Africa, growing production in Kenya and Ethiopia is sufficient to meet increasing domestic demand as well as sustaining a buoyant export market. Although khat is legal in both these countries, and consumption levels are increasing among young people, khat has many detractors (Carrier, 2008; Gebissa, 2008). In East Africa, one way that opponents of khat have attempted to check its popularity is through the introduction of local ordinances or bylaws. Writing of the situation in Ethiopia, Gebissa reports, "Alarmed by the rapid spread of khat cultivation and use, opponents have launched a campaign in favour of proscription. Some regional states, including Tigray, Benishangul, and Gambella, have adopted local ordinances aimed at controlling the deleterious consequences of khat. Interest groups are being organized before, as they say, it destroys the youth and the future of the country" (Gebissa, 2008, p. 785).

Ordinances aimed at controlling khat within specific areas of countries are nothing new, however. In Kenya, during the 1940s and 1950s the British colonial government attempted to restrict the use of khat to the Northern Frontier District (NFD), the area of Kenya dominated by ethnic Somalis. The ordinance, as Carrier reports, was a failure: "The ordinance proved unenforceable, however, and was soon abandoned as smuggling ensured its continued sale; miraa was even smuggled up to Marsabit in the north by the district commissioner's own driver (P. Baxter, personal communication)" (Carrier, 2008, p. 808).

Although the government of independent Kenya appears to be reconciled to the production and consumption of khat, some local authorities in the country, have not adopted such a laissez-faire attitude.

The Lamu Antikhat Campaign

The town of Lamu is well over a thousand years old and is one of the old Swahili city-states that dominated the east coast of Africa between the fifteenth and nineteenth centuries (de Vere Allen, 1993). Within East Africa, Lamu is an important Islamic center and the focus for the annual Maulidi celebrations marking the birthday of the Prophet Mohammed. In 2001 Lamu was declared a United Nations Educational Scientific and Cultural Organization (UNESCO) World Heritage Site, and the main industry is tourism. Khat use in Lamu dates from about 1968, and by 2004, there were an estimated three hundred to five hundred consumers in Lamu town, the majority Swahili men and youth (Beckerelg, 2006).

The campaign to get khat banned in Lamu started in 2001 and included representatives of all the mosques and Islamic groups, youth and women's organizations, the teachers' trade union, officials from the National Museums of Kenya, and community-based organizations in the town. The main objective of the campaign was to introduce a bylaw banning the sale of khat. In a series of letters, campaigners pointed out that khat causes social, medical, economic, and spiritual harm and appealed to individuals and organizations that had the power to curb khat sales in Lamu. In November 2001 a notice concerning a proposed bylaw or ordinance to ban khat was posted in the *Daily Nation* newspaper. If passed, the bylaw would have stipulated that "no person shall carry on the business or trade in Miraa in all areas under the jurisdiction of Lamu County Council." The proposed bylaw was rigorously opposed by the khat traders' welfare association, which enlisted a fellow Meru lawyer from Nairobi. As khat is a legal substance traded and consumed openly throughout the country, their case was strong and the traders won the case (Anderson et al., 2007; Beckerleg, 2006). However, the Lamu community leaders did not give up and continued their campaign of letter writing. In May 2002 the "Anti-Drug Lobby" wrote the minister of local government:

> Due to the miraa menace, the moral, Cultural and social fabric of the Lamu society is being degraded i.e. losing their traditional values. According to the records in the Kadhi's office and children office, Lamu District, miraa is one of the main contributions of divorces, family break-ups and separations. These effects further lead to social crimes such as prostitution, theft and unstable society morally. The high school dropouts of schoolchildren, bad performance and bad discipline among school children now strongly attributed to miraa consumption. . . . All these are signals of community that driving towards doom rather than salvation and prosperity. Hence there is need and very urgent one to put a stop to miraa consumption. In addition the good health of the community is very much at the highest risk e.g. HIV/AIDS etc. Chewing miraa is a drug that leads to the consumption of all other drugs and alcoholism, which subsequently lead to crimes and social problems. (Beckerleg, 2006, p. 225)

This extract from just one letter of many sent between 2001 and 2002 illustrates the ways in which of khat can be used as a scapegoat for all social ills. In Uganda, although similar concerns over khat have arisen, nobody has suggested a link between khat consumption and the transmission of the HIV virus. The Ugandan authorities, on the other hand, are concerned about khat as a cause of violence.

UGANDA BYLAWS

In Uganda, khat is not mentioned in current, national drug legislation. This, in the minds of some law enforcers, puts khat in a class of its own: not illegal but not permitted either. In the southwest of Uganda increasing levels of khat use are a cause of concern to district level officials. The attempted solution to, what they perceive as, the khat problem varies from district to district. In the town of Kasese the police and courts ran an antikhat campaign in 2008, which used a law laid out in chapter 120 of the penal code. Section 167 defines "idle and disorderly persons" and the associated penalties as follows:

> Any person who—
>
> (a) being a prostitute, behaves in a disorderly or indecent manner in any public place;
>
> (b) wanders or places himself or herself in any public place to beg or gather alms, or causes or procures or encourages any child to do so;
>
> (c) plays at any game of chance for money or money's worth in any public place;
>
> (d) publicly conducts himself or herself in a manner likely to cause a breach of the peace;
>
> (e) without lawful excuse, publicly does any indecent act;
>
> (f) in any public place solicits or loiters for immoral purposes;
>
> (g) wanders about and endeavours by the exposure of wounds or deformation to obtain or gather alms, shall be deemed an idle and disorderly person, and is liable on conviction to imprisonment for three months or to a fine not exceeding three thousand shillings or to both such fine and imprisonment, but in the case of an offence contrary to paragraph (a), (e) or (f) that person is liable to imprisonment for seven years. (Penal Code Act, Cap. 120, pp. 2797–2798)

This legislation dates from colonial times, and several senior administrators and a senior police officer in Kampala told me that the section of the penal code concerning being "idle and disorderly" has been cancelled. In the west of the country, such reforms count for little.

The Kasese Crackdown

In July 2008, Kassim, an elderly Yemeni khat trader, was warned by a senior brigade intelligence officer to stop selling khat. He ignored the warning and was arrested and brought before the resident district commissioner who said that Kassim could not be kept in the cells because of his advanced age and high standing in the community. Kassim was released without paying any fine or bribe. He told me after this incident that he had heard that "idle and disorderly" had been abolished but was not sure what this meant. His family continued to sell khat but, for a while, stopped displaying it openly in the kiosk that they had erected courtyard of their home.

Kassim's arrest turned out to be the prelude to a wider clamp down on khat traders across Kasese. A week after his arrest and release, eight more khat traders were arrested and charged with being "idle and disorderly." Several of them, including a mother, were granted bail, while others were remanded in custody. Prominent among those on remand was Anisa, a successful wholesaler and retailer. I visited her in custody.

We found Anisa seated outside in a large compound on the outskirts of Kasese, shelling peanuts with two other women. They were guarded by a sergeant wearing a red cap (military police). The two policemen explained that there had been a crackdown on drugs and that Anisa had been arrested as part of this. We talked to Anisa briefly and commiserated, then left and drove to her nearby shop. At Anisa's shop and residence that same day, khat was being sold in a back room by a young man. Several customers were chewing there and there was a steady trickle of trade. One particularly talkative and articulate young man explained that "eight traders have been arrested by the brigade intelligence officer. They are being charged with 'being idle and disorderly'" and will appear in court the tomorrow. They were arrested as part of a drugs round up. Chewers have been given two hundred lashes (kiboko) "like in Obote's time."

Next, I went to Kasese police station and talked to the district police officer in charge of the criminal investigation department (CID) and a junior officer. They implied that there was some sort of bylaw in force in Kasese, but when I probed, it turned out that "idle and disorderly persons" was being used as the "weapon" of crackdown. The crackdown was the decision of the entire Security Committee, which includes the brigade intelligence officer, who is in charge of security and defense against local insurgency, but is headed by the resident district commissioner, insisted the police officer. The "idle and disorderly persons" charge was made at the advice of a state attorney who had looked into what charges could be made against local khat traders. They told me there is no truth in the rumor that being "idle and disorderly" is no longer a crime. The need to crackdown on khat was, according to the CID officer, because "teenaged groups are involved in chewing and most kids are becoming addicted to khat." He added that there had been "an increase in housebreaking and muggings," that "gangs sit around for many hours plotting these crimes" and that such "castles in the air" leads to crimes committed in order to attain their dreams. He refuted the rumor that some khat consumers had received two hundred lashes. In conclusion, he explained that the "exhibit" (fifteen to twenty sacks of rotting khat) was there at the police station ready for the hearing of the eight traders who were due to appear in court soon. The exhibit was indeed on the veranda of the police station in full view, not locked in a room.

After talking to the police, I sought out Steven, a prominent local khat trader, who had thus far avoided arrest. Steve explained that when a new army officer had been transferred from Bundibuyo (an area to the north where there is periodic insurgency), things got tough. "He's a divisional commander. The word is that he is realistic and wants to reduce the khat trade by 60 percent, as he cannot eliminate it. The remaining 40 percent of traders will be left to do business as usual. At present the price of khat is unstable and currently has gone up from 2,000 shillings to 3,000 shillings ($1–1.5)." Steve further explained that so far, the arrested traders had paid 150,000 shillings ($75) for bail each, while the usual fine for being idle and disorderly is 20,000 to 30,000 shillings ($10–15). Steve's information proved accurate with regard to the bail conditions.

By now Anisa had been released, and I visited her at home, where in the company of several people, she was resting in her living room, which was crowded with sofas and soft furnishings—and with a TV playing loud music videos. Anisa said that upon release, she went straight to the hospital where she got medicine that she needed after sleeping on cement for days. She was out on bail and showed me paperwork, which showed that she had paid 150,000 shillings ($75) "surety" and that she and the other seven arrested had to answer the charge of being idle and disorderly the following Monday.

I also visited the Kasese assistant resident district commissioner who, like most government officials, had strong views on khat:

> The increase in crime is associated with youth gangs who take khat, thereby creating conditions of being idle and disorderly. The idea of the authorities is to disband the idle and disorderly groups and cut crime. Khat is expensive and drives idlers into crime as a small bunch costs 3,000/-. The increase in crime is house breakages and waylaying others, for example in alleyways and generally hunting for money. Arabs chew at home—there is no problem and no public order issue. Mixing drugs leads to a loss of sense of direction. We now have a runaway society, meaning that things are running out of control. We want to "lock the gate." The challenge about khat is about Ugandan society.

The traders duly appeared in court, paid their fines, and continued in business as usual. In Mbarara, it is khat consumers who are usually targeted under the idle and disorderly legislation. In this town, the authorities claim that khat and cannabis are used and sold in together.

During an interview with the Mbarara district police commander, he reported that there is widespread use of khat, especially in the slums where it is consumed by people who are "doing nothing" as they are unemployed. He added that people have started taking khat in combination with cannabis and that the two substances are sold together in the same package, with the cannabis concealed by the khat leaves. Anybody checking these packages sees only khat, which is not classified as a drug in Uganda. Therefore, there is a problem with enforcement in relation to drug use and the solution is to charge khat users with being idle and disorderly. The police do this because of the "outcry from the community" over khat consumption. He added, "When people are high (on khat) they do 'funny things'—rape, petty crime. It makes people high like a drug. . . . More than half the people we arrest are into khat and drugs. . . . These people are robbers and housebreakers and gang rapists. Half or three-quarters of those taking khat are criminals or potential criminals. . . . We are praying hard that a law on mairungi [khat] comes out. . . . Even to arrest them you have to fight them. . . . We wonder if it's worth arresting them."

Although khat traders do not sell profitable khat alongside cheap cannabis, there was a grain of truth in the Mbarara district police commander's assessment of the situation. Observation of trading venues in Mbarara confirmed that cannabis sellers operate in khat retailing areas, while in Kasese Valium was being sold old alongside khat in one retail outlet.

THE BUSHENYI ORDINANCE AND ITS ENFORCEMENT

In 2006, Bushenyi District enacted a bylaw, "The Bushenyi District (*Mairungi*) Trade and Consumption Control Ordinance, 2006." The ordinance prohibits the cultivation, consumption, or sale of khat within Bushenyi District and levies a fine of up to 40,000 shillings ($20) and up to six months imprisonment on those caught in possession of the leaves. Khat grown in the Kaborole plantations passes south through Bushenyi on en route to Mbarara and there is no evidence that the ban is enforceable or has reduced the supply of khat to the district. On the contrary, new rural retailers and consumers have emerged along the main road in last few months. One policeman based in Kabarole District dismissed the ban as unworkable.

MAMA SALIM'S TRAVAILS

Recently widowed, Mama Salim is a long-standing khat trader living in Kasese and selling in Mbarara. Each morning she rises early and travels north to the Kaborole plantations on a public transport. Having purchased her khat, it is rapidly packed in sacks. She then travels south passing through her hometown of Kasese and onto Mbarara where khat is in high demand. In mid-2008 Mama Salim set up business just around the corner from the main line of khat kiosks near the bus station in Mbara in a former butcher shop (see Chapter 6). Shortly after Mama Salim had established her new business venture, I hear that she has been arrested in Bushenyi. When I saw Mama Salim a few days later at her home in Kasese, she explained what had happened. The following is what happened that day:

They were a group of khat traders passing through Bushenyi in a shared minibus taxi transporting their supplies of khat to Mbarara. A senior local government official, the Local Councilor Level Five (LC5), drove past and saw one of the traders selling khat from the stationery vehicle and called the police to arrest them. When the police arrived and stopped the vehicle, which was by then continuing on its journey, several traders ran away, leaving Mama Salim, Abu, and a youth behind. Another female passenger was left to go free as she was an "ordinary passenger," not a khat trader. The three khat traders were taken to the police station along with Mama Salim and the youth and charged with possessing khat. There was no chance of following the normal practice of bribing the police because the LC5 had ordered their arrest. Mama Salim realized that she would have to appear in court the following Monday. She was bailed (for no fee) and went to stay with a relative in Bushenyi where she spent the weekend. The youth, however, was locked up. On the following Monday they both appeared in court. She told the magistrate she was a khat seller, but that she did not know it was crime. She and the youth paid the fine of 20,000 shillings ($11) and were released.

Shortly after Mama Salim's arrest, I met the Bushenyi LC5 in his office. He was talking to an FM radio journalist when we arrived, who was told to stay and listen to the discussion "on marijuana." Despite telling him the subject of my research project was "mairungi" and giving him an information sheet summarizing the study, the confusion between khat and cannabis persisted. Officials who came into the room telling him "the meeting had already started" were also told that I was "researching marijuana." Although unclear about the difference between khat and cannabis, the LC5 had no doubts about the harm of khat. Hence, he confirmed that in his capacity as secretary of production, he was the official who had pushed for the district-wide ban on khat. He enumerated the reasons why he considered the ban necessary:

1. Khat is a "kind of drug" that "kills the mind."
2. Khat is now consumed by the youth who are becoming idle.
3. They use money to buy khat without working. Where do they get the money?
4. When intoxicated by khat they do bad acts: sexual harassment, fighting, beating people.
5. They contribute nothing to society's development. The children do not go to school. There is no meaningful production.

He finished by stating that khat is a "menace." The LC5 went onto to explain, "Last week, we apprehended a vehicle. I was driving from a workshop and saw people selling khat openly from the vehicle. There were six traders, including a lady. Three ran away leaving Hadajti [respectful term for a Muslim woman (i.e., Mama Salim)], her son, and another woman. Ten sacks of khat were handed over to the police." He made no mention of the youth who was also charged, and his interest focused on the arrest of a mature, Muslim woman. Despite this arrest, he conceded, the sanctions would do little to dent the trade. "The fine should be increased to one million—it is not a deterrent at present. We are let down by security officials. They know where it is sold but do not act; they are 'not serious' about khat control."

In 2009 matters in the district escalated when a government official from Bushenyi shot a man who was probably a khat trader, but according to the confused reporting of the incident, may have been a cannabis seller. In the newspaper report of the shooting, either the newspaper reporter or his informant makes the common Ugandan error of confusing khat with marijuana:

> The police in Bushenyi district are investigating circumstances under which the deputy resident district commissioner (RDC) shot at a suspected mairungi vendor, injuring him on the arm. . . . The district police commander, Jimmy Oyuku, said Nickson Kabuye shot at a man, only identified as Kamakoti of Kakanju village in Kakanju sub-county. The incident happened on Thursday at around 2:00pm near Nyakabirizi Trading Centre. Oyuku said Kamakoti and four men were offloading bags of marijuana from a Kasese-Mbarara vehicle when Kabuye spotted

them. "He stopped his car and asked them the source and destination of the toxicant, but they turned unruly. He called the Police to intervene. But before the Police arrived, the group attacked the RDC, who overpowered them. One man was injured, while the rest took off to the bush as the driver sped off with the weed," Oyukuyu said. Kamakoti is admitted at Kampala International University—Western campus teaching hospital, while the rest are on the run. (Ahimbisibwe, *New Vision*, March 22, 2009)

REGULATING KHAT IN THE KABAROLE DISTRICT

In Kabarole District, where most of the khat supplying southwestern Uganda is grown, many government officials and community groups are vehemently opposed to mairungi consumption. In this district, in 2008 and again in 2009, I interviewed all the main stakeholders in the khat industry: government officials, health workers, the police, members of nongovernmental organizations (NGO), and officer holders of the Hakibale Busoro Kicwanba Mairungi (khat) Association, which represents local khat farmers and traders. The views of Maureen, who works for a human rights NGO in Fort Portal, were typical of the group opposing khat:

> It was about late in 1997 that mairungi [khat] started to be used openly used. It is popular amongst disco-goers, transport brokers and drivers. It's also very common amongst chotara [people of mixed race], who are numerous in Fort Portal. Mairungi consumption depends on culture. Chotara do not fear to take mairungi, but Africans see it as bad. We look at mairungi as a drug. Last year, I met an elderly person coming of out Andrews Supermarket. He was chewing. I was shocked and told him off for setting a bad example to the youth and being lacking in self respect. He was embarrassed. He was a chotara and drove off in a good car. A woman overhead me and congratulated me on taking a stand.
>
> You cannot say it's legal or illegal in this country. It is not specified. People who take mairungi are idle and disorderly and cause commotion. Most habitual criminals are mairungi or cannabis users. When we visit people in the police cells they demand that we bring them mairungi as they are in withdrawal and are desperate. [SB Do you bring them mairungi?] Sorry, I meant cannabis. We cannot bring it because it is illegal. As human rights workers, we do not discriminate, and assist all those arrested, including mairungi chewers, with para-legal services. (cited in Beckerleg, 2009, pp. 50–51)

February 2008, working with Andrew Mugisa of the Toro Development Association, a community-based organization, we brought together representatives of the khat industry and local officials in a "consultative meeting." Maureen was invited but did not attend. A policeman, a senior health educator, the local inspector of drugs, a senior town councilor, a local radio journalist, several local NGO representatives, Mama Salim from Kasese representing khat traders, and three khat farmers all attended the meeting. Other khat farmers had been too scared to come to the meeting in case they were arrested and made an example of by the regional police commander, a vociferous opponent of khat. Indeed, there was much discussion among the leaders of the Hakibale Busoro Kicwanba Mairungi Association before they agreed to send three representatives.

The questions and discussion revealed that there were two camps: one pushing for an outright ban and those supporting some kind of regulation. The policeman and the inspector of drugs led the group calling for the banning of khat, although they acknowledged that the bylaw in Bushenyi District banning khat had not worked. The policeman appeared to hope for a voluntary move away from khat and said that "farmers should agree to remove khat. They could plant pineapples [as a cash crop] instead." Much of the discussion concerned how khat is being used in combination with cannabis and alcohol. Participants also discussed the use of spirits and the widely ignored "Enguli law" that requires locally distilled liquor to be sent to Kampala for "purification" (Willis, 2002). They assumed that khat users mix these substances together with khat. The inspector of drugs commented that "we assume they are mixing with cannabis and that it's dangerous." The meeting broke up after three hours uninterrupted discussion.

By late the following year the district council was ready to put together a draft ordinance. "The Kabarole District (Mairungi Control) Ordinance 2008" was posted in the council headquarters in May 2009 and invited public comment. Although the language of the draft ordinance is couched in terms of "prohibition," unlike the Bushenyi legislation, it would regulate rather than ban khat. The draft proposes the following prohibitions:

Prohibition from growing Mairungi without permit
Prohibition from growing Mairungi, outside gazetted area
Prohibition from trading in Mairungi—without permit
Prohibition from consumption of Mairungi in a public place
Prohibition from consumption of Mairungi while driving or riding

Prohibition from adulteration of food, drink or other consumables with Mairungi

Parent or guardian to ensure that minor children do not consume Mairungi. (Draft Kabarole District [Mairungi Control] Ordinance, 2008, p. 1)

Although one of the farmers' who attended the consultative meeting recognized that he would be able to continue with his lucrative business and declared himself happy with the draft ordinance, other farmers were more nervous of regulation. As for the district officials, some were already worrying that the ordinance would be unenforceable. Whether or not the Kabarole ordinance is passed, new legislation at national level on drugs, including khat for the first time, may render the ordinance redundant before it even becomes law.

National Concerns and Reactions

A new drug law been in the making for over ten years has been presented to the Ugandan Parliament. Police officers say they would welcome new legislation, which, although designed to increase sentences for traffickers of heroin and cocaine, will also make khat an illegal substance in Uganda. The Narcotics and Psychotropic Substances Control Bill of 2007 was presented on March 10, 2009. However, opinion among key policy makers, including the police and mental health specialists, differs as to when, or if, the bill will become law. A senior antinarcotics officer told me that it would be law by the end of 2009. Once this happened, producers would be given a "grace period" to uproot their khat before the police start burning the trees, arresting farmers, and fining them up to ten million shillings ($5,000). He added that the maximum penalty for possession of khat would be five years imprisonment. Meanwhile, it was his opinion that district level ordinances "cannot work."

Khat, Alcohol, and Violent Crime

The non-khat-chewing majority of Ugandans have come to see khat a dangerous substance (Klein, Beckerleg, & Hailu, 2009). A recent feature in the leading daily newspaper on drugs and crime in Kampala, the *New Vision*, listed common drugs as "khat, bhang [cannabis] and cocaine" and printed a photo showing "youth preparing mairungi (khat) for sale." The feature lays out the concerns of government officials concerning growing drug abuse and associated violent crimes including "murder, rape and robberies" (Kato, 2008, p. 23).

In Uganda, the linkage of khat consumption to violence is a recent phenomenon. Although the groups of youth who are the cause of concern are in fact multidrug users, the call is for controls on khat and not on alcohol or cannabis. Although illegal, cannabis is cheap, widely available, and is a familiar substance. Alcohol is very widely consumed and is part of the culture of most Ugandans, with many Muslims also drinking discretely. A centuries-old drinking culture (Willis, 2002) enables most Ugandans to consume alcohol without fear of social of condemnation. Indeed, one official commented to me that to regulate alcohol in Uganda would involve "banning the Catholic Church." Alcohol use is far more common than khat use, yet violent crime is linked to khat use rather than to drinking spirits or beer. Khat, which has only gained popularity in Ugandan within the last twenty years, is, for most people, an unknown and alien substance.

The commonly held Ugandan view of khat as a cause of violence is unusual, but not unprecedented, among those claiming the substance to be dangerous. In academic literature khat is not usually strongly linked to violent behavior. However, Graziani et al. (2008) do link khat to violence in rats: "As happens when amphetamine is given at low doses (Miczek & Haney, 1994), both the khat extract and cathinone have been found to enhance the aggressive behaviour in isolated rats (Banjaw et al., 2006)" (Graziani et al., 2008, p. 768).

Such animal studies privilege chemical effects over the power of "set and setting" (Zinberg, 1984). Khat chewed in its traditional setting does not induce violence but the opposite. For example, according to Varisco, writing on traditional patterns of khat use in Yemen stresses that there is no link to violence: "It is important to note that aggressive behaviour is rarely found in qat chews, nor is qat thought locally in Yemen to induce a fighting spirit. People will sit next to each other, at times closely packed, without evident signs of irritation. Passive reflexivity, a mood of introspection, is the ultimate outcome of normal chewing" (Varisco, 2004, p. 109).

Other social studies link khat use to lethargy and demotivation but never to violence. As Gebissa points out, "In the case of khat's alleged negative socioeconomic consequence, the rather popular argument is that which depicts chewers as lethargic individuals who spend most of their days masticating on the leaves. The implication of such an assessment is that their jobs often suffer from neglect. The sight of *bartcha*, the afternoon chew session, inevitably impresses upon observers, including some scholars, that khat is a cause for tardiness to work, absenteeism, and declining productivity" (Gebissa, 2008, p. 891).

According to most detractors of khat, the problem with chewing is not violence but lethargy. Klein found that in Streatham, South London, khat was a subject of concern for local residents worried that its use caused violent behavior. But, members of the Waaberri Somali community group had opposite ideas:

> The key concern of the residents' association, however, was the pharmacological effect of khat and how it increased the tendency to violence. But according to the Waaberri informants, khat made the chewer peaceful and active in clear contrast to alcohol which made the drinker incapable and aggressive. Khat users themselves were surprised by the link, as the first rush brought on by khat was euphoric, followed by a reflective and melancholic phase. Even the detractors explained their opposition to khat because it was demotivating, wasteful and inappropriate in the UK—not because of the violence. (Klein, 2008, p. 824)

A report by the Advisory Council on the Misuse of Drugs (2005) found some reported linkages between khat and violence. Hence, "women were more likely than men to report that khat use was responsible for family breakdown and violent behaviour" (ACMD, 2005, p. 18). Yet overall the report authors concluded, "Very low offending rates were reported in the NARCO report. Of three individuals who reported having committed violence, all were recent khat users. There does not appear to be a link with acquisitive crime. The rates detected are particularly low considering the financial status, social situation and location of many of the khat using communities" (ACMD, 2005, p. 18).

When khat is associated with violence, it appears often to be linked to Somalis often by Somali women activists writing on both their war-torn, debilitated country (Dirie & D'Jeanne, 2002) and on life in the diaspora (Klein & Beckerleg, 2007). Conversely, in the ethnic Somali-dominated North Eastern Province of Kenya where there is no war but many refugees, khat is blamed on underdevelopment (Anderson et al., 2007).

Violence occurring among khat consumers can be linked to difficult and violent social environments rather than to the psychoactive properties of *Catha edulis*, a substance notorious for making people sit around doing nothing. Violent behavior is not one of many concerns of psychiatrists and medical practitioners concerning khat, who point out possible links between khat and psychosis and a host of negative health effects (Anderson et al., 2007).

There is little evidence to support the widespread Ugandan view that khat use causes violent behavior. The Uganda authorities, however, are not the first national representatives of law and order to jump to conclusions about the dangers posed by specific drugs. For example, Chavannes reports that in Jamaica, in the early twentieth century, cannabis (ganja) has been viewed and how it came to be associated with violence: "Another negative reaction that ganja was, at one time, thought to provoke was a proneness to violence. This seemed to have been the reason for Jamaica including ganja in its ratification of the 1912 Hague Opium Convention signed by Great Britain, not on the basis of expert or scientific evidence but on the basis of unsubstantiated allegations. Forty years previously the Governor had mentioned in a report to the Colonial Office that it was believed that ganja had induced an Indian to murder his wife. Forty years later, allegation had become fact" (Chavannes, 2004a, p. 179).

The Jamaican police, like their Ugandan counterparts forty years later, attempted to link specific drug use with rape. Hence, in Jamaica in the early 1960s, "the police force also tried its own version of the United States Bureau of Narcotics campaign in trying, but without much success, to link ganja smoking to with the rise of crime, including rape" (Chavannes, 2004b, p. 69).

The association between ganja and violence persisted, even in the lack of any academic evidence: "In 1962 the vicious murder of two people in the Jamaican resort of Coral Gardens by a Rastafarian led to the further association of ganja with violence, despite contemporary studies showing no link between cannabis use and violence" (Chavannes, 2004b, p. 70).

A similar association between cannabis and violence was constructed in California during the 1930s. According to Feiling, "Newspapers repeated unsubstantiated claims that 'the killer weed' led users, particularly Mexican users, to commit terrible acts of violence, particularly against Anglo-Saxon women."

Across the United States at different times, according to Feiling (2009), various substances have been associated with violence and rape. Scare mongering by U.S. government officials in the twentieth century focused particularly on cocaine and cannabis and had a strongly racist dimension (Feiling, 2009). For example, Feiling reports that in the 1910s, a cocaine panic struck the U.S. southern states: "Dr Christopher Koch of the state Pharmacy Board of Pennsylvania testified before Congress that 'most of the attacks upon the white of the South are the direct result of a cocaine-crazed Negro brain'" (Feiling, 2009, p. 21).

These examples of drug scares in the Americas demonstrate that there is nothing unique or even unusual in the linking of drugs with violence as well as with foreigners or people from specific ethnic groups. In Uganda I have heard Somalis described as "sex fiends" fuelled by khat. Nevertheless, the Ugandan claim that khat makes people violent runs counter to even the arguments of the many campaigners against khat, a substance usually linked to "idling" and lethargy.

CONCLUSION

Uganda is not alone in the search for an appropriate control regime for khat. Internationally, there is considerable pressure to impose a ban on khat, and efforts to achieve this goal are championed by the International Narcotics Control Board, the body established within the UN system with a quasijudicial function to promote compliance drug control treaties (Anderson et al., 2007). Recommendation 45 of the 2006 Annual Report recommends khat to be placed under international control (Klein et al., 2009). Khat for many policy makers is a drug of "abuse" and therefore should be banned. The Ugandan officials working in the west of country have reached a similar conclusion and have decided to act rather than waiting for national legislation. Yet, now that khat plantations have sprung up all over Uganda and consumers are found in every town and many villages, eradicating consumption is likely to be an impossible task.

CHAPTER 10

KHAT AND DEVELOPMENT

Since the end of World War II there have been ongoing efforts by Western governments and charitable organizations, which are now known as nongovernmental organizations (NGO), to "develop" Africa and other poor, nonindustrialized areas of the world. At its most basic, the development process seeks to change the lives of the ordinary Africans and other supposed beneficiaries around the world. According to Kaufmann, "The process of development involves a relationship between the developers—the experts, technocrats, advisors, specialists, volunteers, fieldworkers—and the developed, the recipients of the aid and advice. The developers, whether working at home, 'overseas' or 'in the field,' are caught up in the gargantuan task of changing, shaping, homogenizing, and supposedly improving the lot of the developed" (Kaufmann, 1997, p. 107).

In Africa during the twentieth century, the shift from the application of policies that were designed to promote economic prosperity for colonizers and their subjects alike to the activities of international development agencies has been seamless. From the 1960s onward in most African countries, and particularly in former British colonies such as Kenya and Uganda, colonial administrators, agricultural officers, and medical researchers have been replaced by a set of experts who perform similar functions. Although the rhetoric of development changes rapidly, so that "empowerment" and "participation" are key to success one year, while another year champions "civil society" and "drivers of change," the basic goal of development remains the same (Grillo & Stirrat, 1997; Parfitt, 2002). At its most basic, "development" involves "directed social and economic change" (Grillo, 1997, p. 2). There is an ongoing international debate as to the degree that "development" has been effective. Easterly, a former World Bank economist, leads the recent assault by presenting evidence that, far from reducing global poverty, "development" has become part of the problem (Easterly, 2007).

DRUGS AND DEVELOPMENT

Development experts consider drug economies, trafficking, and substance use to be barriers to both national and personal development. For example, Bourgeois's classic account of drug dealing and use in New York paints a picture of wasted lives and economic deprivation in the wealthy United States (Bourgois, 1995). Less attention has been paid to the links between development and drugs in Africa and other "less developed" regions. Singer, however, suggests that development failures should be attributed, at least partly, to both legal and illegal drugs. "While various theories of the failures of development have been espoused, it is only recently that the role played by psychotropic drugs—including alcohol, tobacco various pharmaceuticals, heroin, cocaine methamphetamine and other mind-altering substances—has been clear" (Singer, 2008, p. 2).

Singer approaches the subject of drugs and development within the framework of the political economy approach, which seeks to analyze the "development of underdevelopment." He argues that in order to "fully realize the complex effects of drug use, addiction, and trade on development, it is necessary to take a comprehensive approach that views these phenomena in historic, social, and political economic contexts" (Singer, 2008, p. 6).

Singer's overview of the role of drugs in development makes no mention of khat, which in global terms is an obscure substance used by a small minority of the world's drug users. However, in countries where khat is produced and consumed, its presence on the local scene has an impact on development. In this final chapter, I explore the relationship between khat and development and show how khat production by African smallholders undermines the ideological foundations of Western-led development aid.

THE SINGULARITY OF KHAT

"Is miraa a drug?" was a question people in Kenya often posed to Neil Carrier (Carrier, 2008). Although there is no doubt that the answer is "Yes, miraa is a drug," khat is a substance like no other. One unique characteristic of khat is the short shelf life of its active main ingredient, cathinone. For centuries khat was confined to some highland areas of East Africa and Yemen. Now, thanks to modern transportation and the high demand for khat by Somalis in their wide flung diaspora, the plant has become a global commodity. Consumption in North America and Europe, however, remains largely confined to the peoples originating from khat-producing areas. Psychologists, social workers, and health experts with khat-using clients have decried khat as a check on personal development and wellbeing, blaming chewing patterns on the failure of whole communities, such as Somalis residing in North Eastern Province of Kenya or in Djibouti, to thrive (Anderson et al., 2007; Borelli & Perali, 2004). Among academics, there is little agreement on the effects of khat in relation to mental health and a host of physical conditions (Ajab & Warsa, 2005; Dhadphale & Omolo, 1988; Odenwald, 2007; Warfa et al., 2007). In 2005 an assessment of the drug by the UK government concluded that khat did not cause sufficient harm either with regard to health or to social factors to warrant making it illegal in Britain.

In Yemen and East Africa khat consumption is often viewed by aid experts as an impediment to development because chewing entails not only a daily expenditure but also sitting around for hours. The detractors of khat claim that these hours are lost time that could be put to productive use. An associated debate has rumbled along for decades over whether the economic benefits of cultivation of and trade in khat outweigh negative effects on consumers. Further concerns, which cannot be dismissed, are voiced over the long-term environmental impact of irrigated khat plants, particularly in Ethiopia and Yemen (Gebissa, 2008; Varisco, 2004).

The controversies surrounding khat use continue to wage on the international scene, in the boardrooms and conference halls where drug policies are negotiated. Most commentators agree that khat does less harm to its users than tobacco and alcohol does to smokers and drinkers but more harm than consuming tea and coffee—these Ugandan-grown beverages being, perhaps, the most benign and socially acceptable "soft drugs" the world over. Khat consumption is not health promoting nor particularly dangerous, except when consumed in great excess in the absence of any cultural controls. Unlike the tobacco industry, there are no powerful lobbyists advocating for khat. Therefore, the international policy direction seems to be toward making khat an illegal substance, as it already is in countries as diverse as the United States and Tanzania. Over the last twenty years, the khat phenomenon has grown so fast that they are seeking to stop the unstoppable. If khat were banned, its use would continue in the same way that illegal cannabis is widely used across the country.

In this final chapter the role of khat and other drugs in impeding or facilitating development in Uganda and other production countries is analyzed. Controversies over khat are set to run and run, and earlier chapters have addressed many of these issues. Here, I consider khat as a subversive substance: a plant grown, traded, and consumed in a manner that undermines many of the principles of international development. Khat is subversive because in East Africa, it has improved the lives of millions of poor people who are not part of development programs. Khat, I contend, renders "development" irrelevant to the lives and livelihoods of independent-minded producers and entrepreneurs.

KHAT PRODUCTION

Khat production is an example of successful indigenous development, undertaken by farmers who decide, without the benefit of expert guidance, to grow a crop for which there is strong local and regional demand. In 1983 Robert Chambers wrote about the often-overlooked importance of local knowledge in agriculture development: "Rural people's knowledge, and especially indigenous knowledge systems, have many dimensions, including linguistics, medicine, clinical psychology, botany, zoology, climate, agriculture, animal husbandry and craft skills. Its validity and range have been neglected in all these" (Chambers, 1983, p. 85).

Although Chambers may have overstated his case, there are many incidences where indigenous knowledge proved more useful than that of the experts. Indeed, clashing knowledge systems have affected agricultural development since colonial times. Carswell has documented the ways that farmers in Kigezi in southwestern Uganda defied colonial attempts at agricultural reform designed to tackle soil erosion and to introduce cash crops and opted instead for food crop production for sale to regional markets (Carswell, 2007). In West Africa, Fairhead and Leach (1997) found that indigenous agricultural practices in Guinea increased forest cover, even though the population was increasing.

Khat production falls into the category of farming using local knowledge that is transmitted by word of mouth. There are no manuals and no government-appointed experts to consult about the best way to grow khat. In the Nyambene region of Kenya, khat farmers have incorporated khat into the traditional mixed agricultural system in ways that does not damage the environment (Goldsmith, 1994), while in southern Ugandan, most khat is grown within similar mixed farming systems. However, the go-it-alone attitude of khat farmers does not always result in good practice. In Yemen and Ethiopia there are widespread concerns about the profligate use of irrigated water in khat cultivation and the long-term effects this irrigation will have on the water table (Milich & Al-Sabbry, 1995). There are also international concerns about the use of pesticides on khat plants in all production areas.

AGRICULTURAL EXTENSION SERVICES

While tea and coffee have been promoted as cash crops by colonialist and postindependence governments, khat production was first ignored and later discouraged in all countries where it is grown (Borelli & Perali, 2004). No agricultural extension service providing advice on cultivation and marketing to farmers, anywhere, promotes khat cultivation, and the crop continues to be ignored and reviled wherever it is commercially grown. For example, in Southern Region, Ethiopia, an area that has only recently started cultivating khat, Anderson et al. (2007) report that "in the Southern Region, officials do not shy away from condemning the khat industry, speaking openly of future strategies to encourage farmers to switch to other produce. Recently the local government considered providing tax incentives for non-khat products, encouraging farmers into areas such as poultry farming, silk farming and livestock rearing. . . . The local government is also experimenting with production of high-quality and economically high-return fruits such as strawberries, apple, mango, avocado, papaya, sugar cane, banana and sweet potato" (Anderson et al., 2007, p. 29).

The Ugandan khat industry has grown up under the noses of the government and of development agencies. Khat is an important exemplar of the ability of African farmers to gain prosperity without any outside assistance. Khat production subverts the notion that extension services, demonstration plots, and capacity building are vital for agricultural development. Even more importantly, khat enables farmers to be independent of agencies offering loans for inputs and dictating the prices of outputs. The National Agricultural Advisory Service (NAADS) was set up in Uganda in 2001 with a mission to "increase farmer access to information, knowledge and technology for profitable agricultural production" (NAADS, 2003, p. 9). The NAADS program is due to run for twenty-five years and operates in a number of administrative districts that are major khat producer areas: Arua, Kabarole, Wakiso (Kasenge), and Makono (Mabira Forest). In none of these "NAADS districts" is khat included as one of the crops to be developed (NAADS, 2003). However, according to an article in the Business Link section of the *Red Pepper* newspaper, the Ugandan government may be changing its mind over khat. Far from calling for its ban, a government minister was reported as encouraging khat production and its possible inclusion in NAADS programs. The newspaper article quotes the minister for agriculture, Hillary Onek, during a visit to the northwest of Uganda: "'Mairungi is good. They keep you awake and add value to life. Whatever brings money and supports the economy, just do.' Onek, who was accompanied by NAADS officials, told farmers in Nyadri" (Muwambi, 2008, p. 1).

LEGAL AND ILLEGAL "NARCOCROPS"

Besides khat, several other legal drugs are grown with government approval in Uganda. Tobacco is far more dangerous to health than khat yet is promoted in areas such as Arua in the northwest of the country and sold to the multinational company British American Tobacco. Before the forests were cleared about twenty years ago, khat grew wild in Rukingiri in the southwest near the border of the Democratic Republic of Congo (DRC). Now, harvesters from the town glean leaves from the few remaining wild khat trees and recently settled farmers to the area are being encouraged to take out loans to produce tea leaves for sale to big corporations. Across the Buganda kingdom and in many other Ugandan areas, khat is grown alongside coffee trees, many of which are suffering from diseases such as "wilt."

As a cash crop, khat should be compared to these legal drugs and not to opium or coca production. In fact, apart from in Bushenyi District, khat is a legal crop in Uganda that has little in common with small scale coca or opium production as part of illicit "narcoindustries" operated by ruthless and wealthy drug cartels in Asia and Latin America (Singer, 2007). Coca and opium were once grown for local use as medicine, in rituals, and for recreation use (Coomber & South, 2004) but have long since been processed into the global illicit-market commodities and sold as cocaine and heroin. Although farmers of opium poppies and cocoa leaves often benefit financially from good economic returns in comparison to growing other legal crops, the narcocrop once sold enters the supply train controlled by global drug traffickers. Farmers are sometimes drawn into the local processing of opium into heroin or coca into cocaine. Nevertheless, the larger profits are made, not by the farmers, but by the criminal gangs that distribute the drug commodities to a global market. As Singer notes, "Drugs, which are readily tradable, constitute *consumable psychotropic commodities*, that is, chemical substances that are industrially produced through a system of wage labor and commercially distributed in a market economy. Notably, in the drug trade, drug commodities acquire greater value the farther they move from the actual hands that first produced them" (Singer, 2008, p. 21).

Industrially produced drugs are sold far from where they are produced. Khat, for centuries consumed near the production areas, is now exported all over the world, primarily from Kenya and Ethiopia. As global demand for khat has expanded, the supply has also increased. Although khat is an illicit drug in Canada, United States, and many European countries, it is a legal crop in most of East Africa. However, khat is not processed and its consumption can be equated with a mild coca leaf experience rather than the snorting of cocaine. Khat, like kola nuts in West Africa and kava in the Pacific region, is produced by smallholders operating outside the control of Western economic enterprises (Klein et al., 2009). Similarly, Kennedy equates khat with coca and betel and finishes his monograph on khat in Yemen with a call for the study of "natural psychoactive substances" in their "traditional settings" (Kennedy, 1987, p. 245). Unlike coffee, khat does not have a worldwide market, but it is with coffee, rather than opium or coca, that the leaves should be compared.

Coffee and Khat Compared

Both coffee and khat trees originate in the highlands of Ethiopia and Yemen, and both contain chemicals that stimulate the central nervous system. Yet only coffee beans were taken up by Europeans to become, eventually, a beverage consumed worldwide. European demand for coffee took off in the eighteenth century and has not abated since. As coffee cannot be grown in Europe, Europeans looked to colonies in tropical Africa, Latin America, and Asia to produce coffee beans. Khat, by contrast, could not be successfully exported because of the volatile content of the cathinone, its main active ingredient. Even if the "need for speed" (Carrier, 2005b) could be met, as it now has been, since road, air, and rail transport have made it possible to send khat quickly around the globe, the chewing of leaves and twigs is still unpalatable and much less attractive to many people than sipping a cup of coffee.

All the main khat-producing countries, Yemen, Ethiopia, Kenya, and Uganda, are also coffee producers. In Kenya and Uganda, Britain, the colonial power, promoted coffee production, and from the 1960s independent governments continued where the colonialist had left off. There is little domestic demand for coffee in either Kenya or

Uganda, and it is grown largely for export. Prices are set on the world market and, in terms of unit price they can expect for their beans, the fortunes of farmers are decided in distant capital cities far beyond East Africa. The governments of the producer countries play their part in perpetuating the system. In the 1970 and 1980s in Uganda, coffee was bought and exported by the Coffee Marketing Board, which also collected export taxes from farmers already hard pressed by ongoing political instability in the country (Ssemorgerere & Wiegratz, 2007, p. 7). During the 1990s in Uganda coffee earnings rose but fell again from $286.90 to $112.20 between 1997 to 1998 and 2000 to 2001. During the same period, the unit price fell from $1.60 to $0.60 (Ssemorgerere & Wiegratz, 2007, p. 17). Coffee farmers in Ethiopia, Yemen and, Kenya are subject to the same external price controls and many no longer find the crop profitable. Price crashes can ruin livelihoods: "When the international coffee price crashed to thirty year lows in 2001, millions of coffee farmers around the world faced hardships and reduced incomes. In countries like Ethiopia where significant portions of foreign revenue come from coffee exports, the crisis left farming families unable to pay for education and health care" (Oxfam International, 2006, p. 4, cited by DeCarlo, 2007).

As khat grows in similar conditions to those that favor coffee production, switching to khat production usually has a profitable outcome. Yet development agencies and academics routinely deplore the spread of khat cultivation and claim that coffee has been the loser. Kennedy, however, refutes the argument that coffee and khat grow in identical conditions and could find no evidence that coffee trees were ripped out and replaced by khat in Yemen (Kennedy, 1987). Even if coffee had been directly replaced by khat, it is hard to understand the reasons for championing the continued production of a crop that earns little for farmers, has no nutritional value, and is rather a source of the stimulant, caffeine. Khat farmers, on the other hand, produce a stimulant that gives good earning at prices not controlled by distant commodity markets.

MANY HAPPY RETURNS

The success of khat as a cash crop depends on supply and demand and the trading and marketing skills of small-scale individual entrepreneurs. There are no multinational "drug barons" in the khat business, and any comparison of khat production to poppy growing in Afghanistan would not stand up to scrutiny. Equally striking is the lack of connection of khat to world markets dominated by multinational companies. Coffee and tea producers sell their crop, whether fair traded or not, to large business concerns that take profits out of the country. Khat is a local cash crop benefiting farmers and traders, who operate entirely without inputs from development agencies.

Although African women are the main agricultural producers, they take little part in the planting and harvesting of khat. On typical small holdings that include khat plants, women grow food crops, often assisted by men and boys in the family, but care of khat seedlings and harvesting is mostly a male activity. Reference to "khat farmers" in Ethiopia (Anderson et al., 2007; Gebissa, 2004) and in Kenya (Carrier, 2007; Goldsmith, 1994) is to men who look after the khat crop and take charge of its sale and of the money received. Anderson et al. (2007) found that Ethiopian farmers put their income from khat to good use: "Khat increases purchasing power, but farmers in the Oromia region express a clear sense of priorities about their patterns of expenditure. Our informants generally used incomes from the first khat harvest to purchase foodstuffs, before assigning money to expenditure on clothing. Repairs and improvements to the household came next in the scale, and it is notable that corrugated iron sheets are now widely used for roofing in this region—a sure sign of prosperity" (Anderson et al., 2007, p. 26).

Khat in Yemen, Ethiopia, Kenya, and Uganda is cultivated on family-run homesteads. There are no large-scale khat producers, farming plantations similar to the large-scale tea gardens found in Uganda. In Uganda, khat farms do not exceed ten acres. Yet, in Uganda, as elsewhere, khat is providing very good returns compared with other cash crops. As khat grows at the same altitudes that are suitable for tea and coffee production, these are the crops with which it competes and wins. In many areas of Uganda, khat is a wonder crop. Hence, according to tea and khat growers in Kabarole District in Uganda, khat yields at least ten times the income that would be derived from selling tea leaves in terms of returns per area of land use. Other farmers across Uganda also enthusiastically compare khat returns to those obtainable from selling coffee, tea, or tobacco, typically claiming a factor of ten times the profit. This compares well with the situation in the Nyambene Hills, as described by Carrier:

> *Miraa* is cultivated on smallholder plots and offers farmers a very good return per acre in comparison with "progressive" crops like coffee and tea: one farmer mentioned in a UNDCP (UN International Drug Control Programme) report of 1999 (p. 27) that every shilling invested in tea brings a return of two shillings; whereas every shilling invested in *miraa*

> gives a return of four shillings. Farmers also appreciate the frequent harvests that *miraa* trees provide (every few weeks or so depending on the season), pointing out that income from crops like coffee is not only depressingly small, but also comes in just one yearly payment. (Carrier, 2005b, p. 540)

Khat returns in Kabarole District and across Uganda also compare well with the situation in eastern Ethiopia, as Gebissa explains: "Harvested at least three times a year, it provided a regular source of income to meet household expenses. Khat also consistently maintained price advantages over other crops. In the early 1980s, it yielded three times the return on sorghum, 10 times the returns on coffee, and nearly twice the returns on low impact management potato. By the mid-1990s this price differential had widened further, with per hectare profit from khat exceeding all other crops, making government-sponsored substitution programs unattractive and unsuccessful" (Gebissa, 2008, p. 976).

"Khat Educates Our Children"

Khat earnings in Ethiopia and Uganda, in particular, have enabled farmers to find a route out of agriculture through education and investment in off-farm enterprises. In the Harerge in eastern Ethiopia, khat has enabled farmers to earn enough money to leave the land in an area where it has become scarce. According to Gebissa, "It seems that Harerge's farmers have identified a successful rural development strategy. Most use their cash wealth to enter nonfarm life, but have limited knowledge of the opportunities that are available. Policymakers could benefit the farmers by helping them develop and invest their money in workable nonfarm economic activities rather than insisting on the perpetuation of smallholder agriculture" (Gebissa, 2004, p. 186).

In the Harerge, khat farmers are moving forward without official government guidance, while viable development policies lag behind. In Uganda, there is less pressure on land for the time being, but here farmers, imbued with respect for Western education, use khat incomes to pay school and university fees so that the next generation can leave farming.

The situation is particularly good for many khat farmers in Southern Uganda, a region that has so much abundant rainfall that it enables farmers to harvest leaves from khat trees and bushes as often as every month. Farmers with a couple of acres planted with khat are able to plan harvesting so sections of their plantation are harvested in rotation, with some of the trees or bushes being plucked of their tender leaves daily. Thus, khat provides a "daily income" for these farmers and one that they asset "educates out children." In Kaborole District, western Uganda, Ahmed Byarufu has helped dozens, perhaps hundreds of small scale farmers become khat producers. As a result, the whole area has prospered as the new nursery schools, churches, and mosques constructed in the area testify. It is not only in Kabarole that khat has brought prosperity. In a country that puts the highest value on education, the claim that khat money is used in this way provides the strongest justification for continued production.

When faced with opposition from representatives of government agencies, Ugandan khat farmers are quick to point out that khat brings development. Even the most vehement campaigners against khat are forced to pause and consider the benefits of a crop that provides school fees. Yet the argument that "khat educates our children" is not sufficient to stop the antikhat movement. Most farmers operate in an atmosphere of uncertainty, aware that their cash crop could be declared illegal and put on par with cannabis production. They possess little or no information on the pharmacology, effects, or arguments for or against consumption.

TRUST AND TRADE

Within Uganda, the distribution of khat operates on the basis of personal contacts maintained through face-to-face interactions and by cell phones, whereby prices and payment modes are agreed verbally. The industry is self-regulating and operates in the face of opposition to khat consumption by many local authorities. Typically, khat is sent on public transportation from the production areas by agents to wholesalers who then distribute to retailers. Cash payments for stock received are sent by the care of bus conductors on the second day or even up to a week later. Such a system requires trust but also opens up the possibility of payments default and sharp practice. Aldridge, in his analysis of the trust in markets, points out the advantages of doing business with people we know: "First, that person has an economic incentive to give us a good service in the hope of repeat business; and, if the service was good, we have an interest in paying promptly in order that he or she will want to deal with us again. It is a straightforward example of the market working to our mutual advantage. Secondly, in addition to the economic calculation there is also the question of social and personal ties, which create expectations of trust and make opportunistic exploitation immoral" (Aldridge, 2005).

There are eighteen links in the average commodity chain that links local producers to consumers of products such as coffee and tea (Brown, 1993, p. 70). At each link there is the potential for middlemen and traders to dominate trade terms by price setting. The fair-trade movement sets out to reduce or eliminate the unfair and exploitative trading terms and to reduce the number of links in the commodity chain so that intermediaries take most of the profits. Nevertheless, fair-trade coffee still passes from farmer to consumer along a chain with at least four links (DeCarlo, 2007). Khat has a shorter value chain, typically just two links: a producer sells direct to a trader who sells to the consumer. In Uganda, some farmers harvest khat leaves and take them straight to town where they sell them directly to consumers. At most, the commodity chain for khat sold on the domestic market has three links: producer to wholesaler to retailer to consumer. This three-link chain is the usual distribution pattern of khat grown in the Nyambene Hills in Kenya (Anderson et al., 2007). Exported khat from the Nyambenes and the money it generates, however, pass through more hands. For example, Kenyan khat form the Nyambenes is rushed to Nairobi (Carrier, 2005b), where it is handed over to wholesalers for repackaging before being loaded on aircraft for the European market. Khat reaching Europe that is sent into Canada and the United States where it becomes a trafficked substance passes through still more links in the commodity chain (Anderson et al., 2007).

As khat in many countries is unregulated or lightly regulated, all transactions depend on trust between sellers and buyers. In a country like Uganda, where violence and civil war marred life for decades, trust is particularly important to the successful operation of business, both in the domestic market place and for exports. Hence, Wiegratz (2008) argues that in Uganda, "the institutional environment, the trust culture of the country, the macro and micro socio-economic conditions (including family) and so on play an important role in shaping the ability of Ugandan economic actors to develop interpersonal trust, with both domestic and foreign actors" (Wiegratz, 2008, p. 10).

Fukuyama (1995), in a major analysis of social cohesion and business in a range of cultures, argues that trust in business depends on a strong civil society through social networks operating at a level lower than the state but a higher level than the family. He writes that "trust is the expectation that arises within a community of regular, honest, and cooperative behaviour, based on commonly shared norms, on the part of other members of that community" (Fukuyama, 1995, p. 26).

Fukuyama's analysis of business, trust, and the strength of civil society in different settings does not cover any African country. Fukuyama is interested in the ways of civil society, for example, in the form of local associations such as church groups and clubs, and how it provides an intermediate level of social organization between the family and the state. However, Chabal and Daloz (1999) do not find the notion of civil society to have much meaning in contemporary African states. The development of social movements and groups that might be called "civil society" is often weak in Africa. They argue that "we ought not lose sight of the basic fact that African societies are essentially plural, fragmented and, above all, organized along vertical lines. Socio-political cleavages are usually a matter of fractions, or factional divisions, which occur primarily because of competition for scarce resources. In general, then, vertical divisions remain more significant than horizontal functional bonds or ties of solidarity between those who are similarly employed or professionally linked" (Chabal & Daloz, 1999, p.20). Hence, according to Chabal and Daloz, people in African countries rely on their families and on members of the same ethnic group rather than associations such as professional bodies or trades union.

Clearly, the khat trade, or any business for that matter, cannot operate without trust. Trade bodies and the police are not brought in to regulate khat commerce. If a buyer defaults on payment or a seller provides old, and therefore worthless stock, there is no comeback. The khat trade operates best when one ethnic group, or even specific clans, monopolizes the trade. In Kenya, the Igembe and Tigania clans dominate the khat trade, but there has been violence when Somalis moved from being a major consumer group into wholesaling (Anderson et al., 2007; Carrier, 2007). In western Uganda, the multiethnic khat trade is characterized by competition that sometimes leads to violence and to informing on competitors to the police. In Ethiopia, too, Gebissa cautions about seeing khat as a wholly positive influence on the social institutions of the Harerge region: "It is important to recognize that the production and distribution of khat have led to conflict between traders, ethnic groups, farmers and officials. Hareri farmers jealously kept the shrub from spreading to the Oromo until the late nineteenth century, when they hired the latter to work their khat orchards" (Gebissa, 2004, p. 179).

Khat across the production areas of Ethiopia, Kenya, and Uganda has not promoted trust between ethnic groups. However, khat production has created wealth and prosperity for millions of people growing and trading in the plant.

CONSUMPTION AND DEVELOPMENT WORK, CREATIVITY, AND DEPENDENCE

Evidence has been presented in this book that chewing khat promotes harmony between people of diverse backgrounds. Individuals from different ethnic backgrounds sit together chewing for hours on end, and the many detractors of khat claim that the personal development of these consumers is being stunted.

Khat consumers, regardless of ethnicity of social class, often describe the effects of khat in similar terms and describe how chewers often hatch unrealistic money-making schemes turn out to be "houses of ice" or "buildings made of spit" that are easy to talk about but impossible to execute (Klein & Beckerleg, 2007). Popular anecdotes center on the disorientation that sometimes occurs after chewing for a number of hours and typically describe a chewer roaming around at night (Beckerleg, 2006; Carrier, 2007).

But long-term khat consumers also often speak about the ill effects that chewing has had on their lives. Some heavy users acknowledge that chewing has harmed their economic standing as their businesses failed and even led to the breakdown of their marriages. Physical symptoms occurring in the absence of a supply of khat were reported by long-term users. The symptoms, including headaches, irritability, shaking, and shivering, point to a degree of physical dependence. Doubts and uncertainty among researchers concerning the degree of dependence that can arise from long-term khat use persist:

> There is no agreement or scientific consensus on whether khat is addictive or not. The pharmacological, chemical and medical findings are inconclusive and contradictory. It is nevertheless well established that cathine and cathinone induce temporary euphoria, enhance, wakefulness, suppress hunger and increase physical energy and concentration. In the past, some scientists and health professionals believed that the active substances were addictive drugs which if used over a long period of time, could lead to massive deterioration in the health of the chewer, to madness and even death. Recent researchers do acknowledge that users may become psychologically addicted, but argue that it is more appropriate to speak of habituation than addiction. (Gebissa, 2004, p. 19)

However, Kennedy did find some evidence among Yemeni consumers of the problems typically associated with drug addiction and physical dependence. He writes, "The mild depressive feelings with lack of energy and experienced powerlessness are probably due to psychological conditions, supporting a notion of psychic dependence;

but the general malaise, trembling and bad dreams appear to be purely physiological responses to drug deprivation. These data support the hypothesis that a mild form of physiological dependence does result from extremely heavy use" (Kennedy, 1987, p. 193).

In 2005 the Advisory Council on the Misuse of Drugs reached similar, measured conclusions to those arrived at by Kennedy over twenty years ago: "Khat is a much less potent stimulant than other commonly used drugs such as amphetamine or cocaine. However some individuals use it in a dependent manner" (ACMD, 2005, para. 9.2).

In the 1970s Kennedy (1987) carried out the only study ever undertaken that compared the health of khat users with nonusers. The study compared seventy-eight nonkhat users with 174 light users and 161 heavy users. He found that "our data point to some negative health effects which may result from heavy or prolonged use" (Kennedy, 1987, p. 235). Yet Kennedy's overall conclusion regarding the health effects of khat chewing is that "most of the severe problems predicted by Western medical authorities were not encountered" (Kennedy, 1987, p. 235).

Controversies about khat are set to continue for the foreseeable future. Khat is not a particularly dangerous drug; on the contrary, many consumers argue, it is useful in promoting good community and interethnic relationships as well as business ideas. The last word goes to Mzamil Karemire, university graduate, khat trader, and daily consumer living in Mbarara, Uganda. This young man filled an exercise book with his thoughts on khat and presented it to me. One section of his handwritten document concerns the building of good relationships in khat. "It [khat] has created friendly relationships between indigenous Ugandans and foreigners from Kenya, Somalia, Ethiopia, Yemen and Djibouti, [be]cause when these people come to Uganda to places where khat is sold they buy the khat, settle and chew with Ugandans whereby they share ideas and promises" (Karemire, 2008).

References

Abdullahi, M. D. (2001). *Culture and customs of Somalia.* London: Greenwood Press.

Adam, H. M., & Ford, R. (1997). *Mending the rips in the sky: Options for Somali communities in the 21st century.* Lawrenceville, NJ: Red Sea Press.

Advisory Council on the Misuse of Drugs (ACMD). (2005). *Khat (Qat) assessment of risk to individual and community in the UK.* Home Office, United Kingdom.

Ahimbisibwe, C. (2009, March 22). RDC shots mairungi vendor. *New Vision.* Retrieved April 24, 2009, from http://www.newvision.co.ug

Ahmed, A. J. (1995). "Daybreak is near, won't you become sour?" Going beyond the current rhetoric in Somali Studies. In A. J. Ahmed (Ed.), *The invention of Somalia* (pp. 135–155). Lawrenceville, NJ: Red Sea Press.

Ahmed, C. C. (1995). Finely etched chattel: The invention of the Somali woman. In A. J. Ahmed (Ed.), *The invention of Somalia* (pp. 157–189). Lawrenceville, NJ: Red Sea Press.

Aldridge, A. (2005). *The market.* Cambridge: Polity Press.

Almeddom, A., & Abraham, S. (1994). Women, moral virtue and chat-chewing. In M. MacDonald (Ed.), *Gender, drink and drugs* (pp. 249–258). Oxford: Berg.

Aluka, P., & Hakiza, G. J. (2001). Tea (*Camillea sinensis*). In National Agricultural Research Organization (Ed.), *Agriculture in Uganda: Volume II Crops* (pp. 437–461). Kampala: Fountain Books.

Anderson, B. (1983). *Imagined communities: Reflections on the origins and spread of nationalism.* London: Verso.

Anderson, D., Beckerleg, S., Hailu, D., & Klein, A. (2007). *The khat controversy: Stimulating the drugs debate.* Oxford: Berg.

Anderson, D., & Carrier, N. (2006). "Flowers of paradise" or "polluting the nation"? Contested narratives of khat consumption. In J. Brewer and F. Trentmann (Eds.), *Consuming cultures, global perspectives: Historical trajectories, transnational exchanges* (pp. 145–166). Oxford: Berg.

Anderson, D., & Lochery, E. (2008). Violence and exodus in Kenya's Rift Valley, 2008: Predictable and preventable? *Journal of Eastern African Studies, 2*(2), 328–343.

Arero, H. W. (2007). Coming to Kenya: Imagining and perceiving a nation among the Borana of Kenya. *Journal of Eastern African Studies, 1*(2), 292–304.

Barnes, C. (2007). The Somali Youth League, Ethiopian Somalis and the greater Somalia idea, c. 1946–48. *Journal of Eastern African Studies, 1*(2), 277–291.

Barnes, C., & Hassan, H. (2007). The rise and fall of Mogadishu's Islamic Courts. *Journal of Eastern African Studies, 1*(2), 151–60.

Beckerleg, S. (2004). Modernity has been Swahilised: The case of Malindi. In P. Caplan & F. Topan (Eds.), *Swahili modernities: Identity and power on the East African coast* (pp. 19–35). Trenton, NJ: Africa World Press.

Beckerleg, S. (2006). What harm? Kenyan and Ugandan perspectives on khat. *African Affairs, 104*(418), 219–241.

Beckerleg, S. (2008). Khat in East Africa: Taking women into or out of sex work? *Substance Use and Misuse, 43*, 1170–1185.

Beckerleg, S. (2009a). From ocean to lakes: Cultural transformations of Yemenis in Kenya and Uganda. *African and Asian Studies, 8*, 288–308.

Beckerleg, S. (2009b). Khat chewing as a new Ugandan leisure activity. *Journal of East African Studies, 3*(1), 42–54.

Beckerleg, S., & Sheekh, N. (2005). A view from the refugee camps: New Somali khat use in Kenya. *Drugs and Alcohol Today, 5*(3), 25–27.

Bell, W. D. M. (1949). *Karamoja safari.* London: Victor Gollancz.

Bennett, N. R. (1986). *Arab versus European: Diplomacy and war in nineteenth-century East Central Africa.* New York: Africana.

Besteman, C. (1995). The invention of Gosha: Slavery, colonialism, and stigma in Somali history. In A. J. Ahmed (Ed.), *The invention of Somalia* (pp. 43–62). Lawrenceville, NJ: Red Sea Press.

Borelli, S., & Perali, F. (2004). Drug consumption and intra-household distribution of resources. In C. Dagum & G. Ferrari (Eds.), *Household behaviour, equivalence scales, welfare and poverty.* Heidelberg: Physica-Verlag.

Bourgois, P. (1995). *In search of respect: Selling crack in El Barrio.* Cambridge: Cambridge University Press.

Boxberger, L. (2002). *On the edge of empire: Hadhramawt, emigration, and the Indian Ocean, 1880s–1930s.* New York: State University of New York Press.

Brettell, C. B. (2008). Theorizing migration in anthropology. In C. B. Brettel & J. F. Hollifield (Eds.), *Migration theory* (pp. 113–159). New York: Routledge.

Brown, M. B. (1993). *Fair trade: Reform and realities in the international trading system.* London: Zed Books.

Bryceson, D. F. (2009). The urban melting pot in East Africa: Ethnicity and urban growth in Kampala and Dar es Salaam. In F. Locatelli & P. Nugent (Eds.), *African cities: Competing claims on urban space* (pp. 242–260). Leiden: Brill.

Burton, R. (1966). *First footsteps in East Africa, or an exploration of the Harar (1854–1856).* New York: Schuster (Original work published 1856).

Bushenyi District (*Mairungi* Trade and Consumption Control) Ordinance. (2006). (Sections 38 and 40 of the Local Government Act, Cap. 243). Kampala: Government of Uganda.

Byabashaija, D. M., Kahembwe, F., & Ndemere, P. (2001). Management of natural forests. In J. K. Mukiibi (Ed.), *Agriculture in Uganda: Volume III, Forestry* (pp. 48–58). Kampala Fountain.

Caplan, P. (2007). "But the coast, of course, is quite different": Academic and local ideas about the East African Littoral. *Journal of Eastern African Studies, 1*(2), 305–320.

Carrier, N. (2003). *The social life of miraa: Farming, trade and consumption of a plant stimulant in Kenya.* PhD dissertation, Department of Social Anthropology, University of St. Andrews, United Kingdom.

Carrier, N. (2005a). Miraa is cool: The cultural importance of miraa (khat) for Tigania and Igembe youth in Kenya. *Journal of African Cultural Studies, 17*(2), 201–218.

Carrier, N. (2005b). The need for speed: Contrasting timeframes in the social life of Kenyan khat. *Africa, 75*(4), 539–558.

Carrier, N. (2007). *Kenyan khat: The social life of a stimulant.* Leiden: Brill.

Carrier, N. (2008). Is miraa a drug? Categorizing Kenyan khat. *Substance Use and Misuse, 43*(6), 803–818.

Carswell, G. (2007). *Cultivating success in Uganda: Kigezi farmers and colonial policies.* Oxford: James Currey.

Chabal, P., & Daloz, J.-P. (1999). *Africa works: Disorder as political instrument.* Oxford: James Currey.

Chambers, R. (1983). *Rural development: Putting the last first.* London: Longman.

Chavannes, B. (2004a). Criminalizing cultural practice: The case of Jamaica. In A. Klein, M. Day, & A. Harriott (Eds.), *Caribbean drugs: From criminalization to harm reduction.* London: Zed Books.

Chavannes, B. (2004b). Ganja and the road to decriminalization in Jamaica. In R. Coomber & N. South (Eds.), *Drugs in the global context: Comparative perspectives on cultures and controls.* London: Free Association Press.

Child, K. (2009). Civil society in Uganda: The struggle to save the Mabira Forest Reserve. *Journal of Eastern African Studies, 3*(2), 240–258.

Clarence-Smith, W. G. (2002). The rise and fall of Hadhrami shipping in the Indian Ocean, c.1750–c.1940. In D. Parkin & R. Barnes (Eds.), *Ships and the development of maritime technology in the Indian Ocean* (pp. 227–258). London: Routledge/Curzon.

Cook, A. (1945). *Uganda memories (1897–1940).* Kampala: The Uganda Society.

Coomber, R., & South, N. (2004). *Drug use and cultural contexts: Beyond the West.* London: Free Association Books.

Cowan, J. M. (1976). *Hans Wehr: A dictionary of modern written Arabic* (3rd ed.). Ithaca, NY: Spoken Language Services Inc.

Date, J., Tanida, N., & Hobara, T. (2004). Qat chewing and pesticides: A study of adverse health effects in people of the mountainous areas of Yemen. *International Journal of Environmental Health Research, 14*, 405–414.

DeCarlo, J. (2007). *Fair trade: A beginner's guide.* Oxford: Oneworld.

Declich, F. (1995). Identity, dance and Islam among people with Bantu origins in riverine areas of Somalia. In A. J. Ahmed (Ed.), *The invention of Somalia* (pp. 191–222). Lawrenceville, NJ: Red Sea Press.

de Vere Allen, J. (1993). *Swahili origins: Swahili culture and the Shungwaya phenomenon.* Oxford: James Currey.

Dhadphale, M., & Omolo, O. E. (1988). Psychiatric morbidity amongst khat chewers. *East African Medical Journal, 65*(6), 355–359.

Dirie, W., & D'Haem, J. (2002). *Desert dawn.* London: Virago.

Easterly, W. (2007). *The white man's burden.* Oxford: Oxford University Press.

Eaton, D. (2008). The business of peace: Raiding and peace work along the Kenya-Uganda border (Part 1). *African Affairs, 107*(426), 89–110.

Eggeling, W. J. (1951). *The indigenous trees of the Uganda protectorate* (2nd ed.). London: Crown Agents.

El Zein, A. H. M. (1974). *The sacred meadows: A structural analysis of religious symbolism in an East African town.* Evanston, IL: Northwestern University Press.

Esegu, J. F. O. (2001). Forest tree genetic resources in Uganda. In J. K. Mukiibi (Ed.). *Agriculture in Uganda: Volume III, Forestry* (pp. 1–33). Kampala: NARO, Fountain.

Fabian, J. (2000). *Out of our minds: Reason and madness in the exploration of Central Africa.* London: University of California Press.

Fairhead, J., & Leach, M. (1997). Webs of power and the construction of environmental policy problems: Forest loss in Guinea. In R. D. Grillo & R. L. Stirrat (Eds.), *Discourses of development: Anthropological perspectives* (pp. 35–57). Oxford: Berg.

Farley, O. W. (1959). *The Sudanese troops in Uganda from Lugard's enlistment to the mutiny, 1891–97.* Paper presented at Conference of East African Institute of Social Research, Makerere College, January 1959. Accessed from Uganda Society Archives, Kampala, Uganda.

Feiling, T. (2009). *The candy machine: How cocaine took over the world.* London: Penguin.

Fortt, J. M. (1973). Land tenure and the emergence of large scale farming. In A. I. Richards, F. Sturrock, & J. M. Fortt (Eds.), *Subsistence to commercial farming in present-day Uganda: An economic and anthropological survey* (chap. 3). Cambridge: Cambridge University Press.

Fortt, J. M., & Houghton, D. A. (1973). Environment, population and economic history. In A. I. Richards, F. Sturrock, & J. M. Fortt (Eds.), *Subsistence to commercial farming in present-day Uganda: An economic and anthropological survey* (chap. 1). Cambridge: Cambridge University Press.

Fukuyama, F. (1995). *Trust: The social virtues and the creation of prosperity.* New York: Free Press, Simon and Schuster.

Gardner, K. (2002). *Age, narrative and migration: The life course and life histories of Bengali elders in London.* Oxford: Berg.

Gebissa, E. (2004). *Leaf of Allah: Khat and agricultural transformation in Harerge, Ethiopia 1875–1991.* Oxford: James Currey.

Gebissa, E. (2008). Scourge of life or an economic lifeline? Public discourses on Khat (*catha edulis*) in Ethiopia. *Substance Use and Misuse, 43*(6), 784–802.

Gellner, G. (2000). Trust, cohesion and the social order. In D. Gembetta (Ed.), *Trust: Making and breaking cooperative relations* (pp. 142–157). Oxford: Basil Blackwell, 1988. Republished in 2000 as an electronic edition. Retrieved October 2006 from http://www.sociology.ox.ac.uk/trustbook.html

Gerholm, T. (1977). *Market, mosque and mafraj.* Stockholm: Department of Anthropology, University of Stockholm.

Ghaidan, U. (1975). *Lamu: A study of the Swahili town.* Nairobi: East African Literature Bureau.

Giddens, A. (1991). *Modernity and self-identity: Self and society in the late modern age.* Cambridge: Polity Press.

Goldsmith, P. (1994). *Symbiosis and transformation in Kenya's Meru District.* PhD thesis, University of Florida.

Goldsmith, P. (1997). The Somali impact on Kenya, 1990–1993: The view from the camps. In H. M. Adam & R. Ford (Eds.), *Mending rips in the sky: Options for Somali communities in the 21st century* (pp. 461–483). Lawrenceville, NJ: Red Sea Press.

Goodman, J., Lovejoy, P., & Sherrat, A. (2007). *Consuming habits* (2nd ed.). Abingdon: Routledge.

Government of Uganda. (n.d.). *Penal code act CAP.120 Uganda.* Kampala: LDC.

Grillo, R. D. (1997). Discourses of development: The view from anthropology. In R. D. Grillo & R. L. Stirrat (Eds.), *Discourses of development: Anthropological perspectives* (pp. 1–33). Oxford: Berg.

Grillo, R. D., & Stirrat, R. L. (Eds.). (1997). *Discourses of development: Anthropological perspectives.* Oxford: Berg.

Hailu, D. (2005). Supporting a nation: Khat farming and livelihoods in Ethiopia. *Drugs and Alcohol Today, 5*(3), 22–24.

Hailu, D. (2007). Should *khat* be banned? The development impact. *One Pager. Number 40. International Poverty Centre.* Brasilia, Brazil: UNDP.

Halliday, F. (1992). *Arabs in exile: Yemeni migrants in urban Britain.* London: I. B. Tauris.

Hanson, H. (2003). *Landed obligation: The practice of power in Buganda.* Portsmouth, NH: Heinemann.

Hanson, H. (2007). Stolen people and autonomous chiefs in nineteenth-century Buganda. In H. Medard & S. Doyle (Eds.), *Slavery in the Great Lakes Region of East Africa* (pp. 161–173). Oxford: James Currey.

Heald, S. (1999). *Manhood and morality: Sex, violence and ritual in Gisu society*. London: Routledge.

Hersi, A. A. (1977). *The Arab factor in Somali history: The origins and the development of Arab enterprise and cultural influence in the Somali peninsula*. Unpublished PhD thesis, University of California, Los Angeles.

Hodd, M., & Roche, A. (2002). *Footprint Uganda handbook*. Bristol: Footprint Books.

Horton, M., & Middleton, J. (2000). *The Swahili: The social landscape of a mercantile society*. Oxford: Blackwell.

Ihunwo, A. O., Kayanja, F. I. B., & Amadi-Ihunwo, U. B. (2004). Use and perception of the psychostimulant, khat (*Catha edulis*) among three occupational groups in south western Uganda. *East African Medical Journal, 81*(9), 468–473.

Jenkins, R. (2004). *Social identity* (2nd ed.). London: Routledge.

Johnson, D. H. (2009). Tribe or nationality? The Sudanese diaspora and the Kenyan Nubis. *Journal of Eastern African Studies, 3*(1), 112–131.

Johnson, F. (1979). *Madan's a standard Swahili-English dictionary*. Nairobi: Oxford University Press.

Karemire, M. A. (2008). Research Report. Mbarara: Handwritten Report, Mbarara.

Kassim, M. M. (1995). Aspects of the Benadir cultural history: The case of the Bravan Ulama. In A. J. Ahmed (Ed.), *The invention of Somalia* (pp. 29–42). Lawrenceville, NJ: Red Sea Press.

Kasozi, A. B. K. (1996). *The life of Prince Badru Kakungulu Wasajja*. Kampala: Progressive.

Kato, J. (2008, July 17). Drug abuse behind Kampala's high crime rate. *New Vision*, 23.

Kaufmann, G. (1997). Watching the developers: A partial ethnography. In R. D. Grillo & R. L. Stirrat (Eds.), *Discourses of development: Anthropological perspectives* (pp. 107–131). Oxford: Berg.

Kawoya, V. F. K. (1985). Kiswahili in Uganda. In J. Maw & D. Parkin (Eds.), *Swahili language and society* (pp. 35–45). Vienna: Beitrage zur Afrikanistik.

Kennedy, J. G. (1987). *The flower of paradise: The institutionalized use of the drug qat in North Yemen*. Dortrech: D. Reidel.

Klein, A. (2005). Chewing it over: Reviewing the legal status of khat. *Drugs and Alcohol Today, 5*(3), 12–13.

Klein, A. (2008). Khat in the neighbourhood—local government responses to khat use in a London community. *Substance Use and Misuse, 43*(6), 819–831.

Klein, A., & Beckerleg, S. (2007). Building castles of spit—the role of khat in ritual, leisure and work. In J. Goodman, P. Lovejoy, & A. Sherrat (Eds.), *Consuming habits* (2nd ed., pp. 238–254). Abingdon: Routledge.

Klein, A., Beckerleg, S., & Hailu, D. (2009). Regulating khat—dilemmas and opportunities for the international drug control system. *International Journal of Drug Policy, 20*(6), 509–513.

Kusow, A. M. (1995). The Somali origin: Myth or reality? In A. J. Ahmed (Ed.), *The invention of Somalia* (pp. 81–106). Lawrenceville, NJ: Red Sea Press.

Landa, J. T. (1995). *Trust, ethnicity and identity: Beyond the new institutional economics of ethnic trading.* Michigan: University of Michigan.

Lautze, S. (2008). Social dynamics in militarized livelihood systems: Evidence from a study of Ugandan Army Soldiers. *Journal of Eastern African Studies, 2*(3), 415–438.

Le Guennec-Coppens, F. (1989). Social and cultural integration: A case study of the East African Hadramis. *Africa, 59*(2), 185–195.

Le Guennec-Coppens, F. (1991). Qui epouse-t-on chez les Hadrami d'Afrique orientale: Les reseaux d'alliances. In Le Guennec- Coppens F. et Caplan P. (Eds.), *Les Swahili entre Afrique et Arabie* (pp. 145–162). Paris: Karthala.

Lonsdale, J. (2008). Soil, work, civilisation and citizenship in Kenya. *Journal of Eastern African Studies, 2*(2), 305–314.

Leopold, M. (2005). *Inside West Nile.* Oxford: James Currey.

Leopold, M. (2007). Legacies of slavery in North West Uganda: The story of the "One-Elevens." In H. Medard & S. Doyle (Eds.), *Slavery in the Great Lakes Region of East Africa.* Oxford: James Currey.

Lovejoy, P. E. (2007). Kola nuts: The "coffee" of central Sudan. In J. Goodman, P. Lovejoy, & A. Sherrat (Eds.), *Consuming habits* (2nd ed., pp. 98–120). Abingdon: Routledge.

Maitai, C. K. (1996). *Catha edulis (miraa): A detailed review focusing on its chemistry, health implication, economic, legal, social, cultural, religious, moral aspects and its cultivation.* Nairobi: National Council for Science and Technology.

Mansur, A. O. (1995). The nature of the Somali clan system. In A. J. Ahmed (Ed.), *The invention of Somalia* (pp. 117–134). Lawrenceville, NJ: Red Sea Press.

Martin, B. G. (1976). *Muslim brotherhoods in nineteenth-century Africa.* Cambridge: Cambridge University Press.

Martin, E. B., & Martin, C. P. (1978). *Cargoes of the East: The ports, trade and culture of the Arabian seas and the Western Indian Ocean.* London: Elm Tree/Hamish Hamilton.

Matthee, R. (1995). Exotic substances: The introduction and global spread of tobacco, coffee, cocoa, tea, and distilled liquor, sixteenth to eighteenth centuries. In R. Porter & M. Teich (Eds.), *Drugs and narcotics in history* (pp. 24–51). Cambridge: Cambridge University Press.

Maunda, P. M. (1999). *Traditional food plants of Kenya.* Nairobi: KENRIK, National Museums of Kenya.

Mazrui, A. M., & Shariff, I. N. (1994). *The Swahili: Idiom and identity of an African people.* Trenton, NJ: Africa World Press.

Meneley, A. (1996). *Tournaments of value: Sociability and hierarchy in a Yemeni town*. London: University of Toronto Press.

Meredith, M. (2006). *The state of Africa: A history of fifty years of independence*. London: Free Press.

Milich, L., & Al-Sabbry. M. (1995). The "rational peasant" vs. sustainable livelihoods: The case of Qat in Yemen. Retrieved August 22, 2005, from http://ag.arizona.edu~lmilich/yemen.html

Ministry of Agriculture Animal Industries and Fisheries. (2008). National Agricultural Advisory Service: Annual report, 2006–2007. Unpublished report. Kampala: Uganda National Agricultural Advisory Service.

Mkutu, K. A. (2007). Small arms and light weapons among pastoral groups in the Kenya-Uganda border area. *African Affairs, 106*(422), 47–70.

Moyse-Bartlett, H. (1956). *The King's African Rifles: A study of the military history of East and Central Africa, 1890–1945*. Aldershot: Gale and Polden.

Mukhtar, M. J. (1995). Islam in Somali history: Fact and fiction. In A. J. Ahmed (Ed.), *The invention of Somalia* (pp. 1–27). Lawrenceville, NJ: Red Sea Press.

Mukiibi, J. K. (Ed.). (2001). *Agriculture in Uganda: Volume III, Forestry*. Kamapala: NARO, Fountain.

Musoli, P. C., Hakiza, J. B., Birikunzira, J. B., Kibirige-Sebunya, I., & Kucel, P. (2001). Coffee (coffea spp). In National Agricultural Research Organization (Ed.), *Agriculture in Uganda: Volume II, Crops* (pp. 376–436). Kampala: Fountain Books.

Muwambi, S. (2008, July 3). Gov't to support brisk mairungi trade. *Red Pepper*, p. 1.

NAADS. (2003a). *Consultative workshop on vanilla sub-sector*. Kampala: Uganda National Agricultural Advisory Service.

NAADS. (2003b). *National agricultural advisory service: Facts and figures*. Kampala: Uganda National Agricultural Advisory Service.

Nabusoba, I. (2007, October 29). Somalis demand recognition. *New Vision*, p. 14.

National Agricultural Research Organization (NARO). (1999). *Catalogue of plants in Entebbe Botanical Gardens 1999*. Kampala: National Agricultural Research Organisation.

National Agricultural Research Organization (NARO). (2001). *Agriculture in Uganda: Volume II, Crops*. Kampala: Fountain Books.

Oded, A. (1974). *Islam in Uganda: Islamization through a centralized state in pre-colonial Africa*. Jerusalem: Israel Universities Press.

Odenwald, M. (2007). Chronic khat use and psychotic disorders: A review of the literature and future prospects. *SUCHT, 53*(1), 9–22.

Onzima, R. J., & Birikunzira, J. B. (2001). Tobacco (*Nicotiana tabacum*). In National Agricultural Research Organization (Ed.) *Agriculture in Uganda: Volume II, Crops* (pp. 500–529). Kampala: Fountain Books.

Oxfam International. (2006). *Grounds for change: Creating a voice for small coffee farmers and farmworkers with the next international coffee agreement.* Junta Nacional del Café and Oromia Coffee Farmer Cooperative Union [Newsletter], p. 5.

Parfitt, T. (2002). *The end of development? Modernity, post-modernity and development.* London: Pluto Press.

Peake, R. (1989). Swahili stratification and tourism in Malindi Old Town, Kenya. *Africa, 59*(2), 209–220.

Perham M. (1956). *Lugard: The years of adventure. 1858–1898.* London: Collins.

Perham, M. (1959). *The dairies of Lord Lugard, Uganda* (Vol. 1). London: Faber and Faber.

Posnansky, M. (1975). Connections between the Lacustrine peoples and the coast. In N. Chittick & R. Rotberg (Eds.). *East Africa and the Orient* (pp. 217–225). London: Africana.

Randall, T. (1993). Khat abuse fuels Somali conflict, drains economy. *Journal of the American Medical Association, 269*(1), 12–14.

Ray, B. C. (1991). *Myth, ritual and kingship in Buganda.* Oxford: Oxford University Press.

Reid, R. (2007). Human booty in Buganda. In H. Medard & S. Doyle (Eds.), *Slavery in the Great Lakes region of East Africa* (pp. 145–160). Oxford: James Currey.

Reid, R., & Dirar, U. C. (2007). Experiencing identities: Making and remaking African communities. *Journal of Eastern African Studies, 1*(2), 234–237.

Richards, A. I., Sturrock, F., & Fortt, J. M. (1973). *Subsistence to commercial farming in present-day Uganda: An economic and anthropological survey.* Cambridge: Cambridge University Press.

Roscoe, J. (1965). *The Baganda.* London: Frank Cass.

Scmittter Heisler, B. (2008). The sociology of immigration. In C. B. Brettel & J. F. Hollifield (Eds.), *Migration theory* (pp. 83–111). New York: Routledge.

Seligman, A. (2000). *Problem of trust.* Princeton, NJ: Princeton University Press.

Sex and mairungi. (2008, July 13). *Red Pepper*, pp. 7–9.

Singer, M. (2008). *Drugs and development: The global impact on sustainable growth and human rights.* Long Grove, IL: Waveland Press.

Snoxall, R. A. (1985). The East African Interterritorial Language (Swahili) Committee. In J. Maw & D. Parkin (Eds.), *Swahili language and society* (pp. 15–24). Vienna: Beitrage zur Afrikanistik.

Soghayroun, I. (1981). *The Sudanese Muslim factor in Uganda.* Khartoum: Khartoum University Press.

Ssemorgerere, G., & Wiegratz, J. (2007). Is export-led growth a possibility? A qualitative assessment of Uganda's export policies over the last 15 years 1990/91–2005/06; with suggestions for non-distorting but selective interventions to enhance the export and growth agenda. Report presented at the National Policy Conference in Sustaining growth in Uganda, Kampala.

Stacey, T. (2003). *Tribe*. London: Stacey International.

Stark, O. (1991). *The migration of labor*. Cambridge, MA: Basil Blackwell.

Steinhart, E. L. (2007). Slavery and other forms of social oppression in Ankole, 1890–1940. In H. Medard & S. Doyle (Eds.), *Slavery in the Great Lakes region of East Africa* (pp. 189–209). Oxford: James Currey.

Sztompka, P. (2000). *Trust: A sociological theory*. Cambridge: Cambridge University Press.

Taylor, C. (1999). *Sacrifice as terror: The Rwandan genocide of 1994*. Oxford: Berg.

Tefera, T. L., Kirsten, J., & Perret, S. (2004). Market incentives, farmers' response and a policy dilemma: A case study of chat production in the eastern Ethiopian Highlands. Presented at the Workshop on Khat and the Ethiopian Reality: Production, Consumption, and Marketing, Addis Ababa University.

Tushemereirwe, W. K., Karamura, D., Ssali, H., Bwamiki, D., Kashaiji, I., Nankinga, C., . . . Ssebuliba, R. (2001). Bananas. (*musa spp*). In National Agricultural Research Organization (NARO) (Ed.) *Agriculture in Uganda: Volume II, Crops* (pp. 281–319). Kampala: Fountain Books.

Trimmingham, J. S. (1989). *Islam in East Africa*. Oxford: Clarendon Press.

UNEP/GRID-Arendal. (2008). Forest vs. Agriculture—the case of the Mabira forest reserve, Uganda. UNEP/GRID-Arendal Maps and Graphics Library. Retrieved June 14, 2009, from http://maps.grida.no/go/graphic/forest-vs-agriculture-the-case-of-the-mabira-forest-reserve-uganda

Valeri, M. (2007). Nation-building and communities in Oman since 1970: The Swahili-speaking Omani in search of identity. *African Affairs, 106*(424), 479–496.

Van Hear, N. (1998). *New diasporas: The mass exodus, dispersal and regrouping of migrant communities*. London: UCL Press, Taylor and Francis.

Varisco, D. M. (1986). On the meaning of chewing—the significance of qat (Catha-edulis) in the Yemen-Arab-Republic. *International Journal of Middle East Studies, 18*(1), 1–13.

Varisco, D. M. (2004). The elixir of life or the devil's cud? The debate over qat (*Catha edulis*) in Yemeni culture. In R. Coomber & S. Nigel (Eds.), *Drug use and cultural contexts: "Beyond the West."* London: Free Association Books.

Uganda Protectorate. (1951). *Report on the census of the non-native population of Uganda Protectorate taken on the night of 25th February, 1948*. London: Crown Agents.

United Nations International Drug Control Programme. (1999). *The drugs nexus in Africa*. Vienna: ODCCP Studies on Drugs and Crime.

Walls, M. (2009). The emergence of a Somali state: Building peace from civil war in Somaliland. *African Affairs, 108*(432), 371–389.

Warfa, N., Klein, A., Bhui, K., Leavey, G., Craig, T., & Stansfeld, S. (2007). Association between khat use and mental disorders: An emerging paradigm. *Social Science and Medicine*, *65*(2), 309–318.

Weir, S. (1985a). Economic aspects of the qat industry in north-west Yemen. In B. R. Pridham (Ed.), *Economy, society and culture in contemporary Yemen* (pp. 65–82). London: Croom Helm.

Weir, S. (1985b). *Qat in Yemen: Consumption and social change*. London: British Museum.

Wiegratz, J. (2008). Beyond harsh trade!? The relevance of "soft" competitiveness factors for Ugandan enterprises to endure in global value chains. *The African Journal of Business and Law*, *2*(1), 1–23.

Willis, J. (2002). *Potent brews: A social history of alcohol in East Africa 1850–1999*. Oxford: James Currey.

Zinberg, N. E. (1984). *Drug, set, and setting: The basis for controlled intoxicant use*. New Haven, CT: Yale University Press.

Index

UNIVERSITIES AT MEDWAY LIBRARY